DATE DUE

GAYLORD			PRINTED IN U.S.A

WORK SIMPLIFICATION IN DANISH PUBLIC LIBRARIES

LTP Publication • No. *15*

WORK SIMPLIFICATION

IN DANISH PUBLIC LIBRARIES

The report
of *The Work Simplification Committee*
of the *Danish Library Association,*
by *Henning Gimbel,* Study Director.
An abridged version.

Translated from the Danish by *Rudolph C. Ellsworth*

Library Technology Program | American Library Association
Chicago

Originally published in full as: *Rationalisering i danske folkebiblioteker,*
Copenhagen: Bibliotekscentralen, 1964

Standard Book Number 8389-3094-8 (1969)
Library of Congress Catalog Card Number 69-15862
Copyright © 1969 by the *American Library Association*
Printed in the United States of America

Contents

Efficiency in getting a socially needed job done is the fundamental basis of the economic, social, and political power of the world's leading nations.

Efficiency and doing a job, however, are two distinct things. One can do a job, inefficiently, and yet provide society a very valuable service. Or one can do another job, efficiently, and contribute nothing to society. In the first case people needed what was produced, however inefficiently. In the second case nobody needed the output, however efficiently it was produced. The ideal situation is, of course, to combine efficiency with a socially desirable end.

Recognition of these simple propositions led to the development of "scientific management," an art peculiar to the twentieth century and which has been, probably, an important ingredient in the almost fantastic rate of modern industrial development.

Credit should be duly given to the innovators: Frederick Winslow Taylor for his time and motion studies, to Frank Gilbreth for his refinements of Taylor's methods, and to Gilbreth's wife, Dr. Lillian Gilbreth, for emphasizing the importance of human factors, attention to the latter being given further impetus by Elton Mayo. Harrington Emerson probably deserves special recognition for adding the capping element: the importance of clearly defined goals. Probably the greatest pioneer of all was Henri Fayol, who began his career as a mining engineer and who, with characteristic French incisiveness of thought, perceived the causes of approaching bankruptcy facing the large coal and steel combine of which he became Director in 1888. He applied his concept of "administrative science" and raised the company to a solid and profitable venture by 1918. His viewpoint was so fundamental and theoretical that he transcended his more mundane contemporaries to a point where he should probably be considered more of a political scientist than a management engineer.

During the somewhat irresponsible years between World War I and the depression, the rationalists were more or less dismissed to the sidelines. They came into their own in the crisis of World War II when efficient management of their resources meant life or death to the great nations of the world. The

practitioners were so numerous that they became anonymous. They refined
the art of getting the needed job done with the utmost efficiency to a point
where their communications became almost esoteric. (In the process, unfortunately, some of them began to strangle, impoverish, and degrade their
native tongues.) Their appellation of their own art changed frequently. The
term was "operations research" in World War II; in the 1950's it was known
as "systems analysis"; by the late 1960's it was "cost effectiveness." But
regardless of what their skill is called, these specialists have developed
methods which, if properly applied, can enable society to get the maximum
return for its efforts.

It was logical, in view of the demonstrated success of such methodology
during World War II, that such specialists would offer their services (for
good fees) to industry during its short period of adjustment after the war
and its spectacular expansion since. These experts became known as (though
there are several other designations) "management consultants."

A sure sign that any new group has established itself solidly on the scene
is attention in the form of attempted ridicule. Thus, it is said, a management
consultant is a person who borrows your watch and then tells you what time
it is. As with all good jokes there is an element of truth in this quip. It
would lose its humor, for example, if the owner of the watch could not,
for one reason or another, see its dial as clearly as the management consultant
who borrowed it.

Herein, precisely, lies one of the most important capabilities of the management consultant. His vision is not distorted by the emotional, personal,
irrational factors which constantly beset the manager of an enterprise. The
management consultant can study the operation without the involvement of
his own emotions. In short, he can be objective, free of the myopia often
induced by bias, preconceived ideas, or tradition, and capable of seeing both
forest and component trees.

In addition, of course, he possesses a general theory of management which
he can adapt and apply to a specific operation.

The skills of the management consultant were for a number of years
applied almost solely to industry. Only relatively recently have they been
brought to bear on activities whose primary goals were not monetary profit.
The U.S. Department of Defense is a notable example. Even libraries have,
in recent years, with increasing frequency engaged management consultant
firms, and a few such enterprises actually specialize in library problems.

Some of the studies of library procedures have introduced a somewhat
novel technique: do-it-yourself systems analysis. One of the pioneers was
the Library Technology Project (now the Library Technology Program)
which hired George Fry and Associates to study first the problems of circulation control and later of reproducing catalog cards. In both cases the consultant firm provided, and LTP published, a detailed guide to procedures and

precise formulae which any library could use to determine the most efficient methods and equipment suited to its particular needs. [LTP Publication No. 1, *Study of Circulation Control Systems,* 1961; and LTP Publication No. 9, *Catalog Card Reproduction,* 1965.] Built into the fact-finding and analytical systems devised by the team of management consultants were investigative techniques designed to eliminate the subjective bias which is nearly always present in self-studies.

Alert to the value of systems analysis for libraries, the staff of LTP discovered two Scandinavian studies on "work simplification," both of which employed the do-it-yourself mode of operation with built-in protection against the hazards of subjectivity. One was a study carried out in Sweden during 1958-60 devoted to circulation control. Following closely on its heels, and deriving much benefit from its methodology, came the work presented in the following pages: a detailed analysis of the procedures involved in "processing"—i.e., book selection, cataloging, indexing, and preparing the book for shelving and circulation—performed by The Work Simplification Committee of the Danish Library Association.

The greatest value of this work, now being made available to American libraries by the Library Technology Program, is its guidance toward the simplification of working routines and the reallocation of duties in accordance with training and experience in order to alleviate the serious manpower shortage in American libraries—all this without undergoing the expense of calling in a management consultant.

During a decade of work at the Council on Library Resources, and during a year of intensive exposure to a great variety of library problems while working as the Executive Director of the National Advisory Commission on Libraries, I have become convinced that inadequate attention to management either causes or exacerbates the most troublesome of those problems. Mr. Henning Gimbel, his Committee, the State Inspection for Public Libraries in Copenhagen, and the Library Technology Program all deserve commendation for bringing the text that follows into the English language literature of librarianship. Even if the particular pattern set forth were not followed, a perusal of the book would be valuable because of the point of view it reveals. Simplification of work, streamlining of routine procedures, assignment of duties to appropriately trained personnel, or indeed sometimes to machines, would free professional librarians to perform more of the creative and intellectually stimulating functions for which they are suited by qualification and training.

> MELVILLE J. RUGGLES
> Program Officer
> Council on Library Resources, Inc.

Washington, D.C.
November, 1968

EDITOR'S PREFACE

In consultation with the author of this report and with E. Allerslev Jensen, Head of the Danish State Library Inspection, we have slightly abridged or condensed some sections of the original report as published in Denmark in 1964. The matter thus deleted or condensed related mostly to data on individual Danish libraries or to specific findings or recommendations of the Danish Library Association's Work Simplification Committee which would apply solely to the Danish library system, and which would not necessarily be of interest to readers outside of Denmark. We have also reduced the number of tables, charts, and graphs, preserving only those which we felt to be absolutely necessary to the reader's understanding of the purposes, methods, and results of the study. Other minor changes affecting the format and arrangement of the material in the original Danish edition have been made. Basically, however, we have tried to preserve the entire scope and content of the original study in the belief that it is essentially a study in technique and methodology which has applications to library systems everywhere.

Library Technology Program

AUTHOR'S PREFACE

At its annual meeting at Odense, September 5-6, 1959, the Public Librarians' Association (Group C of the Danish Library Association) arranged a series of discussions on work simplification problems in public libraries. The discussions were conducted by E. Allerslev Jensen, Viggo Bredsdorff, and Ole Koch. After the meeting the Public Librarians' Association proposed to the Danish Library Association (DLA) that a committee on work simplification [the title of this committee—"Rationaliseringskomite"—translates literally as "Rationalization Committee," but it shall be referred to throughout this text as the "Work Simplification Committee"]—be established. The DLA concurred with this request, and appointed a five-man committee consisting of Rudolf Jensen (Århus) and R. Lysholt Hansen (Nykøbing, Member of Parliament), representing the library trustees; Astrid Hoffmeyer (Hillerød) and Frode Jensen (Copenhagen), representing the librarians; and E. Allerslev Jensen, the Library Director (head of the State Library Inspection). This Committee was later supplemented by Svend Esbech of the Danish Library Association and two representatives of the Association of Danish Towns, O. Ingvartsen and O. Mitchell.

At the Committee's first meeting January 31, 1961, E. Allerslev Jensen was elected chairman, Ole Koch was appointed secretary, and Bengt Holmström (Malmö) was retained as consultant because of his experience as director of the Swedish work simplification survey made during 1958-60. At a later meeting Henning Gimbel was appointed to direct the work simplification study which began August 1, 1961. The Committee held a total of 16 meetings.

During the course of the inquiry the Committee received advice from a number of institutions, organizations, and individual experts, and it is thankful for this willing assistance. In particular, the Committee would like to thank the secretariat of the Administration Commission of Copenhagen, which made one of its staff, S. Kitaj, available as an advisor during the entire inquiry.

The Committee's investigation could not have been carried out without

1

the cooperation of the full-time libraries and the library service organization Bibliotekscentralen and its affiliated bindery service, Indbindingscentralen. All the full-time libraries answered the questionnaires received from the Committee, and in addition, several of these libraries took part in the various time studies, analyses of procedures, and special investigations conducted by the Committee. The Committee feels a special obligation to acknowledge the assistance received from the 14 libraries that participated in the very demanding work load analysis conducted during September-October, 1961.

By and large, the work of the Committee was financed from the "public library availability fund" [an amount of $2\frac{1}{2}$ percent of the annual state grants for public libraries set aside to support special library and bibliographical projects], but grants were also received from Groups A and C of the Danish Library Association.

Systematic application of work simplification has been put to the greatest use in the private enterprise sector of the economy, where strong and obvious interests have encouraged this type of approach. Public institutions do not have the same apparent incentives to apply work simplification, and this sector of the economy has come to recognize somewhat later than private industry the desirability and necessity for its use. Recently, however, both the central government and the larger municipalities have become quite interested in work simplification. Both the central government and the City of Copenhagen now have permanent offices for work simplification. The Danish Hospital Association has also set up a work simplification office that makes its services available to all members of the association.

The first work simplification studies in libraries were undertaken in the United States at the beginning of the present century. Several comprehensive work studies of a general character, as well as studies of individual libraries, have been carried out there in recent years. In Sweden, several investigations were conducted in individual libraries during the 1940's and 1950's, and a nationwide study was made in 1958-60.

No actual work simplification studies, either of individual libraries or of a more general character, had been undertaken in Denmark prior to the establishment of the Work Simplification Committee after the annual meeting of Public Librarians' Association in 1959, although farsighted individual librarians had previously tried to win support for work simplification ideas. During the 1930's, Thomas Døssing, then the Library Director, and Georg Krogh-Jensen, then City Librarian of Frederiksberg, spoke and wrote of the need to simplify library work. Døssing was concerned with the possibilities of carrying out a better division of work and the centralization of certain processing activities. As the head of a library, Krogh-Jensen was able to put some of these theories into practice. His ideas about simplifying library tasks greatly influenced the layout of the main library of Frederiksberg from the mid-1930's on. However, these two pioneers found only minimal interest in their ideas, and only slight improvements were made in the distribution and methods of work in libraries prior to the establishment of the Work Simplification Committee.

Today, the public library system is undergoing an expansion which, with the enactment of the new library law [the Public Libraries Act of May 27, 1964], can be expected to be even further augmented. The problems of education have become increasingly urgent. In the solution of these problems, the role of the library is a fundamental one, through its services to students, young or old, engaged in acquiring academic or vocational training or retraining, and for its services to those library patrons who are concerned with acquiring general knowledge or better employment qualifications through private study. Increased leisure is also bringing about greater opportunities for mass participation in cultural activities. The demands upon libraries are therefore constantly increasing, and as a result, the traditional areas of library activity must constantly be enlarged and improved, and new areas must be explored. The government's awareness of this was demonstrated in its revision of the library law in 1964.

The degree of recent public library development is indicated by the increase in the annual expenditures for these libraries in the last few years. In 1960-61 the total expenditures were about 50,000,000 kroner, while the expenditures for 1964-65 were budgeted at about 95,000,000 kroner, and it is estimated that they will be about 120,000,000 kroner for 1965-66.[1]

With constantly increasing annual expenditures of this size, the interest of the central government and the municipalities[2] in efficient and effective library operation becomes obvious. The organization, distribution, and methods of library work must therefore now also include positive efforts towards economical operation; and appropriate methods and division of work, based on the training and qualifications of different types of workers, are today essential conditions, both for providing more effective service, and for enabling the staff to derive satisfaction from its work. It is not surprising, therefore, that the first step toward creating the Work Simplification Committee was taken by the Public Librarians' Association.

From the background outlined above, the task of the Work Simplification Committee now becomes clear: to investigate the methods and the distribution of work in libraries having full-time staffs in order to make proposals which when carried out can contribute to the ability of those libraries to accomplish their objectives most effectively, and at the least possible cost. It has not, however, been the aim of the Committee to make proposals which might result in a decrease in state and municipal funds for the

1[The official exchange rate in 1964 was 6.93 kroner to the U.S. dollar.]
2[Denmark is divided for purposes of local government into 22 counties, 88 "urban municipalities," and over 1200 "rural municipalities."]

3

operation of the libraries, and a consequent decrease in their growth and development. It is to be expected that expenditures will continue to rise as a result of the ever greater tasks facing the libraries and the rising demands being made upon them. The essential objective of work simplification is to enable libraries to meet as economically as possible the increaséd demands being made upon them by both the central government and the municipalities.

In fulfilling this objective, the Committee has found it appropriate to arrange its inquiry so that the Danish and Swedish studies supplement each other. The Swedish study carried out during 1958-60 resulted in the report: *Organisation och arbetsmetoder vid kommunala bibliotek* [*Organization and Working Methods in Public Libraries*], published in 1960. This study was the model for the work of the Danish Committee. While neither study includes all activities of the public libraries, both are especially concerned with the problems of the distribution of library work. However, the two studies are quite different. The Swedish Committee studied circulation control in detail, while the Danish Committee has been particularly concerned with processing activities, that is, methods of book selection, cataloging, indexing, and the procedures involved in preparing books for library use. The division of the areas of investigation between these two Committees means that the Danish public libraries can derive benefit not only from the present report, but from the Swedish report as well. The Danish Committee has consequently found it useful in the present study to refer briefly to the Swedish Committee's principal conclusions and to adapt some of the Swedish data to Danish conditions.

However, even these two reports together do not cover all areas of library activities, and, because the results of work simplification studies become rather quickly outdated and must be constantly kept in line with current developments in library procedures and work simplification techniques, the Committee has decided to establish a permanent work simplification ["rationalization"] section within the State Library Inspection. A proposal to this effect was approved by the Association of Danish Towns and the Association of Rural Municipality Councils and approved by the Ministry of Cultural Affairs on September 21, 1963. The future work simplification section of the State Library Inspection will be able to continue the work of the Work Simplification Committee's investigations on a current basis and to advise libraries on the application of work simplification procedures, both those proposed by the Committee and those that it may itself develop in the future.   *Copenhagen, September 23, 1964*

Members of the Work Simplification Committee are: E. Ellerslev Jensen, Chairman, Svend Esbech, O. Ingvartsen, Frode Jensen, Astrid Hoffmeyer, Rudolf Jensen, R. Lysholt Hansen, Ole Mitchell, and Ole Koch, Secretary.

HENNING GIMBEL, Study Director

4

Part I contains a description of the development of full-time libraries since 1945 insofar as this development is relevant to this study. Part-time libraries are discussed only as they are directly related to the liaison activity of the county libraries. Matters irrelevant to the study, even though they may affect the entire public library movement, such as the controversy over circulation fees, the matter of bookstore discounts, and the problems peculiar to the combined public and research library, are not considered.

The full-time libraries in Denmark fall into four natural groups or classes which are treated for the purposes of our study as statistical entities: county libraries (excluding Gentofte); large city or metropolitan libraries (Copenhagen, Frederiksberg, and Gentofte); suburban libraries; and "other full-time libraries." Each of these groups differs in a number of significant ways from the other groups, while the individual members of each group have many characteristics in common. (The three large metropolitan libraries show such wide differences from each other that treating these libraries as a single group may be misleading. These three libraries do not, however, fit into any other group.)

The general notes to the tables in Part I are listed on pages 219 to 222.

1 Purpose of the Public Libraries

The purpose of the public libraries is stated in the first paragraph of the library law. In the Public Libraries Act of 1950, this paragraph read: "The purpose of public libraries is to promote the general diffusion of knowledge and information by means of fiction and nonfiction books which lead to the general development of culture."

In the Public Libraries Act of May 27, 1964, the objectives clause was changed to read: "The purpose of the public libraries is to promote the spread of knowledge, education, and culture by making books and other suitable materials available free of charge."

The Public Libraries Act, and the rules and regulations which arise out of its administration, also prescribe the means by which this purpose is to be accomplished.

The purpose of the public libraries has changed considerably, of course, since the establishment of the first parish libraries in Denmark about 200 years ago; but no really basic changes have been made since the enactment of the first Public Libraries Act in 1920.

At the general cultural level, it is now generally agreed that the libraries are to be vital instruments for the dissemination of thoughts, ideas, experiences, and information in literary form.

At the social and political level, agreement on the purpose of the libraries is an obvious result of agreement upon democracy as the social structure, and of the necessity for attaining a broad and high level of culture and education as the basis for effectively maintaining that form of social order.

7

Thus defined, library service is, for the individual citizen, one of the necessary conditions for acquiring and maintaining the knowledge required to make decisions on matters of general welfare, thereby exercising the rights and obligations of a democracy. Library service is also a primary source of general cultural information and influence, intellectual as well as aesthetic, and thus is a part of the foundation for the culturally full life for which it is the task of democracy to provide the framework. In the nation's effort to increase the material living standards of the people, the task of the libraries is to make facts and information available to commerce and industry to help bring about a climate of favorable working conditions and a more vigorous economic system.

Public libraries must be accessible to all persons in the community and their activities must be comprehensive and well-balanced. That is, the book stock must include all fields of interest, represent all opinions, and contain materials suitable for all ages and levels of education.

The law places the public libraries among the cultural and educational institutions of the country, and they must therefore be accessible to any person who wishes to maintain and develop his knowledge and training received through the schools.

The difference between public libraries and research and special libraries is of a functional nature and not in principle due to a difference in their users. This difference is expressed mainly in the acquisition by the public libraries of that literature which does not require specialized knowledge on the part of the patrons, and acquisition by the research and special libraries of specialized and scholarly literature. Because this difference is merely a formal or functional one, however, the public libraries have an obligation to obtain material which they do not possess from the research and special libraries for their patrons upon request.

According to the provisions of the library law and its associated rules and regulations, six main tasks must be accomplished to fulfill the purpose of the public libraries:

1. Literature is to be selected in accordance with library objectives. That is, a general book collection must be assembled from that part of the available literature which meets the requirements of the objectives clause of the Public Libraries Act regarding the diffusion of knowledge, information, and general cultural values.

2. The literature selected must be made available for use, through, among other things, the processes of indexing and arranging library materials in such a way that library patrons can find, or be helped to find, the specific material they desire.

3. The library patrons, if they so wish, must also be guided to the desired literature where their interests are vague or not clearly defined.

The purpose of this advisory service is to further extend the services made available by the technical library processing described in main task number 2 above.

4. Provisions must also be made to protect books and other library materials, and to ensure that circulated literature is returned. Rules for use of the library are to be laid down in such a way that the individual borrower may have the most favorable conditions possible for using circulated material, while at the same time the maximum number of borrowers may have access to this material.

5. Knowledge of the usefulness of library service is to be disseminated and the promotion of the understanding of the role of the library in the community is to be furthered (through publicity, extension work, and public relations).

6. These five main tasks necessitate the sixth: the organization and administration of library work.

In addition, for the county libraries there is the special liaison work with the libraries within their respective regions.

2 Development of full-time libraries since 1945: legislation, organization, and activities

LIBRARY LAW

In the years prior to the enactment of the first library law in 1920, the main lines of public library organization were established by Hans Ostenfeldt Lange at the first general library meeting at Århus in 1909. The most important changes in the Public Libraries Act before 1945 occurred in 1931 when children's libraries were included in the law. However, it should be noted that, with the accompanying regulations for state grants, this actually resulted in public and children's libraries having their own independent organizations, at least in theory, in most of the larger cities.

Since the 1945 Act, the library law has been amended in 1946, 1950, 1959, and 1964. In 1946, a withholding of 2½ percent of state grants to individual libraries was enacted. (This withholding had actually been started as early as 1937-38 with a provision in the Finance Act.) From this 2½ percent comes the so-called availability fund which is used for financing projects of common interest to all public libraries. In this same amendment, the provision for compensating Danish authors for the use of their works in libraries was first introduced.

The amendments of the 1950 Act mark the end of the pioneer era of the public libraries. As of that year, the Act refers to "public libraries" and not "state-supported libraries," and the principle was established that the municipalities are obliged to give "adequate grants." (The term "adequate grants" is defined in the "Ministry of Education Instruction Concerning the Financial Bases for Public Libraries of October 23, 1951" and the comparable "Ministry of Education Instruction Concerning the Financial Bases for Children's Libraries of March 18, 1953.") The Act of 1950 also introduced the provision that 10 percent of the electorate of a municipality can demand (by the so-called force paragraph) the establishment of a library, and in the same Act, the responsibilities of the county libraries to the residents of their regions were extended to include children as well as adults.

The amendment of 1959 improved the financial basis of county library work significantly. State grants for the liaison work of the county libraries henceforward were based directly on the population of the library region.

The rules for calculating the state grants for the public libraries (the basic grant as well as the special state grant for county libraries) were changed considerably by the revisions of 1931, 1950, and 1959, but the general principle remained the same as in 1920, that is, state grants are made in relation to the local grants. Since 1931, however, these grants have been made according to a graduated scale which is most advantageous for the small, part-time libraries.

With the provision in the Act of 1959 for the special grant for furniture, and the further rules concerning this in the Ministry of Education regulation of January 1, 1960 ("Special State Grants for Equipment Expenses in New Construction or Extensive Rebuilding of Public Libraries") the practice of making state grants according to the principle of reimbursement for expenses incurred came into being.

The library law was again amended in 1964. The principal changes brought about by the new Public Libraries Act of May 27, 1964 are as follows:

Every local authority, either on its own or in conjunction with others, is now obliged to maintain a public library with both adults' and children's departments. Every public library shall be open to all persons living in Denmark. Municipalities with a population of 5,000 or over must appoint a qualified librarian as well as any assistants necessary.

In the future, state support to public libraries will take the form of a reimbursement based on a percentage of the annual individual library budget. This will be paid out in the same year as that covered by the budget and will be calculated at the end of the year. Forty-five percent of all expenses up to 275,000 kroner, and 30 percent of any sum above that, will be reimbursed. All expenditures necessary to maintain the library qualify for reimbursement. This includes the cost of books purchased, salaries, premises, office expenses, furniture, mobile libraries, etc. Audiovisual aids are now eligible for state grants. The provision made in earlier Acts that 2½ percent of the basic state grants be withheld, and that

11

this sum be made available for projects common to all public libraries, remains.

Further, the new Act makes available 100,000 kroner to individual libraries for trying out new methods, and for other special expenditures. The work done by the county libraries which serve as headquarters for libraries within their area will in future be paid jointly by the state government and county authorities, so that the towns in which these county libraries are situated will not have to bear this expense. The special grant for this purpose may be up to 60,000 kroner plus 2 kroner per resident of the region, and is to be regulated by the cost of living index. County districts are to be consolidated, and the number of county libraries is to be decreased.

The 1964 Act also contains legislation on school libraries for the first time. These libraries come under the supervision of the Ministry of Education, while the public libraries are under the supervision of the Ministry of Cultural Affairs. School libraries are not made compulsory but "all efforts should be made to establish them." They form part of the local educational system, although they cooperate with the public libraries in matters of budget, book selection, and in library techniques. The Act also aims at future cooperation with other types of schools. As a further consequence of the new Act, the State Library Inspection will in future serve more and more in an advisory and consultative capacity instead of merely acting as an agency for inspection and supervision as it had in the past.

ORGANIZATION

The fundamental structure of the public library system, which, as we said before, has not undergone any basic changes since 1920, is characterized by:

1. Independent libraries, each of which serves its own area, which is a municipality as a rule, but sometimes a parish in rural areas.

2. Cooperation between libraries.

Cooperation

The most important elements of the nationwide public library system are: (1) the individual libraries, with the county libraries as separate groups; (2) the State Library Inspection; (3) the Public Library Information Office; (4) the Royal Danish School of Librarianship; (5) the library service organization Bibliotekscentralen; (6) the Danish Library Association; (7) ancillary library activities.

Library cooperation occurs in a number of areas, and the degree of this cooperation determines to a great extent the effectiveness of the individual libraries. Interlibrary loan cooperation, for example, is shown in the following diagram. (The arrows show the direction in which the loan requests are forwarded.)

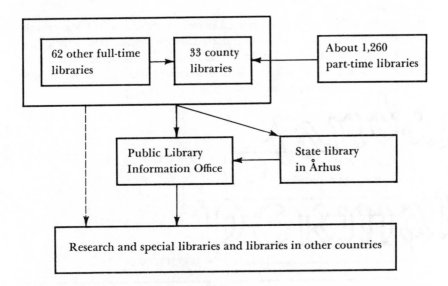

The 33 county libraries are the focal points for library service in the rural areas, because through their separate county library departments they "supplement the work of the local general libraries within a large region, in part by making available informative literature for circulation free of charge, in part by supporting the local libraries with guidance in technical library processing activities, and in other ways" in addition to serving as general libraries for their own municipalities.

Institutions
The State Library Inspection "undertakes the necessary calculation and disbursement of the state grants according to the regulations established for this purpose and provides the libraries with advice and guidance."

On April 1, 1961, the Public Library Information Office was separated from the State Library Inspection. It takes care of interlibrary loan activity.

In 1956, the Royal Danish School of Librarianship was also separated from the State Library Inspection. It is the country's training facility for librarians and library assistants in public libraries as well as research and special libraries. The school also conducts courses for part-time librarians.

The library service organization Bibliotekscentralen was established in 1939 [under a different name—see Chapter 6] for the purpose of "assisting

Danish libraries by undertaking bibliographical and technical processing activities, including publishing, binding, and the furnishing of equipment and office supplies."

Associations

In addition to the institutions named above, cooperation in library work is also manifested through the Danish Library Association which has as its object "to further Danish librarianship in public as well as in research and special libraries." The organizational structure of the Danish Library Association is shown in the diagram below.

The Danish Library Association (DLA)
SECTION 1

	SECTION 2
Group A Large public libraries	
Group B Smaller public libraries	
Group C Public Librarians' Association	*Group D* Danish Research and Special Libraries Association
Group F Part-time Librarians' Association	*Group E* Librarians' Association for Research and Special Libraries

The Danish Library Association also appoints committees to accomplish special tasks.

The Danish School Library Association, whose membership consists of the county school library associations, the children's and school libraries, and the school centrals, is an important factor in cooperation between school and library.

Other important organizations for cooperation between libraries are the Revolving Library for Foreign Literature for the Public Libraries, the Study Group Center, and the New Danish Literary Society.

Special library activities

Special tasks are carried out through the following organizations:

Libraries at military installations are serviced by the local public libraries through agreements between the Armed Forces Welfare Service and the State Library Inspection.

The Danish Merchant Marine Library has charge of library work on private and state-owned merchant ships.

The Central Library for Tuberculous Patients, whose activity includes service to both institutional and home-care patients.

Library work in Greenland is managed from the Greenland Central Library at Godthåb, is administered by the governor of Greenland, and is directed by the State Library Inspection.

The work in South Schleswig which is directed from the Danish Central Library for South Schleswig in Flensborg.

EXTENT AND TYPE OF ACTIVITIES

Since the end of World War II, both full-time and part-time libraries have gone through a period of rapid development. This has been particularly true of the large public libraries. The areas of activity have increased, in many respects the quality of service has improved, and various new tasks have been undertaken. Functions which were formerly performed rather poorly, such as service to children and young people, have been improved and now constitute important parts of the complete library operation. On the whole, the stock of material with which libraries work has also slowly but surely improved in quality, due in part to publishers' attempts to keep pace with the general improvement in formal educational and training facilities, and in part to the influence which voluntary educational radio, television, and library programs have had on the public's needs and requirements for higher cultural (including literary) quality. This gradual transition, which may not be apparent from one day to the next, becomes obvious over a period of years. It is evident, for example, in the difference between the descriptive book annotations published in the Danish library journal *Bogens Verden* (*Book World*) during the 1920's and those of today. It can also be seen in the difference in quality between the books a library discards at present and the new ones it buys. Even since 1945 this transition is apparent. During these years there has been a distinct upgrading of the quality of fiction used for recreational reading. Also, the demands for nonfiction have increased significantly. These changes have influenced the general quality of the books in libraries, and, more especially, the extent and coverage of the nonfiction holdings which formerly were considered to be too specialized to be of interest to public libraries.

Buildings

The total lack of library construction during World War II resulted

15

in the fact that by the end of the war many library buildings erected or remodeled for library use in the 1920's and 1930's literally bulged with overflowing collections, the demands for which had at the same time grown enormously. Library construction has continued to be slow since the war, which has meant that the space problems of the full-time libraries for the country as a whole are even worse today than they were in 1945. Since 1952 a number of modern and well-furnished library buildings have been built, and some libraries have moved into larger, remodeled quarters, but the great majority of full-time libraries have not had their premises enlarged or remodeled to any noticeable extent since the 1930's. Many of these buildings appear poorer, gloomier, and more crowded each year, because of their increased activity due to the general rise in the standard of living with its accompanying increase in leisure and cultural activity.

Book stock

By 1945 the stock of the libraries had deteriorated physically to a certain extent because of extremely high use during the war and because of the poor quality of the available wartime paper and binding. Today, however, these wartime effects are noticed only occasionally, and in most libraries only in those books which are held in the storage collections.

Book stock for adults. From 1946 to 1961, the total holdings in the adult departments of all full-time libraries almost doubled [from approximately 2.1 million to approximately 4.1 million volumes—an increase of 93 percent]. Per capita, the overall increase was almost 50 percent. The figures for the growth of the book stock during the period, however, show fairly large differences for the various types of libraries. For example, the increase in the total number of volumes held was greatest in the suburban libraries and "other full-time libraries." However, because of the more rapid growth of the population in the areas served by these libraries, the increase in volumes per capita for these libraries was less than the nationwide average. The large increases in the total holdings of suburban libraries [adult holdings increased 328 percent] and "other full-time libraries" [adult holdings increased 104 percent], should therefore be viewed in relation to the population increase in the areas served by these libraries, and also to the large number of libraries of this type which became full-time units during this period [the number of suburban libraries increased from 9 to 18, "other full-time libraries" from 28 to 41].

If the adult book stock per capita for each class of library is compared with the requirement set forth in the "Ministry of Education Instructions Concerning the Financial Bases for Public Libraries," it can be seen that this requirement was fulfilled only by the county libraries. Because detailed statistics are not available for the special central book collections of the county libraries, and because these collections cannot be differentiated from those parts of the book collections which these institutions must maintain to fulfill their own local library obligations, it cannot be stated categorically, however, that even the county library collections are really adequate. It is fair to state, however, that during this period all four types of full-time libraries have come noticeably closer to achieving the book stock required by the Ministry of Education Instructions.

The ratio of total holdings to volumes circulated has also shown some progress for all types of libraries. The figures show that the average yearly circulation per book for all full-time libraries as a group, 1945-61, was between 3 and 4. This circulation ranged from a high of 6 times the holdings in the large city libraries (Copenhagen, Frederiksberg, and Gentofte) in 1945-46, to a low of 2½ times the holdings in the "other full-time libraries" in 1960-61. It cannot, however, be determined whether the increase in total holdings per capita and total holdings per books circulated indicates a real improvement in the book stock and of the assembling of a collection which now meets, to a greater extent than previously, more varied and different needs, or whether the rise may be due in part to increases in parts of the collection which are dead and should be discarded.

Book stock for children. Collections for children have grown more rapidly than those for adults. For the entire group of full-time libraries the total growth in children's collections has been more than 300 percent, and for the suburban libraries it has been just under 600 percent. The per capita increases for these collections are also large: 200 percent for all of the full-time libraries, more than 250 percent for the county libraries, and 100 percent for the suburban libraries. However, only in the county libraries could the book stock adequately keep pace with the loans to children; in the other libraries the ratio of total holdings to circulated books was less in 1961 than in 1946. In the suburban libraries during 1960-61, circulation was 6 times the total stock; in all of the other types of libraries about 3 times the stock.

The great increase in the children's collections, however, should be viewed against the background of the modest extent of these collections at the beginning of the period. For the full-time libraries as a group the children's book stock in 1946 was 0.3 volume per capita, and as the number of children of school age was somewhat more than 10 percent of the total population, the book stock was thus not quite 3 volumes per child. In 1961 the children's book stock had increased to 0.9 volume per capita or 7 to 8 volumes per child. (In 1961, children of school age were 12 to 14 percent of the total population in the cities.) Increases in the children's book stock per capita were more or less uniform in the different types of libraries (however, it should be noted that by 1961 the book stock had only risen to 0.6 volume per capita in the municipalities of Greater Copenhagen). The requirement in the "Ministry of Education Instruction Concerning the Financial Bases for Children's Libraries" for 8 to 10 volumes per child were apparently close to being achieved by the county libraries, but as the classroom sets were also counted in their figures, it should be noted that none of the types of libraries in 1961 actually fulfilled the standards of the Instructions for the size of children's book collections. A very substantial improvement has, however, taken place since 1946.

In this Part and in Part II, all figures for the activities of the children's departments (unless otherwise noted) include the children's and school library departments in elementary schools. Towards the end of the period considered here, vigorous development began in the school libraries as a result of the publication by the Ministry of Education of the so-called blue report: "Instructions for Teaching for Elementary Schools" (1960-61, 2 vols.).

Circulation

The total circulation to children and adults by full-time libraries increased from just over 10 million volumes in 1945-46 to not quite 21 million volumes in 1960-61.

Circulation to children. The greatest progress has been in children's departments. This progress has been almost explosive. From a total circulation of a little over 1.5 million volumes in 1945-46, it rose to more than 7 million volumes in 1960-61, an increase of 353 percent. The per capita increase was 213 percent.

The special loans to schools [of from 10 to 30 copies of individual titles and referred to as "class sets"] consisted of only about 5,000 volumes in 1945-46, but more than one-half million volumes in 1960-61. If the county libraries' circulation of children's books to non-resident borrowers (both individual loans and deposit loans) as well as the loan of class sets are deducted, total circulation in 1960-61 would still be about 6.5 million volumes.

This immense increase in the circulation of the children's libraries is by no means due only to the increased number of children of reading age. The principal reason for greater circulation is to be found in the improved service of the children's libraries. For the majority of libraries, service to children only really began after the war. In many localities an effective children's library organization with departments in the public library and the schools was first established after the war using the so-called Frederiksberg System of 1937 as a pattern.

The improvement and extension of children's library service during the years since 1945 has been, however, somewhat uneven. When the development of individual libraries is considered, it is characterized by intermittent bursts of activity and by great differences between libraries. In 1945-46, nearly all libraries reported a circulation to children of less than 2 volumes per capita. During the 15-year period that followed, one library after another reorganized its work with children: children's librarians were employed in more and more places, modern children's departments—with reading rooms as well as circulation departments— were established in the schools, and the holdings of children's books in the main libraries were enlarged. By 1960-61 almost half [46 out of 94] of the full-time libraries reported a per capita circulation to children of 3 or more volumes. The development within the different types of libraries corresponds fairly closely to that of the full-time libraries as a whole, although the growth has been a bit faster and gone somewhat further in the county libraries than in the others.

In 1960-61, while just under one-fourth [23 out of 94] of the full-time libraries had a per capita circulation to children of 4 or more volumes, 17 libraries, or just under one-fifth, continued to have a per capita circulation to children of less than 2 volumes. Should it become possible to bring these comparatively undeveloped children's departments up to a standard corresponding to that reached by the best libraries, circulation to children in the full-time libraries will be greatly increased.

Work with children's libraries as well as library construction has become one of the special interests of the State Library Inspection, and in 1957 it appointed an inspector to work exclusively with these interests. In the latter part of the period under review, work with children has been hampered by a shortage of children's librarians, but for the period as a whole, professional guidance in children's libraries, considering all the large libraries together, has been greatly improved. Instruction in school classes on how to use the library, for example, is now included as a regular feature of school and library work in more and more localities. In 1956 and 1961 nationwide children's book weeks were held with the cooperation of libraries, schools, bookstores, and publishers. These promotions, as well as the generally increased interest in children's books, have brought about a greater supply of quality books for children.

Circulation to young people. Service to young [teen-age] people became a subject of serious concern during the mid-1950's, primarily due to the challenges raised by the "large year classes"—children born during the war and now in their teens—who, in many places had received better service in children's libraries than their predecessors, and who had also been taught how to use the library so that they were library-oriented to an extent that was previously unknown in library work.

19

The answers of the libraries to this challenge were: (1) the training of librarians with young people's reading interests as a specialty, (2) training in the use of libraries for groups of young people now out of school, (3) the setting up of young people's collections or departments in the public libraries, and (4) the preparation of special reading lists. In addition, the Danish Library Association appointed a committee to work out the problems involved with serving young people. Improvement in service was at first hampered by the lack of suitable material, but during the mid-1950's a special young people's literature became available. In work with both young people and children much progress has been made, and although there are still libraries which do not provide satisfactory service in these areas, most of the libraries are moving steadily to improve their service.

Circulation to adults. The total full-time library circulation to adults rose from 8.9 million volumes in 1945-46, to 13.7 million volumes in 1960-61 (or if the county libraries' non-resident circulation is not considered, from 8.3 million to 12.7 million volumes), or over 50 percent. Circulation per capita to adults (for the county libraries again only loans to borrowers in their home municipalities are included) increased from 4.0 to 4.8 volumes, or 20 percent. This rate of increase was comparatively uniform among the different types of libraries. Circulation per capita in the suburban libraries in 1945-46 was somewhat less than in the other libraries, but an especially large recent increase has now raised the circulation per capita of these libraries to the level of the other libraries. How large a part of the increase in circulation of the full-time libraries is due to young adults cannot be documented, but there is no doubt that during the fairly stable circulation of the past five or six years [the per capita circulation of all full-time libraries remained at 4.8 from 1955 through 1961] there has been a shift in the pattern of circulation, with a relatively large increase in circulation to young adults, and a corresponding decline in circulation to older persons. At the same time a noticeable change has taken place in the type of material circulated, with a documented increase in the circulation of nonfiction and a decline in the circulation of fiction. A shift has also occurred—not documented, but quite apparent—from light to more substantial fiction.

Television is usually blamed for the decline in circulation of lighter fiction and the corresponding drop in circulation of recreational reading, since it now provides the type of entertainment which previously may have come from the libraries, and consequently it may have exerted some pressure against the circulation of the lighter reading material in the library book collections.

At the same time, however, television may be included among those factors which have stimulated the library circulation of the more important and "serious" fiction, literature of general cultural interest, and nonfiction material, and which have brought about the circulation of an increasingly sophisticated and diverse literature. The extent to which this development may be attributed to television cannot be accurately determined; it can only be said that it is one of many factors which have worked in this direction.

The noticeable change in the age distribution of readers has already been noted. The most frequently cited explanations for this are the expansion of the paperback book market, the rising standard of living, full employment, and increased leisure time. Possibly more obscure factors are involved, but one remaining cause of uncertain dimensions may be sought in the effects that libraries (including the children's libraries), and the general adult-education movement have had on the public during the past generation.

While it is not possible to determine accurately the extent of the changes in the pattern of library circulation, the relatively stable per capita circulation of the last few years indicates that the decrease in the circulation of light reading material is just about balanced by the increase in the circulation of more substantial fiction and nonfiction.

Interlibrary loan

The increasing need for various kinds of literature as well as the general improvement in library service is indicated by the vigorous increases in interlibrary loan activity. This increase cannot be accurately estimated for public libraries as a whole, but the figures for loans to other public libraries from the State Library in Århus and for the requests processed by the Public Library Information Office may serve as an example. (See Table 1).

The loans among all full-time libraries and the individual loans of

Table 1. Århus State Library loans to public libraries and number of interlibrary loan requests processed through the Public Library Information Office

Year	Århus State Library loans to public libraries	Interlibrary loan requests processed through the Public Library Information Office
	volumes	requests
1945	35,754	11,950
1950	40,004	14,837
1955	47,950	17,715
1960	64,322	25,450

county libraries to full- and part-time libraries within their regions cannot be accurately estimated, but reports indicate that the extent of interlibrary loan activity varies widely among the individual libraries. The variations cannot be accounted for solely by differences in the size and content of the individual collections. They also depend upon the service the individual library offers through its advisory work. Table 2 shows the extent to which a rural library with a limited collection can make use of interlibrary loans when the library has a full-time librarian who has the time and interest to clarify the literature needs of his patrons and to attempt to meet these needs by means of obtaining interlibrary loans.

Table 2. Interlibrary loans to Niløse-Stenlille parish library

Year	Loans	Population	Loans per 100 residents
	volumes		volumes
1955-56	729	2,500	29.2
1956-57	876	2,500	35.0
1957-58	1,427	2,500	57.1
1958-59	1,445	2,500	57.8
1959-60	1,131	2,500	45.2

Note: In 1955 a full-time librarian was appointed in this parish. In 1960, however, the position was again vacant. This undoubtedly explains the decrease in activity in 1959-60.

Reference service

The reference services of full-time libraries have not been stated in figures which can be entirely accepted as a valid statement of the extent of this activity, but this entire function has undergone a new appraisal. It was apparent for some time prior to 1950 that the role of the reference room was not to become that which had been anticipated for it during the pathfinding days of 1920. The new evaluation occurred at the beginning of the 1950's in connection with, and as a result of, investigations undertaken, first at reference rooms in Copenhagen, and subsequently in 15 other reference rooms throughout the country. The results of these investigations were summarized in *Bibliotekaren* (*The Librarian*), p. 76, in 1951 as follows:

". . . the reading room of the future should have three parts:

"1. A newspaper room, if one is to be maintained. If there is one, it should be separated from the other areas.

"2. A large and complete collection of reference works with emphasis on quick-reference material and periodicals, that is, a reference department in its proper meaning, with reading positions near the circulation area where the enforcement of silence or any other formalities of reading room discipline are not required.

"3. A smaller reading or study room where books from both the circulation and reference departments may be used."

Library construction since the early 1950's has shown the effects of this reassessment. The reference room is comparatively smaller than in the library buildings from the 1920's and 1930's, and is frequently not separated from the circulation area, while separate study rooms have been provided.

However, only the reference rooms of the larger cities are busy information centers which meet the current demand for facts. Reference rooms in the smaller towns usually cannot afford the expenditure involved in maintaining an adequate reference collection. This means that cooperation between libraries should also be extended to include supplying information from the large reference rooms to those in the libraries of the smaller towns.

Liaison work of the county libraries

Individual loans. Individual loans from the county libraries to the full- and part-time libraries within their regions have already been mentioned, as well as the work involved in handling them. This, and other phases of liaison work have developed rapidly since the end of World War II.

Bookmobiles.[1] Bookmobile service, which had been in operation for several years before the war in some localities, is now provided by practically all the county libraries. Bookmobile service has been described as one of the most important and valuable forms of liaison service, and has been of great significance, both in furnishing the small, permanent collections of the part-time libraries with changing loan deposits from the county libraries, and in the increased contact which this has created between the staffs of these libraries. However, the holdings of the part-time libraries are now often so large that these loans, which usually consist of 50 to 75 volumes, have become of questionable importance. Bookmobiles are no longer a necessary means of bringing about contacts between Danish libraries, and they will therefore probably be replaced by a smaller vehicle for the delivery of individual loans, new books, etc., from the county libraries to the part-time libraries.

Joint book collections. Book collections owned jointly by part-time

---

1[In the Danish library system, a "bookmobile" does not have quite the same function as in the American or British systems. It does not serve as a traveling collection or branch library for the circulation of books to individual borrowers, but simply as a means of transporting small, supplemental collections, or "loan deposits," between the county libraries and the part-time libraries; and, as the author here points out, even this function is undergoing a change.]

libraries in the area serviced by a county library exist in two forms: supplementary collections for the permanent, local collections in the part-time libraries, and joint children's libraries.

The first type of joint book collection came into being during the mid-1930's for the purpose of making available as varied a collection as possible in the part-time libraries. Collections were organized for rotation among voluntary associations of small, independent units within a county library region, resembling the method used in the English county library system. Where they existed, these joint book collections provided the associated part-time libraries with a changing stock which the county libraries could not then have provided by other means because of the small grants available for this phase of county library work. The importance of this type of joint book collection, however, has greatly declined. There are two reasons for this. First, with larger grants for work with the part-time libraries, the county libraries have become more able to meet the requirements for individual and deposit loans as stated in the library law. Second, there have been administrative problems within the plan itself; it has not been possible, for example, to work out dependable measures to place them on an effective financial basis. Therefore, with one exception, they have been steadily disbanded in recent years.

The joint children's libraries originated at a time when a general lack of children's literature prevailed in the part-time libraries, and when the county libraries' responsibilities within their regions did not extend to books for children. (The first joint library was established in 1937.) The organizational principle here was the same as with the supplementary joint book collections mentioned above, but with a more extensive application. In their original form, the joint children's libraries were to be responsible for *all* children's work in the area served by the affiliated part-time libraries. As with the supplementary joint book collections, their significance has been dwindling, but it must be conceded that as a result of the establishment of such libraries the part-time librarians themselves, at first gradually, and then to an increasing extent, took over the task of buying children's books for their own collections. As this latter development got underway, loans from the joint children's libraries declined. However, during their most active period these joint libraries provided better children's service in the outlying areas than that provided by non-affiliated part-time libraries. The existing joint children's libraries are used mostly to supplement children's collections which are constantly being enlarged by the part-time libraries themselves, and their finances are entirely inadequate.

Book selection and budget preparation. Aid in book selection by the county libraries to the part-time libraries has increased in scale, particularly during the last 10 to 15 years. It has included group book selection meetings for the entire county library district, written proposals, and book selection meetings held at individual part-time libraries. No less important has been the aid provided in recent years in preparing budgets for part-time libraries.

Book care. The county library departments of the county libraries provide assistance to part-time libraries in the care and repair of the book stock, as well as in its updating and in the revision of shelf lists and catalogs that result. This assistance, however, is established on a regular schedule in only a few places.

Technical processing. During the period from 1945 to 1960, the county library departments have also performed a series of technical processing services for the part-time libraries. These activities have included preparing book cards, date slips, shelf lists and sometimes catalog cards, organizing binding procedures, and also, on occasion, making purchases resulting from local book selection meetings.

Public relations

The public libraries have been slow in perceiving the significance of public relations work. They are now, however, apparently on the threshold of an immense development in this field. The most long-standing public relations work has been with children and has included exhibits and instruction in the use of the library. (The children's book weeks held in 1956 and 1961 were noted earlier.) During the course of the period from 1945 to 1960, increasing use was made of group sessions to introduce the library to both children and adults, of literature evenings and similar events, of exhibitions, and of colorful and attractive posters inside and outside the library. The Danish Library Association became involved in this work in 1950 by establishing the Committee for Better Use of the Library (a report by this Committee was published in 1961), and by setting up a public relations office in 1960 to facilitate the centralized coordination of library promotion and the dissemination of exhibition material to improve the hitherto largely amateur efforts of the libraries. The importance now being given to this work is also shown in the provision of lecture and meeting rooms in most of the library buildings which have been erected since the mid-1950's. Still it must be admitted that the "out-reaching activities" of libraries remain among the most underdeveloped of the library tasks.

Hospital libraries

Among the ancillary special library tasks, work with hospitals and military installations have been developed most extensively. Hospital work is the oldest. It was started in 1926. As shown in Table 3, it has improved steadily since 1945.

Table 3.   Hospital libraries

Year	Number of libraries with circulation to hospital patients	Number of hospitals with library staff	Circulation from hospital libraries (volumes)	Number of beds in hospitals with library staff	Hours per week of hospital library service	
					Librarians	Assistants
General hospitals						
1945-46	57	67	587,175	12,563[a]	Total 751[b]	
1950-51	68	89	628,468	16,359	Total 788½	
1955-56	71	94	863,667	20,082	1,100	355
1960-61	73	106	904,109	23,591	1,301½	291
Mental hospitals						
1945-46[c]	—	—	—	—	—	—
1950-51	11	12	70,226	8,806	Total 80½	
1955-56	10	10	72,704	7,026	105	65
1960-61	13	15	94,831	8,636	190½	127

aFigures missing from 11 hospitals.
bFigures missing from 1 hospital.
cStatistics not available.

Military libraries

During the first years of the war, library books began to be circulated to troops at various local installations. Since 1945, through the cooperation between the Armed Forces Welfare Service and the local public libraries, service has gradually been established at the larger military installations. Figures for this work first became available in 1949-50 and the development since then is shown in Table 4.

Table 4.   Libraries at military and civil defense installations

Year	Installations	Reading room visits	Circulation	Borrowers	Circulation of re-cordings	State grant
			volumes		records	kroner
1949-50	15	42,337	32,169	—	—	—
1950-51	27	68,758	52,685	—	—	—
1955-56	64	335,000	244,200	24,291	—	228,800
1960-61	81	400,000	277,351	25,716	2,656	260,849

Note: In 1950-51 trained civilian librarians served at 15 defense installations; in 1955-56 at 43 defense installations; and in 1960-61 at 44 defense installations. In 1960-61 seven installations had full-time, and three half-time, professionally trained librarians.

3 Full-time library development since 1945: finances

BACKGROUND

As a result of the changed attitude of both civil authorities and citizens towards public libraries, the finances of libraries have improved markedly in recent years. The earlier view was that public libraries were institutions with worthy and lofty intentions, but were of little practical importance in the daily life of the community. Public support for library affairs was expressed largely through the work of private associations. Libraries are today considered as necessary for the growth of the community as school and other educational, informational, and cultural institutions. This attitude is expressed by the current legislative provisions for the financial obligations of municipalities to the libraries. The change has been particularly noticeable since World War II, and more especially during the last five years, and has become so widespread today that it is rare to meet objections on principle to library appropriations from public funds. The sudden increase in financial support for libraries is, of course, also closely associated with the general economic development of the country.

Financial development of the full-time libraries since 1945 is shown in Tables 5 and 6.

Table 5. Finances of all full-time libraries per capita (in kroner)

Year	Total income	State grants	Municipal grants	Book funds	Salaries
1945-46	3.82	0.92	2.14	1.14	1.66
1950-51	6.54	2.06	3.64	1.95	3.06
1955-56	9.92	3.01	5.94	2.64	4.99
1960-61	15.59	4.77	9.49	3.99	8.23
Percent increase	300	430	344	250	396

Note: For general notes to this, and all the following tables in Part 1, see page 219.

Table 6. Finances of all full-time libraries per circulated volume (in kroner)

Year	Total income	State grants	Municipal grants	Book funds	Salaries
1945-46	0.75	0.18	0.42	0.22	0.33
1950-51	1.23	0.39	0.69	0.37	0.58
1955-56	1.33	0.40	0.79	0.35	0.66
1960-61	1.94	0.61	1.21	0.50	1.05
Percent increase	159	238	188	127	218

FINANCIAL FIGURES

Differences between the financial resources of the various types of libraries is not primarily due to differences in the quality of service among these groups, but rather to the basic differences in their function or type of service. The county libraries undertake special functions for part-time libraries within their regions, for example, while the larger full-time libraries perform extensive reference services. Smaller libraries concentrate to a greater extent on circulation work.

Total circulation figures can only be used with certain reservations in making comparisons between types of libraries. The most reliable library "production unit" is still the total number of volumes circulated. This figure makes comparisons of the general level of activity of libraries possible—but they must, of course, be libraries of the same type and relative size. Perhaps a more significant figure, especially for those libraries which are undergoing a period of rapid growth and development, as are many of the suburban libraries, would be the per capita circulation.

Differences in per capita book budgets and income reflect two types of libraries—libraries which have an inadequate collection which they are now attempting to enlarge, and libraries which already have a fairly adequate book collection. Libraries actively expanding their collections generally have larger per capita book budgets than libraries which already have adequate collections, because their book funds must cover enlarging the collection as well as maintaining it.

INCOME

In 1945-46, total financial resources (including municipal, state, and other grants; income from other sources; and the value of premises) were just under 8 million kroner. In 1960-61, this figure had increased to more than 41 million kroner (see Table 7). These figures include public and children's libraries, plus the children's and school library departments in elementary schools, as well as the income of county libraries from county liaison work. In this period, the total income increased more than 400 percent. The increase was greatest for the suburban libraries, least for the large city libraries.

The per capita increase, figured at a constant price level (based on the cost of living index of January 1, 1946), was 158 percent—3.82 to 9.87 kroner (see Table 8). The percentage increase was greatest in the large city libraries and least in the "other full-time libraries."

Total income per circulated volume calculated at the 1946 price level showed an increase of 64 percent—from 0.75 to 1.23 kroner (see Table 9). Again the increase was greatest in the large cities and was least in the "other full-time libraries." It is interesting to note that while the per capita income steadily increased, the income in the first half of the 1950's was not able to keep pace with the increase in circulation. Income per circulated volume in 1955-56 was less than in 1950-51.

Municipal grants

The home communities or municipalities are responsible for the operation of the municipal as well as the independent [society or association] libraries within their jurisdiction. For the municipal libraries they determine, within the legislative framework, both policies and extent of activities. They have some influence on the independent libraries because of their representation on the boards of these institutions, and also because of the dependence of these institutions on municipal appropriations. The municipalities cover the greater portion of the expenses of the full-time libraries. During the period from 1945 to 1960, the share of total library expenditures borne by these communities increased from 56.1 percent to 60.9 percent (see Table 10). (When the value of the premises, which are made available without charge to the libraries, are excluded, however, their share of the total library expenditures remained almost constant—64.8 percent in 1945-46, and 64.6 percent in 1960-61.)

29

Table 7. Finances of full-time libraries (in kroner)

Year	Total income	State grants	Municipal grants	Book funds	Salaries
All full-time libraries					
1945-46	7,816,969	1,874,861	4,386,451	2,335,429	3,404,040
1950-51	14,974,358	4,718,981	8,322,065	4,453,576	7,007,870
1955-56	24,806,238	7,525,547	14,841,629	6,611,159	12,468,031
1960-61	41,290,331	12,636,787	25,153,640	10,572,637	21,806,039
Percent increase	428	574	473	353	541
County libraries (less Gentofte)					
1945-46	3,387,781	948,608	1,711,224	1,091,390	1,420,011
1950-51	6,835,451	2,456,029	3,402,309	2,017,031	3,114,005
1955-56	10,702,335	3,384,512	5,963,650	2,963,076	5,301,799
1960-61	16,968,385	5,868,970	9,216,006	4,270,253	9,085,996
Percent increase	401	519	439	291	540
Large city libraries (Copenhagen + Frederiksberg + Gentofte)					
1945-46	2,881,564	447,854	1,917,385	737,281	1,405,302
1950-51	5,220,866	1,205,036	3,468,382	1,461,138	2,665,605
1955-56	8,444,044	1,748,685	5,669,478	1,861,493	4,600,200
1960-61	12,471,781	3,178,118	8,555,443	2,655,169	7,030,466
Percent increase	333	610	346	260	400
Suburban libraries					
1945-46	594,398	174,006	331,720	195,545	246,793
1950-51	1,482,208	489,776	824,257	508,692	616,524
1955-56	3,023,140	882,443	1,948,303	952,625	1,387,208
1960-61	7,216,031	1,932,743	4,892,451	2,265,165	3,439,239
Percent increase	1,114	1,011	1,375	1,058	1,294
Other full-time libraries					
1945-46	953,226	304,393	426,122	311,213	331,934
1950-51	1,435,833	568,140	627,117	466,715	611,736
1955-56	2,636,719	995,309	1,260,198	833,965	1,178,824
1960-61	4,634,134	1,656,956	2,489,740	1,382,050	2,250,338
Percent increase	386	444	484	344	578

Table 8. Finances of all full-time libraries per capita at 1946 price levels.
(Price index January 1, 1946 = 100)

(in kroner)

Year	Total income	State grants	Municipal grants	Book funds	Salaries
1945-46	3.82	0.92	2.14	1.14	1.66
1950-51	5.50	1.73	3.06	1.64	2.58
1955-56	6.75	2.14	4.21	1.87	3.54
1960-61	9.87	3.02	6.01	2.53	5.21
Percent increase	158	228	181	121	214

Table 9. Finances of all full-time libraries per circulated volume
at 1946 price level. (Price index January 1, 1946 = 100)

(in kroner)

Year	Total income	State grants	Municipal grants	Book funds	Salaries
1945-46	0.75	0.18	0.42	0.22	0.33
1950-51	1.03	0.33	0.58	0.31	0.49
1955-56	0.94	0.28	0.56	0.25	0.47
1960-61	1.23	0.39	0.77	0.32	0.66
Percent increase	64	117	83	45	100

In the large city libraries, the municipal grants (excluding value of the premises) in 1945-46 made up 66.5 percent of all income, and in "other full-time libraries," the home municipalities' share was 44.7 percent, or more than 20 percent less than in the large libraries. In 1960-61, however, the difference had decreased to 15 percent.

The total grants from the municipalities to the full-time libraries increased from 4.4 million kroner in 1945-46 to somewhat over 25 million kroner in 1960-61, or 473 percent. Per capita (at 1946 prices), the municipal grants rose from 2.14 to 6.01 kroner, or 181 percent. Per circulated volume, the increase was 83 percent—0.42 to 0.77 kroner. (See Tables 7, 8, and 9.) The value of the premises is not included in these figures.

State grants
In 1945-46 state grants made up 24 percent of the income of full-time libraries. In 1960-61, this share increased to 30.6 percent. During the

Table 10. Finances of full-time libraries—sources of income (percent)

Year	State grants	Municipal grants	Value of premises	All other income
All full-time libraries				
1945-46	24.0	56.1	8.7	11.2
1950-51	31.5	55.6	6.8	6.1
1955-56	30.3	59.8	3.9	6.0
1960-61	30.6	60.9	3.7	4.8
County libraries (less Gentofte)				
1945-46	28.0	50.5	7.8	13.7
1950-51	35.9	49.8	5.6	8.7
1955-56	31.6	55.7	4.2	8.5
1960-61	34.6	54.3	4.8	6.3
Large city libraries (Copenhagen + Frederiksberg + Gentofte)				
1945-46	15.5	66.5	8.4	9.6
1950-51	23.1	66.4	7.4	3.1
1955-56	20.7	67.1	2.8	9.4
1960-61	25.5	68.6	2.7	3.2
Suburban libraries				
1945-46	29.3	55.8	12.0	2.9
1950-51	33.0	55.6	9.5	1.9
1955-56	29.2	64.4	4.2	2.2
1960-61	26.8	67.8	3.6	1.8
Other full-time libraries				
1945-46	31.9	44.7	9.5	13.9
1950-51	39.6	43.7	6.8	9.9
1955-56	37.7	47.8	5.6	8.9
1960-61	35.8	53.7	4.0	6.5

entire period, this percentage was greatest for the smallest libraries (the "other full-time libraries"), even though the county libraries received special grants for their county library department work in addition to the general state grants. (See Table 10.)

State grants to the full-time libraries in 1945-46 amounted to 1.8 million, and in 1960-61, to 12.6 million kroner, an increase of just under 600 percent. Per capita (at 1946 prices), the state grants increased from 0.92 to 3.02 kroner, and per circulated volume, the figures were 0.18 and 0.39 kroner. (See Tables 7, 8, and 9.)

In addition to the state grants proper, total state expenditures for public library activities include the so-called availability fund, and from 1959-60 on, special funds for reimbursing expenditures for equipment made in connection with new construction or extensive remodeling. In 1960-61, 372,246 kroner were expended from the availability fund, and the reimbursements for equipment amounted to 583,450 kroner.

EXPENSES

For all practical purposes, total expenses during the period from 1945 to 1961 were the same as total income. During the entire period, the largest items were salaries and book funds. In 1945-46, salaries constituted 43.5 percent of the expenses of the full-time libraries. In 1960-61 the percentage increased to 52.8. The book funds fell from 29.9 percent in 1945-46 to 25.6 percent in 1960-61, while payments for premises and all other expenses fell from 26.6 percent to 21.6 percent. (See Table 11.)

Salaries

The total expenditures for salaries increased from 3.4 million kroner in 1945-46, to 21.8 million kroner in 1960-61, or 540 percent. Per capita (at 1946 price levels), salaries increased from 1.66 to 5.21 kroner, or 214 percent. Per circulated volume, the figures are 0.33 and 0.66 kroner, or an increase of 100 percent (see Tables 7, 8, and 9). It cannot be determined how much of the latter increase is due (1) to the total increase in real wages of staff members, (2) to changed categories of staff, (3) to the allocation to other library work of an increasing share of total work time at the expense of circulation duties, or (4) to increased staff time (including advising readers) per circulated volume as a result of the change in the pattern of circulation discussed previously.

Book budget

Although the book budget's percentage share of the total expenditures declined during the entire period, its total amount increased from 2.3 million to 10.5 million kroner, or 350 percent. In terms of 1946 prices, the book budget per capita increased from 1.14 to 2.53 kroner, or 121 percent. The figures per circulated volume were 0.22 and 0.32 kroner, or an increase of 45 percent (see Tables 7, 8, and 9). There is no special price index for books and binding, therefore it is not possible to determine if prices for these items have increased more or less than the general cost of living index. If the increases in prices for books and binding

Table 11. **Finances of full-time libraries—distribution of total expenses (percent)**

Year	Book funds	Salaries	Rent and other expenses
All full-time libraries			
1945-46	29.9	43.5	26.6
1950-51	29.7	46.8	23.5
1955-56	26.7	50.3	23.0
1960-61	25.6	52.8	21.6
County libraries (less Gentofte)			
1945-46	32.2	41.9	25.9
1950-51	29.5	45.6	24.9
1955-56	27.7	49.5	22.8
1960-61	25.2	53.5	21.3
Large city libraries (Copenhagen + Frederiksberg + Gentofte)			
1945-46	25.6	48.8	25.6
1950-51	28.0	51.1	20.9
1955-56	22.0	54.5	23.5
1960-61	21.3	56.4	22.3
Suburban libraries			
1945-46	32.9	41.5	25.6
1950-51	34.3	41.6	24.1
1955-56	31.4	45.9	22.7
1960-61	31.4	47.7	20.9
Other full-time libraries			
1945-46	32.6	34.8	32.6
1950-51	32.5	42.6	24.9
1955-56	31.6	44.7	23.7
1960-61	29.8	48.6	21.6

considered together follow the general price index, however, the increase for books per volume circulated, converted to the same price level at the beginning and end of the period, indicates the actual improvement in the book budget. Substantial increases in book budgets are, of course, becoming increasingly necessary for making more diversified purchases and for a general quantitative and qualitative improvement of the book stock.

VARIATIONS BETWEEN LIBRARIES OF THE SAME TYPE

All the financial figures cited are averages, either for all the full-time libraries, or for one of the four groups of these, collectively. They therefore do not indicate the minimum and maximum sums necessary to maintain and enlarge libraries in the individual municipalities. Table 12 shows the per capita book and salary budgets for those libraries which in 1960-61 had both the lowest and highest book and salary budgets. The table also shows the per capita circulation for the same libraries. It includes suburban and "other full-time libraries," and the figures cover children's and public libraries together.

The figures show wide variations in library support, and also an apparent connection between the financial support of the library and its degree of use. For all five of the libraries with the lowest book and salary budgets (one has both), service, as judged by per capita circulation, was inadequate.

Table 12. **Per capita circulation in libraries with highest and lowest per capita book and salary budgets — 1960-61**

3 libraries with lowest book budget		3 libraries with highest book budget	
Book budget per capita	Circulation per capita	Book budget per capita	Circulation per capita
kroner	volumes	kroner	volumes
1.55	2.62	8.27	10.20
1.68	5.16	7.12	11.71
1.73	4.27	6.86	11.08
3 libraries with lowest salary budget		**3 libraries with highest salary budget**	
Salary per capita	Circulation per capita	Salary per capita	Circulation per capita
kroner	volumes	kroner	volumes
2.42	5.37	13.36	11.33
2.48	2.62	12.81	8.64
3.08	4.88	11.59	9.64

Source: *Bogens Verden*, 1961, pp. 272-73.

4 Development of full-time libraries since 1945: staff

SIZE AND COMPOSITION OF STAFF

Statistics for the staffs of the full-time libraries are available from 1949 on. The size and composition of the staffs of these libraries prior to 1949 are not recorded.

As of April 1, 1949, a total of 791 staff units (staff units are defined as full-time equivalents, excluding janitorial and maintenance staff) were employed in the 70 public libraries which then had full-time staffs. Of these, 390 were librarian, 155 were trainee, and 246 were "other staff" units. ("Other staff" includes trained clerical staff, pages, messengers, etc.) As of April 1, 1961, a total of 1,355 staff units were employed in the 94 libraries then having a full-time staff. Of these, 661 were librarian, 94 trainee, and 600 "other staff" units. The size and distribution of staff from 1949 to 1961 is illustrated in Table 13.

The change from 1949 to 1961 has not been uniform, either in regard to the total size of the staff, or to the proportion of the staff made up by the three categories of librarians, trainees, and "others."

In the four years from 1949 to 1953, the total staff increased by 94 units, or 12 percent, while during the four years from 1956 to 1960, the total staff increased by 303 units, or 30 percent.

From 1949 to 1953, the proportion of librarians on the staff rose from 49.3 to 55.6 percent. The proportion of trainees fell from 19.6 percent to 14.7 percent, and "other staff" from 31.1 percent to 29.7 percent during the same period.

A marked change took place after 1955. The proportion of librarians fell from 55.5 percent in 1956 to 48.8 percent in 1961. At the same time,

Table 13. Staff of full-time libraries

Year	Number of libraries	Librar-ians (staff units)	Library trainees (persons)	trainees (staff units)	"Other" (staff units)	Total (staff units)	Percentage composition of staff (librar-ians)	(trainees)	("other")
1949	70	390	155	155	246	791	49.3	19.6	31.1
1950	74	419	153	153	214	785	53.3	19.5	27.2
1951	74	445	168	168	236	849	52.5	19.8	27.7
1952	74	472	160	160	251	883	53.4	18.1	28.5
1953	74	492	130	130	263	885	55.6	14.7	29.7
1954	76	538	—	—	—	—	—	—	—
1955	76	534	96	96	317	947	56.4	10.2	33.4
1956	86	561	119	119	332	1,012	55.5	11.8	32.7
1957	89	610	131	61	426	1,097	55.6	5.6	38.8
1958	90	616	147	70	475	1,161	53.1	6.0	40.9
1959	91	633	169	81	493	1,207	52.4	6.7	40.9
1960	92	655	187	89	570	1,315	49.8	6.8	43.4
1961	94	661	198	94	600	1,355	48.8	6.9	44.3

the figures for the trainees went from 11.8 percent down to 6.9 percent. The "other staff" rose from 32.7 percent to 44.3 percent during those years.

This development has been far from uniform in the different types of libraries, but the overall trend is clear. The total staff employed increased more rapidly in the latter half of the period than in the first. This is due only in part to the fact that the total number of libraries with full-time staff increased more rapidly during that time.

Of the total increase of 24 full-time libraries from 1949 to 1961, 15 were "other full-time libraries," while 9 were suburban. For the suburban libraries, this led to a doubling of the number of librarians and, as could be expected, these libraries also show the comparatively largest increase in total staff—from 50 to 210, or 320 percent.

The largest staffs are, of course, in the county libraries and the large city libraries. The 41 "other full-time libraries" in 1961 had a total staff of 141, or only one-third of the 423 persons employed in the libraries of Greater Copenhagen (Copenhagen, Frederiksberg, and Gentofte) alone. Thus most of the "other full-time libraries" are quite small. In 1949, they had an average staff of only 2.9, and in 1961, this figure was still only 3.4. In 1949, only 7 of the 26 "other full-time libraries" had more than two librarians, and 15 had only one. In 1961, these figures were 6 (with more than two librarians), and 22 (with only one librarian), out of a total of 41 "other full-time libraries."

The distribution of the three classes of staff: librarians, trainees, and "others," shows a wide variation among the different types of libraries. The three libraries of Greater Copenhagen have gone through a development quite unlike that of the other libraries. Their percentage of librarians has sometimes been more and sometimes less than that of "other staff." None of the other libraries has, at any time, had more "other staff" than librarians.

The proportion of librarians on the staff showed the greatest change in the suburban and "other full-time libraries." In 1955, in both of these groups librarians made up 76.8 percent of the total. By 1962, this percentage had been reduced to 52.6 for the suburban, and 57.8 percent for the "other full-time libraries."

Over the same period, "other staff" in county libraries as well as in suburban and "other full-time libraries" increased from between 20 and 25 percent to more than 40 percent.

It is only possible to guess about the causes affecting the changes in the distribution of staff among the various categories, but it would not be entirely wrong to assume a connection between the increasing proportion of librarians on the staffs during the period from 1949 to 1955 and low salaries and unemployment among librarians in general. These factors tended to increase the availability of librarians and to decrease their cost to the library. The declining number of trainees during the same period was probably also a factor.

Discussions began as early as the 1930's about the desirability of allocating different types of staff for different kinds of library work, but the idea advanced slowly. Still, it should be noted that, while in most libraries during the mid-1930's, the percentage of librarians on the staff was often almost 100, by the end of the 1940's it had dropped to about 50. The proportion of librarians began to again increase, however, during the first half of the 1950's, and the problem of work distribution once more became a subject of discussion and study. An added factor was that during the last half of the 1950's the shortage of librarians became increasingly acute. One can assume that ideas about a "proper" distribution of staff and the shortage of librarians are together the main reasons why the proportion of librarians on the total staff has again declined in recent years. In many instances, the persistence of professional staff vacancies has forced the employment of nonprofessionals for these positions, and this has been coupled with deliberate attempts by libraries to employ nonprofessional personnel in positions formerly held by professionals.

Whatever the reasons, the percentage of librarians in 1960 was again down to about that of 1949.

What is more significant is that a definite distinction has now been made between trained librarians, library trainees, and "other staff." The Swedish work simplification study provided, for the first time, a complete review of the work done by the "other staff" members.

As of January 1, 1962, the staff of 95 of the 96 full-time public libraries could be divided into more closely defined classes (see Table 14). (One county library did not answer the questionnaire upon which this information is based and its staff is not included in the presentation.)

The table shows that on January 1, 1962, in the 95 full-time libraries the personnel units consisted of: 696 1/42 trained librarians or persons serving as trained librarians (categories 1 and 3), 95 library trainees (category 4a), and 616 19/42 other staff. [The fractional figures are due to the fact that staff units are given in terms of full-time equivalents.] The percentage distribution of these categories was: librarians or persons

Table 14. Staff in 95 of 96 full-time libraries as of January 1, 1962

	Full-time equivalent staff units	Percent
1. Librarians	678$\frac{9}{42}$	48.2
2. Unfilled librarian positions	24	—
3. Persons with only partial library training, or none (excluding library trainees themselves), who serve as librarians	17$\frac{34}{42}$	1.3
4. Library trainees	204	—
4a. Library trainees converted to full-time equivalents	95	6.7
5. Trainees (from 4) attending basic courses at library school	71	—
6. Clerical staff with at least 3 years training	198$\frac{3}{42}$	14.1
7. Clerical staff (from 6) trained in the libraries	96$\frac{24}{42}$	—
8. Persons without office training who work as clerical staff	59$\frac{10}{42}$	4.2
9. Clerical trainees	94$\frac{20}{42}$	6.7
10. Assistants, messengers, pages	222$\frac{32}{42}$	15.8
11. Janitors, drivers	25$\frac{24}{42}$	1.8
12. Cloakroom attendants	16$\frac{14}{42}$	1.2
Total (less 2, 4, 5, and 7)	1,407$\frac{20}{42}$	100.0

Source: Questionnaire sent to all full-time libraries by the Work Simplification Committee in January, 1962.

serving as librarians 49.5 percent, trainees 6.7 percent, and "other staff" 43.8 percent. If persons who served as librarians, but who had no training, or only partial training, for the position (excluding library trainees themselves) are not included, the percentage of librarians becomes 48.2.

The 43.8 percent "other staff" consisted of clerical staff (18.3 percent), clerical trainees (6.7 percent), assistants, messengers, and pages (15.8 percent), and custodial staff (3.0 percent).

STAFF IN RELATION TO POPULATION AND CIRCULATION

The population served by individual libraries (non-resident regions of the county libraries not included) in relation to the number of staff members varies widely. This also applies to circulation. These variations depend upon the effectiveness of the staff, the organization of the work, and the services provided by the library.

It is not possible to give completely reliable figures for circulation either per member of the entire staff, or per librarian. If the figures were to be based on total circulation, this would mean that loans would be included which are handled by school librarians (who are not included in the total staff). If the figures were to be based on a circulation figure which excluded classroom sets and the circulation from children's departments handled by school librarians ("net loans"), the remaining figures would be distorted by such work of the children's departments as technical processing (purchasing, accession, binding, cataloging), and by administration work, all of which is done by staff who would thereby be included in the total number of personnel. The "actual" circulation per member of the entire staff and per librarian is somewhere between "total circulation" and "net circulation" (the figures for these are given in Table 15).

In 1960-61, each member of the staff in the full-time libraries had an average of 2,000 persons to serve, and each librarian about 4,000. The "actual" number of volumes circulated ranged between 13,000 and 16,000 per member of the entire staff and between 25,000 and 30,000 per librarian.

Table 15 shows that circulation per member of the entire staff was highest in the "other full-time libraries" and the suburban libraries. This is probably one reason why these libraries could not spare staff for reference and advisory work to the extent that the large city libraries could.

Circulation per librarian was highest in the large city libraries which, presumably because of their size, are able to make the most effective use of the working time of the librarians. Still, it should be noted that these libraries also show the lowest per capita circulation.

Table 15. Total staff and librarians in relation to population and circulation

Year	Population served		Total circulation (in volumes)		Net circulation (in volumes)		Per capita circulation (in volumes)
	Per staff member	Per librarian	Per staff member	Per librarian	Per staff member	Per librarian	
All full-time libraries							
1950-51	2,910	5,470	15,480	29,010	13,540	25,390	5.0
1955-56	2,640	4,680	19,830	35,150	16,420	29,110	7.6
1960-61	2,050	4,040	15,850	30,800	12,780	25,630	7.5
County libraries (less Gentofte)							
1950-51	2,270	4,160	14,340	26,260	12,160	22,270	5.6
1955-56	2,060	3,430	17,710	29,520	14,700	24,510	7.7
1960-61	1,640	3,300	14,510	29,530	11,910	24,250	7.8
Large city libraries							
1950-51	3,480	7,490	15,730	33,830	14,630	31,500	4.5
1955-56	2,680	6,240	18,750	43,660	15,740	36,650	7.0
1960-61	2,210	4,850	15,160	33,260	12,200	26,770	6.8
Suburban libraries							
1950-51	3,980	6,050	17,770	27,060	15,180	22,910	4.5
1955-56	4,100	5,340	26,320	34,300	21,450	27,920	6.4
1960-61	2,340	4,300	17,800	32,840	14,410	26,510	7.6
Other full-time libraries							
1950-51	3,110	5,090	18,300	29,370	15,030	24,120	5.8
1955-56	4,150	5,390	29,750	38,730	23,830	30,990	7.2
1960-61	2,590	4,340	20,630	34,680	15,860	26,570	8.0

Note: All figures except those for volumes circulated per capita are rounded off to the nearest amount divisible by 10. Total circulation includes circulation to adults and children, loans of class sets, and non-resident loans of the county libraries including individual and deposit loans to part-time libraries. "Net circulation" excludes class set loans and loans from children's libraries where circulation work is done by school librarians. Source: applications for state grants and questionnaire from State Library Inspection to individual libraries during April, 1962.

The figures in Table 15 also reveal that in 1960-61, all libraries had a significantly lower population to serve per member of entire staff and per librarian than in 1950-51. This was undoubtedly one of the factors that resulted in the improvement in service during the period.

41

5 Work simplification efforts since 1920

Methods of work in the public libraries have remained extraordinarily stable and difficult to change over the years. Except for the recent introduction of photocharging in some libraries, it is correct to say that only slight modifications have been made in work methods during the last 30 to 40 years.

Only in recent years have work simplification efforts in public libraries become generally recognized as useful and necessary. This does not mean that changes in working methods were not proposed and discussed earlier. A few pioneer advocates of work simplification continued to make suggestions even though they were seldom accepted and carried out; or if they were, only at an agonizingly slow pace.

The history of work simplification will be considered mainly in four areas: cataloging and other technical processing work, circulation methods, standardization, and work distribution.

Work simplification in cataloging and other technical processing work will be discussed in Chapter 6 in connection with Bibliotekscentralen as these activities form an important part of the early history of that organization.

CIRCULATION METHODS

The oldest circulation system in the public libraries is the "circulation ledger" system. In this system, each borrower had his own page in a record book where the call numbers of the books borrowed were entered. Lines were drawn through these numbers when the books were returned.

42

It is not possible to determine exactly when the Newark system was introduced, but this system was already in general use when the Detroit system appeared in 1930.

In its original form, the Newark system consists of stamping a date slip already in the book, date stamping the borrower's card (one stamp for each book), and date stamping and writing the borrower's number on the book card. The book cards are then sorted and placed in the circulation file. When the books are returned, the book cards are replaced in the books before they are shelved, and the borrower's card is stamped in the date due column. This system originated in 1890, and is a simplification of a previous system which also included writing the call number on the borrower's card.

In the Detroit system, the borrower's card is used only for identification. The patron writes his number on the book card. The book, the borrower's card, and the book card with the borrower's number filled in are shown at the loan desk for verification, where cards or slips already stamped with the due date are placed in the books. The book cards are then arranged as in the Newark system. When the books are returned, the book cards are replaced in the books and the date due cards are removed. No stamping is done at the loan counter in charging or discharging.

In the 1930's, there were lengthy discussions about the relative merits of the Newark and Detroit systems. In 1931, the Detroit system was introduced in Gentofte, with the modification, however, of continuing to stamp a date slip which had already been placed in the book prior to the transaction. Later Gentofte returned to the Newark system, and the Detroit system apparently was used in only a few places. Variations of both systems came into use, but the Newark system with its variants appears to have predominated. Advocates of the Newark system have emphasized its ability to prove whether or not books have actually been returned. Supporters of the Detroit system state that the security of the Newark system is probably no greater in practice than that of the Detroit system, and that the Detroit system releases librarians from circulation duty more often, thus allowing them more time for helping readers.

It is not possible to report how many main circulation departments of the full-time libraries currently use the Newark and Detroit systems. For one thing, variations of these systems are too prevalent.

The introduction of photocharging in 1958 at the main library in Copenhagen, after several years of use in American and British libraries, was the next innovation in the circulation systems used in Denmark. As of January 1, 1962, four libraries had introduced photocharging in the main adult departments.

Other circulation systems were divided as follows: 72 libraries used pasted-in date slips, and 19 used loose date cards. In charging out books, 73 libraries stamped the date slip or date card, 71 stamped the book card, and 34 stamped the borrower's card (some of these libraries, of course, used various combinations of these systems). In 21 large and medium-size libraries, stamping routines at the main circulation desk for adults have been discontinued. (Included among these 21 libraries are the four with photocharging systems.)

STANDARDIZATION

Except for the adoption of more or less uniform catalog rules and the use of printed catalog cards, standardization in the public libraries really only began with the appointment in 1938 of the Standardization Committee of the Danish Library Association.

The tasks of the Standardization Committee since its appointment have been:

1. To work out standard regulations so that the rights and obligations of the patrons of all libraries may conform with the provisions of the library law.

From 1957 to 1961, the Committee worked on a new edition of the model library regulations. This work was greatly delayed by the legislative action amending the library law in 1959 and the subsequent revision of the pertinent ministerial directive in 1961. In 1961, the Committee ceased to operate directly under the Danish Library Association and became responsible to Bibliotekscentralen.

2. To work out standard rules for library statistics as the basis for making comparisons between libraries and for the nationwide collection of library statistics.

The present rules for keeping library statistics are undoubtedly too detailed, and have unfortunately resulted in the accumulation of much unnecessary statistical data. They must be simplified.

3. To work out standardized forms to be produced and sold to libraries through a central agency (Bibliotekscentralen) in order to save the individual libraries much time and expense by centralizing the production and sale of these forms.

During the first decade of the Committee's work, 43 forms were standardized. In 1953, the Danish Standards Committee published DS 912 "Basic Principles of the Design of (Document) Forms," thereby providing the DLA Standardization Committee with a basis for revision and coordination so that its works could be brought into line with a standard, modern design of documents better suited for use with typewriters. Since 1955, the Standardization Committee has designed many new standardized forms and revised several of the old. By 1961 the number of forms standardized had increased to 58, and included most of the forms in general use and several that are used less frequently.

WORK DISTRIBUTION

During the discussions about circulation systems held some 35 years ago, the employment of non-librarians for routine circulation work was frequently mentioned. Dissenting voices were not lacking, but when Thomas Døssing suggested, in 1932, that the Gentofte City Library should divide routine circulation work and advice to readers by staffing the circulation desk with non-library trained personnel, the suggestion was promptly put into practice in that library. The circulation desk was moved to another part of the public service area and the librarians then had more time to devote to reader's advisory work. In the main building of the Frederiksberg City Library in 1935, one of the basic ideas behind the layout and design of the circulation, reading, and reference rooms was the functional separation of professional assistance from routine control activities. The Frederiksberg example had a great influence on librarians—even more than Gentofte.

In a talk entitled "Work Simplification in Libraries," given at the Scandinavian Library Meeting at Oslo in 1933, Thomas Døssing advocated the increased use of staff without library training. He said:

"Such a division of work can also be carried out in the public libraries, at least in the larger ones with a staff of more than three or four persons. Three categories of staff may be distinguished:

"1. Staff with library training for book selection, supervision of cataloging, classification, reference service in circulation and reading rooms, etc.

"2. Clerical staff for book ordering, bookkeeping, routine cataloging work, compiling statistics, correspondence, etc.

"3. Staff for the routine tasks of circulation control and for filing, shelving, etc.

"Of course in the larger libraries there is a fourth category of janitorial and maintenance staff.

"Some of the work done by categories 2 and 3 is of such a nature that it is unnecessary, even unfeasible, that it be done by trained librarians; but it must be emphasized that in a small installation, where the entire staff must necessarily come in contact with the public, such a separation of duties obviously cannot and should not be carried out."

The first attempts to divide all library work operations into categories according to the qualifications required to perform the tasks did not attract great attention. The campaign against librarians doing clerical work, begun by Georg Krogh-Jensen in 1937, was also received without widespread comment. In 1954, Sigurd Möhlenbrock made a report on the work simplication study of the Norrköping Public Library, in which he referred to the Swedish adaptation by A. Waldner of the American Library Association's *Descriptive List of Professional and Nonprofessional Duties in Libraries*. [Preliminary draft. Prepared by the Subcommittee on Analysis of Library Duties of the A.L.A. Board on Personnel Administration. Chicago, 1948. Mimeographed.], and since that time work simplification has received increasing attention.

In 1949, librarians made up about 50 percent of the total staff of the full-time libraries and this proportion, after increasing up to 1955, was, by 1960, again about 50 percent. The demand for dividing circulation work by separating routine control activities from reader's advisory work has resulted in the fact that, as of January 1, 1962, special advisory service points or "information desks" staffed by librarians were provided in the main circulation section for adults in 35 of the 94 full-time libraries from which data was received. However, it should be noted that not all of these 35 libraries have worked out a really effective division between the advisory and control aspects of circulation, that none of the smallest full-time libraries have an "information desk," and that in cities of more than 30,000 population, 5 of 18 libraries do not maintain such desks.

To summarize, it may be said that work simplification was discussed actively during the early 1930's and that this discussion was primarily concerned with circulation methods and the allocation of work associated with these methods. Actual work on the standardization of library forms started in 1938. About 1955, the basis for standardized library forms was noticeably improved, and, at about the same time, interest in work simplification became more intense, inspired particularly by the work being done in Sweden. At the annual meeting of the Danish Library Association in 1959, there was much discussion about work simplification, and the deliberations at this meeting led directly to the appointment of the Work Simplification Committee.

It is, however, no exaggeration to conclude that the debates on work simplification prior to 1959 produced extremely modest results.

6 Bibliotekscentralen

EARLY HISTORY

Before the establishment of Bibliotekscentralen (under another name) in 1939, developments in the field of technical services were characterized by many idealistic and well-meaning proposals and efforts, few events of great significance, and reluctance among libraries to affiliate in an attempt to find joint solutions for problems of cataloging and other technical services.

The earliest event of importance in the effective development of library technical processing was the creation of a common classification system and common catalog rules for the public libraries during the years prior to 1920, just as the formation of modern public library service was getting underway within the country. In 1913, the first edition of the author table appeared; in 1915, the first edition of the Danish Decimal Classification (DDC) was issued; and in 1917, the first catalog rules were published. This foundation for the organization and cataloging of the collections of public libraries was largely the creation of Thomas Døssing. Today, it is difficult to imagine what difficulties a delay in the establishment of this common base could have meant for the progress of cooperation in the field of library technical processing. However, the degree of dissension during the past 25 years over the relative merits of the alphabetical and classified subject catalogs, and whether author or title marks should be done away with, gives some indication of what could have happened if the development of our large libraries had begun with individual classification systems and cataloging rules.

Starting in 1916, the DDC has been used in the Danish national bibliography, *Dansk bogfortegnelse,* from which it was a logical, if somewhat daring, idea to extend the common foundation for classification and cataloging by mass-producing printed catalog cards for common use by the public libraries. This was attempted in 1916 by the publishing firm of G. E. C. Gads, and cards were made available on a subscription basis through the State Library Committee. The project, however, was discontinued in 1917 after some months of operation.

During the reorganization of the libraries of North Schleswig following the return of this territory from Germany in 1920, printed catalog cards were produced for a short time by the State Library Inspection.

It proved to be a single library, however, which carried out the pioneer work of centralized catalog card production. In 1928, the printed cards of the Gentofte City Library were made available for purchase through the Library Supplies Section of the Danish Library Association, and, since that time printed cards have been continuously available. However, this did not mean that a complete breakthrough for the principle of cooperation and standardization was made in 1928.

An excerpt from a spirited article by Jørgen Banke in *Bogens Verden* in 1929 gives some impression of the lack of interest which characterized the reception of this kind of reform by most libraries:

"When library staff members at meetings all over the country have tried to present the ideas of the modern library movement to the public, there have been many discussions in which one person or another has taken the floor to ask how our catalog cards are produced.

"The answer is always that each individual library makes its own cards. This always causes great surprise as every layman can see immediately how uneconomical and what a waste of time this is.

"Therefore it is very embarrassing when explaining how profitably and economically our library organization can work when we cooperate from top to bottom, we must go on to reveal that cooperation concerning the card catalog is totally lacking, when the latter should so obviously be a work of centralized production, distribution, and storage.

"The situation became even more distressing after January 1, 1928, because it was then decided that the problem was solved; but as it turned out, most of the libraries did not make use of the centrally produced cards available after this date.

"This solution to a problem which has been debated for 15 years, has somehow again suddenly slipped out of the picture. Individual cataloging goes on, and tray after tray continues to be filled with handwritten or typed cards without a murmur of dissent."

Why has the development of centralized cataloging been so slow? It could be pointed out that every reform which requires a change of attitude on the part of individual libraries and local and regional library associations has been slow to gain ground. At any rate, the attitude of conservatism has prevailed, and it has been difficult to convince librarians of the necessity for reforms which would release staff members in the individual libraries for duties demanding a more personal involvement with the library public.

In areas other than classification and cataloging, the decades of the 1920's and 1930's were also marked by pioneer work in activities which were later brought together under Bibliotekscentralen.

During this period the Association of County Librarians published printed catalogs intended for use in more than one library. In 1923, the first edition appeared of the list of recommended books for smaller libraries, *Bogfortegnelse for mindre biblioteker,* and, in 1927, the first edition of the list of recommended books for larger libraries, *Faelleskatalog for større købstad-biblioteker.*

The sale of library supplies had been started before 1920 by the Association of Popular Libraries in Denmark and included stamps, forms, cabinets, and the like. In 1921, this activity was taken over by the Library Supplies Section of the Danish Library Association.

The idea of establishing an institution in which the centralized production and sale of supplies to the libraries could be handled was advanced in various ways during the 20 years prior to the establishment of the organization which later became known as Bibliotekscentralen. In 1920, Jørgen Banke proposed that the Library Supplies Section become a "library cooperative society" which would sell supplies, solve the problem of printed cards, publish standard catalogs, and oversee the basic collection of books to form the nucleus of new libraries. Working capital was to be guaranteed by the sale of subscriptions to participating libraries. Only 85 libraries supported the plan, however, and it was abandoned.

In 1933, Thomas Døssing suggested a purchasing and binding enterprise which (1) would be authorized by the libraries to undertake centralized purchasing for two-thirds of their book budgets, and through such large purchases to obtain special discounts, (2) would bind such purchased books centrally, thereby achieving economies by large volume operation, and (3) would also produce and sell printed cards and standard catalogs. It is not clear, however, whether Døssing had intended that all these tasks be carried out by one institution.

In 1935, Åge Bredsted replied to the negative attitude towards centralized cataloging and production of printed cards—which was usually stated as, "No, I don't agree because the problem is not solved in the way I would like it to be"—with the slogan, "A task done for one of us is, at the same time, done for all of us." Bredsted himself considered his suggestion of setting up a Danish Bibliographic Institute as impractical at that time, but pointed out that many problems could be solved eventually by such an institute. The same data, he said, could be used to prepare the national bibliography, printed cards, standard catalogs, and book lists. Such an institute could also, he pointed out, serve bookstores as well as libraries.

These and other such ideas were utopian, however, because of the prevailing lack of cooperation between libraries and the shortage of operating funds. Thomas Døssing's idea of retaining 2½ percent of the total state grants to the public libraries as an availability fund to solve common library and bibliographical problems, and the implementation of this idea in 1937, led to the further development of cooperation in processing activities among libraries. The establishment of this fund was one of the most significant events in this area of librarianship since the establishment of the common classification system and cataloging rules.

After the availability fund became a fact the road was clear for the events which led directly to the founding of Bibliotekscentralen. In 1937, the State Library Inspection took over preparation of the printed catalog cards and the stock of 200,000 cards from the Gentofte City Library, and, in 1939, the Bibliographical Center for Public Libraries was established for the purpose of "carrying out bibliographical work of particular concern to the public libraries, including advice on cataloging and classification."

BIBLIOTEKSCENTRALEN AND INDBINDINGSCENTRALEN

The Bibliographical Center for Public Libraries (FBK) began its work April 1, 1939. Its activities during the first years were limited to issuing publications intended for library patrons and staff. The main part of its production consisted of standard (and other) catalogs, but during the first year of operation an advanced copy of the third edition of the Danish Decimal Classification was also issued. It was only an administrative formality that limited FBK's activity to issuing publications. E. Allerslev Jensen was the first chief of the FBK, and as he was at the same time head of the Section for Printed Cards of the State Library Inspection, and because this section and the FBK shared the same quarters, the activities of the two organizations became fully coordinated. In 1942, the Section for Printed Cards was formally made a part of the FBK.

The next expansion was in 1944 when the FBK took over the then defunct Library Supplies Section of the Danish Library Association, which had earlier functioned autonomously. This sales organization handled various supplies, forms, and pamphlets.

In 1949, the FBK was enlarged to include a department for the centralized binding of library books. The actual binding was done at the Edvard Pedersen Bindery, but the arrangements with the libraries were handled by the FBK. In 1957, the agreement with the bindery was changed to set up the partnership known as Indbindingscentralen.

As early as 1939, a committee of the DLA began to prepare and sell basic collections of books needed to form the nucleus of new libraries. This work was taken over by the FBK in 1950, and the books for the "start" libraries as they are called, were then bound through the centralized binding facility.

In 1954 the name of the FBK was changed to the Danish Bibliographical Office (DBK) because the activities were now extended to bibliographical work of interest to research and special libraries as well as to public libraries.

The latest expansion occurred in 1961 with the establishment of the new department for library furniture and equipment known as Inventarcentralen. This continuous expansion has resulted in changes in the articles of incorporation and the most recent enlargement also involved a change of name, this time (in 1963), to Bibliotekscentralen.

The expansion of Bibliotekscentralen and its predecessors has not been limited to the acquisition of new functions. As appears in Table 16, the total sales within each of the existing functions has also shown a very substantial increase over the years.

A closer scrutiny of the individual activities, however, reveals that increases in sales could have been much greater. The work of this organization has been hampered by two significant factors. The first has been the uncooperative attitude of the libraries towards finding common

Table 16. Bibliotekscentralen—sources of income (in 1,000 kroner)

Year	Subsidy from avail- ability fund	Sale of printed cards	Sale of publica- tions	Sale of supplies	Sale of equip- ment	Share of profit from Indbindings- centralen	Other Income
1939-40	9	—	19	—	—	—	—
1944-45	23	24	45	18	—	—	18
1949-50	54	57	104	35	—	—	17
1954-55	67	74	167	53	—	39	5
1959-60	169	118	289	95	—	119	77
1963-64	320	263	778	265	1,321	83	169

Source: *Biblioteksårbog (Library Yearbook)* and information from Bibliotekscentralen. "Other income" includes fees for items sold on commission, subsidies other than from the availability fund and the finance bill, various other minor sources of income, and operating deficits.

solutions for technical problems; the second is a matter of finances.

Standardization by means of centralized operations is necessary to solve a number of library problems, and opposition to standardization was not by any means overcome in 1928 when the Gentofte City Library began to produce printed cards. Resistance still exists today even though it is less than it was. The effects of this resistance can be felt in every one of the activities now carried on by Bibliotekscentralen.

The increase in the sales of publications has not occurred solely as a result of gradually increasing size of the editions of the standard catalogs, book lists, and other catalogs. For several of these there have been steady or even decreasing press runs during the past 25 years, even though some publications have had, of course, larger press runs. These larger runs can be attributed to the interplay of many factors, but one factor has been the improved content and appearance of these publications, which has been at least partly due to the influence of the libraries through their representatives on the committees which edit them. This, plus the great increase in library activities generally, would naturally bring about marked increases in the size of many of the editions. Other factors have played a part in the increased income from publications, however, such as the generally upward trend in their prices and the expansion and diversification of the publications program itself. New catalogs and book lists in new attractive formats are being issued, and large and small bibliographies, both current and retrospective, are being published in increasing numbers. Considering the size of the language area it serves, Bibliotekscentralen has developed a bibliographical publishing activity of impressive dimensions.

Catalog card production has shown great increases, both in sales and in the number of cards produced and titles cataloged (see Table 17). The advantages of using centrally produced printed cards are so great and so obvious that these cards are now used by almost all of the public libraries. The quality of Bibliotekscentralen's cataloging is such that only a few libraries can offer anything comparable, and by virtue of grants from the availability fund for this centralized cataloging, and the advantages of mass production, no library (with the possible exception of the Copenhagen City Library) can perform cataloging work in an economically feasible way without using the services of Bibliotekscentralen. In 1962, all the full-time libraries with four exceptions used these printed cards, and it may be assumed that even these four made use of Bibliotekscentralen's cataloging to some extent.

There is therefore at the present time fairly wide agreement as to the usefulness of Bibliotekscentralen's printed card system. However, there is a considerable amount of contention about the layout or design of the cards, revolving around the question of whether they should be

Table 17. Printed catalog cards

Year	Catalog cards printed	Catalog cards sold	New titles for adults cataloged	New titles for children cataloged	Total number of titles cataloged
	(1,000 cards)	(1,000 cards)	(titles)	(titles)	(titles)
1937-38	274	98	682	500	1,423
1939-40	625	277	734	90	3,514
1944-45	518	429	1,118	191	1,609
1949-50	688	644	1,044	205	2,408
1954-55	904	750	1,021	203	1,543
1959-60	1,235	933	1,133	276	1,536
1963-64	2,175	1,526	2,226	500	4,641

Source: *Biblioteksårbog* and information from Bibliotekscentralen. Figures for 1937-38 are from State Library Inspection's Section for Printed Cards. Number of cards sold in 1937-38 and 1939-40 (both years inclusive) also include sale of Gentofte cards. In addition to recently published titles for adults and children, the total number of titles cataloged also includes older titles, titles for school materials centers, and from 1960 on, recataloging. In the last four years the number of recataloged titles has been considerable: 1960-61—1,754; 1961-62—1,384; 1962-63—1,585; 1963-64—1,737.

in the form of a unit card without a printed classification number or entry word. It may be worth pointing out that the classification and cataloging practices of libraries continue to be so different that Bibliotekscentralen has not yet dared to replace its unit cards with prepared sets.

The supplies sold by Bibliotekscentralen are varied and include numerous forms and other small supplies. Table 16 also shows a great increase in sales volume in this area. The increasing standardization of library forms was discussed in Chapter 5, but the use of the standardized forms in the libraries is still too limited. Libraries continue to devise individual forms for a large number of purposes, and not all of these meet even the most elementary requirements of modern form design. Counting only the processing slips and shelf list cards used in the full-time libraries in 1962, there were still about 200 different forms in use.

Table 18 shows the sales for centralized binding in number of volumes sold to the libraries and number of titles available from the collective binding service. As of 1963, standardization of the collective binding had not been carried out completely, as the classification numbers and other lettering on the spine were still being done according to individual library specifications, including their placement. However, by means of an effective flow of materials and work processes, and due to the advantages derived from the large volume of work, Indbindingscentralen has been able to supply library bindings of high quality at prices which have been

Table 18. Indbindingscentralen

Year	Number of orders for binding individual volumes	Number of volumes ordered through collective binding			Titles available through collective binding	
		Adult	Children	Total	Adult	Children
	(1,000 volumes)	(1,000 volumes)	(1,000 volumes)	(1,000 volumes)	(titles)	(titles)
1949-50	—	—	—	28	— 171 —	
1950-51	—	24	22	46	—	—
1951-52	—	34	22	56	366	61
1952-53	—	46	23	69	462	57
1953-54	—	40	33	73	410	94
1954-55	—	53	55	108	417	129
1955-56	—	58	60	118	420	113
1956-57	—	55	69	124	379	119
1957-58	—	62	67	129	387	124
1958-59	45	62	79	141	539	142
1959-60	55	71	75	146	531	159
1960-61	62	68	68	136	562	140
1961-62	61	69	71	140	586	146
1962-63	88	58	44	102	575	112
1963-64	79	90	48	139	563	129

Source: Information from Bibliotekscentralen. Volumes ordered through collective binding do not include books supplied through the New Danish Literary Society or the "start" libraries. Number of titles offered does not include those subsequently offered at reduced prices.

advantageous not only to the libraries that have used its service, but also, because of the competitive effect of its prices on the trade, to libraries that use other binderies as well. The actual number of volumes ordered by the libraries through the collective binding service, however, has not increased markedly since 1954-55, and the collective binding service has been used for only about 15 percent of the total accessions of the libraries in recent years. The complete utilization of the collective binding service would result in increasing the present sales figures for this activity several times over.

In 1961, Carsten Tofte Hansen made a survey of library usage of joint service enterprises, that is, primarily the services of Biblioteks-centralen and Indbindingscentralen. In an article in *Reol* (1963, pp. 131-153), he concluded that the responsibility for the modest use of this joint technical service facility must be shared by both the libraries (particularly their leaders) and Bibliotekscentralen and Indbindingscen-

Table 19. Bibliotekscentralen—sources of income (percent)

Year	Subsidy from availability fund and finance bill	Sale of printed cards	Sale of publications	Sale of supplies	Sale of equipment	Share of profit from Indbindings-centralen	Other income
1939-40	32.6	—	66.4	—	—	—	1.0
1944-45	18.3	18.9	35.4	13.8	—	—	13.6
1949-50	20.6	21.6	39.8	13.3	—	—	4.7
1954-55	16.4	18.3	41.2	13.0	—	9.5	1.6
1959-60	19.5	13.7	33.3	11.0	—	13.7	8.8
1963-64	10.0	8.2	24.3	8.3	41.3	2.6	5.3

Note: Figures are based on financial reports of Bibliotekscentralen. "Other income" includes fees for items sold on commission, subsidies other than from the availability fund and the finance bill, various other minor sources of income, and operating deficits.

tralen themselves. In the libraries, he said, "a considerable conservatism can be traced with respect to using common processing services, particularly where these result in changes in prevailing practices," and that, "it can be shown at present that contact is lacking between the processing installations and their clients."

Bibliotekscentralen's development has been impeded not only by the opposition of libraries and their associations to centralized solutions of library tasks, but also by the pricing and other financial policies of the organization itself.

When Bibliotekscentralen was started in 1939 (as **FBK**), its financial policy was that the publications produced should be sold at prices which covered only the expenses of printing, while editorial and other expenses were to be covered by grants from the public library availability fund. In 1942, when the organization took over the production and sale of the printed catalog cards, a similar financial policy was outlined—grants from the availability fund were to pay for the actual cataloging while sales receipts were to cover only the expenses of printing and selling the cards. At the time, this seemed to be the only practical policy to follow in Bibliotekscentralen's two first areas of operation, and it is still in effect for the cards, and in part for the publications.

The efforts of Bibliotekscentralen to supply the libraries at cost in all the traditional areas of activity has meant that the organization's financial position has been under a constant strain. Investments in new machines and equipment and the other capital expenditures necessary for expanding operations cannot be adequately financed from general operating income. Therefore, expansion has generally taken place only when sales can be assured in advance. No margin has been available for short-term financial risks.

This has meant that Bibliotekscentralen's rising volume of sales has involved great financial problems. Thus in 1962-63, the volume (nearly double that of the previous year) resulted in a record deficit of about 180,000 kroner. The immediate financial crisis was relieved during 1962 by a guarantee from the Danish Library Association of a cash credit of 250,000 kroner. This credit is to be replaced during the next few years by a capital deposit to be raised jointly by the DLA and the public library availability fund.

In spite of the fact that full use has not been made of the services provided by Bibliotekscentralen and Indbindingscentralen, and in spite of the financially restricted development of Bibliotekscentralen, the activities of these two institutions represent the greatest progress that has been made in the working methods of libraries in cataloging and book processing since 1920.

PART II

Methods and Results of the Work Simplification Committee's Investigations

The first half of Part II (Chapters 7-9) describes the methods and the results of the Work Simplification Committee's investigations of the composition of library work and of the distribution of this work among the various categories of staff. The second half (Chapters 10-12) describes the methods and the results of the Committee's investigations of procedures and working methods, time required, and amount of work involved in processing work.

Appendices 1 and 2, which contain the written instructions to the participants in the investigations into the composition of library work and its distribution among the categories of staff, should be read in connection with the first half of Part II.

Appendix 4 is a flow chart diagram of the present work flow of processing activities as carried out in one of the libraries investigated, and should be read in connection with the second half of Part II. The list of abbreviations and code symbols for the diagram are given in Appendix 3. Appendix 4A shows the information provided by forms, etc., used in the flow of work outlined in the diagram.

7 Composition and distribution of work in full-time libraries: methods of investigation

The attempt to fulfill the objectives of full-time public libraries has been made by means of the activities, and with the financial and personnel resources, described in Chapters 2, 3, and 4 of Part I.

A more detailed description of the use of the staff, which by itself uses up a very substantial portion of the financial resources of libraries, requires an investigation of the composition of library work, its distribution among the staff, and of working methods; and is necessary as a basis for working out concrete proposals for future changes and improvements.

WORK SURVEYS AND WORK SAMPLING STUDIES

Methods appropriate for investigating the composition of library work and its distribution among the different types of staff include work surveys (sometimes called work counts, or time and work unit measurements), and work sampling studies.

Work surveys are made by having the staff members themselves record the amount of time used to do their tasks. This is done according to more or less detailed rules, and usually by following a more or less detailed list of the tasks to be completed and recorded. Compilation of the results of the work survey consists of checking to see where the work recorded fits into the list of activities (which may be assigned code numbers), and totaling the time used by each type of staff for each individual task. The percentage of the total work time spent on each task and by each category of staff may be calculated from this data.

Work sampling studies are made by having an outside observer record the activity of workers at periods selected at random during the time of investigation. This record is also usually made according to a list (again possibly coded) of individual tasks. The percentage occurrence of each individual task in the total number of observations is then calculated. As these studies are random samples, and therefore are based on the calculation of probabilities, the percentages are reliable only to a certain degree. This degree can be fairly well determined in advance, however, and thus the extent of the investigation can be adjusted to achieve a degree of reliability that is acceptable to the investigators. The time spent on a particular task is calculated on the basis of the total working time and the percentage of this total spent on this task. Similarly, the distribution of each separate task among the categories of staff may be calculated.

Sources of error

There are, of course, many possibilities for errors in both work surveys and work sampling studies.

The degree of accuracy of the work survey depends upon the care with which the workers record their work, upon the rules used, and upon the accuracy and comprehensiveness of the list of activities on which the survey is based. In that type of work survey where the record is taken only at certain intervals, every 15 minutes for example, activities which occur only momentarily will tend to be disregarded or under-reported. It must also be remembered that, in a work survey made over a limited period, activities which occur only periodically or irregularly will perhaps be under- or over-represented during the period of investigation. Finally, if the results of a survey of individual libraries are to be taken as expressing the composition and distribution of work in all libraries, the representativeness of the libraries selected is important for the degree of accuracy.

Work surveys have the advantage of not being particularly demanding on the investigators (other than in calculating the final results). They can, however, be very demanding upon the workers.

On the other hand, work sampling studies cause only slight inconvenience to the workers whose tasks are being investigated. They do, however, require the presence of an observer during the entire period of the investigation for each of the libraries investigated, and are therefore very demanding on the time of the observer.

The degree of the reliability of work sampling studies can be fairly well calculated mathematically, based on the number of observations made, but the effect of certain factors, including the carefulness of the observer, the representativeness of the selected libraries, and the period of investigation, as well as the magnitude of all the uncertainty factors which also apply in work surveys, can only be approximately estimated. The accuracy of work sampling studies has not been thoroughly investigated nor has it been fully determined whether the accuracy of work surveys or of work sampling studies is greater.

Both work surveys and work sampling studies were used in the work simplification study of the Swedish public libraries during 1958-60. Considering the extent of the investigations, the differences between the results obtained by the work survey method and by the work sampling method were not significant.

Only the methods of the work survey, however, were used in investigating the composition of work and its distribution among the types of staff in the Danish studies. This is due in part to the lack of any significant differences in the results obtained by the use of the two methods in the Swedish investigation, and in part to the fact that work sampling investigations carried on simultaneously in a number of libraries, as would be required in using this method, would have required a large number of observers, and would have been prohibitively expensive.

RELIABILITY OF THE RESULTS OF THE INVESTIGATION

In judging the accuracy of the results of the work surveys the following factors must be taken into account:

1. The actual performance of the work survey, including the degree of adherence to the rules and the amount of care on the part of the participants in recording their duties.

2. The representativeness for the entire year of the period of investigation.

3. The representativeness of the particular libraries selected for investigation.

4. The extent of the investigation.

Conducting the work survey

The work survey was made in 14 libraries for four weeks during September-October, 1961, and a supplementary survey was made in two of these libraries for two weeks in February, 1962.

The proposed four-week work survey was presented to the heads and assistant heads of the participating libraries at a meeting between them and the Work Simplification Committee on August 12, 1961. At this meeting the organization of the study of time and work units was discussed on the basis of (1) a draft of the written instructions to the workers in the participating libraries, and (2) a list of the library duties to be recorded.

At meetings held at each of the 14 libraries from August 19 to September 9, 1961, the library boards, representatives of the municipal councils, and the local press were informed about the objectives and methods of the work survey, and the library staffs were oriented on the basis of the written instructions sent in advance of these meetings (see Appendix 1).

Trial runs and practice exercises were conducted for from two to five days in the individual libraries. The four-week work survey then took place simultaneously in all of the 14 designated libraries beginning September 18 and concluding October 14, 1961.

After again rehearsing the instructions, an additional two-week work survey was carried out in two of the libraries from February 12 to February 24, 1962.

On the basis of the results of the four-week survey, and additional written and verbal instructions, every staff member in 6 of the 14 libraries also prepared an estimate of the composition of his work load for one whole year, based on the list of duties used in the survey (see the written instructions for making this estimate in Appendix 2).

The rules for carrying out the four-week time and work measurement study were more detailed than is normal for such studies, and the observations of the participants were as extensive as it was possible to make them without allowing the task of recording to become so burdensome that it would noticeably influence the work which was being recorded.

The material from the survey indicates that almost all of the workers in the participating libraries did their record keeping very carefully.

Period of the work survey

The time for carrying out the four-week work survey was selected on the assumption that it was the most representative period of the entire year for the composition of library tasks and their distribution among the staff.

For the public services of advising readers and circulation control, the period chosen covers the transition from the comparatively low activity during summer to the comparatively high activity during winter.

During the same period, the total processing services of book selection, purchasing, accession, classification, cataloging, indexing, and binding, are changing from summer work, which consists mostly of making replacement and supplementary purchases, and other clean-up work suitable to a time when little publication takes place, to the winter work which is marked by more frequent publication and by a heavier purchasing of new books.

During the four-week work survey, the 14 participating libraries circulated a total of 221,995 volumes from those departments in which the staff took part in the survey (that is, excluding departments at the schools where circulation is handled by school librarians). The average daily circulation of the 14 libraries during the reporting period was 9,250 volumes. These libraries circulated a total of 2,890,720 volumes from the same departments during a twelve-month period in 1961-62. Considering the number of days per year the libraries are open to be 303, the average daily circulation was 9,540. The difference between the two figures is only 3 percent. Thus for circulation, to the extent that these figures can be verified, the reporting period was quite representative for the year.

The period for the additional two-week work survey was selected to occur after the peak-load time for public services.

Selection of participating libraries

Fifteen libraries were initially chosen to take part in the four-week work survey. However, because of delays in remodeling its building during the period of the survey, one library withdrew from the study, leaving a total of 14.

The libraries were selected so that different sizes and different types of collections were represented, and also so that libraries with both large and small per capita expenditures and with both high and low per capita circulation would be included.

Even though the differences were comparatively small, neither with respect to size (computed on the basis of the population of the area served), nor to type, were the 14 libraries as a group completely representative of the 96 full-time libraries which were then in existence. However, this is significant only if the results of the work survey show pronounced differences between the different types and sizes of libraries included in the survey.

The average activity and the average resources in almost all areas are higher in the 14 libraries which took part in the work survey than the averages of the full-time libraries considered as a whole. The differences between the average figures for the 14 libraries and the nationwide averages are less, however, than the differences among the 14 libraries themselves.

For each of the resources and activities reported, some of the survey libraries in the investigation were above and some were below the nationwide average for the type of library concerned.

Even though it is not possible to distinguish from the results of the work survey the exact extent of the individual library's differences from the averages for the type of library to which it belongs in size, type, extent of activity, and resources, the results of the survey appear to indicate that differences between the averages for the 14 libraries investigated and those for all the full-time libraries in the country as a group did not have any significant effect on the results of the present study.

63

Extent of the investigation

The extent of the investigation is important for the degree to which the results of the work survey can be accepted as accurately reflecting the composition of library work and its distribution among the different types of staff in all of the Danish full-time libraries. During the four-week work survey a total of 2,323,312 minutes of working time were recorded, corresponding to a total of 230½ staff units. About one-sixth of the total staff units in the 96 full-time libraries then in operation were therefore included in the survey. This may be taken to indicate that the size of the sample under investigation was quite satisfactory.

CODE OF LIBRARIES AND CATEGORIES OF LIBRARY WORK

In this report, the 14 libraries that took part in this investigation are designated as: C1, C2, C3, C4, C5, C6, F1, F2, F3, K1, K2, K3, K4, and K5. The C-libraries are county libraries, F-libraries are suburban libraries, and K-libraries "other full-time libraries." The code number indicates the size of the library within the group, the largest library in each group having the lowest number.

The list of activities used during the work survey, and according to which the results of the investigations are presented, was partly made up from the activity list in *Organisation och arbetsmetoder vid kommunala bibliotek* (Stockholm: 1960), partly from that in *Descriptive List of Professional and Nonprofessional Duties in Libraries* (Chicago: American Library Association, 1948), and partly from that in Watson O'Dell Pierce, *Work Measurement in Public Libraries* (New York: Social Science Research Council, 1949). The Danish list differs considerably, however, from each of these.

The Danish list used in the investigation was readjusted somewhat during the preparation of the material obtained from the investigation and describes the individual activities as follows:

List of library activities

0	*Total book selection*	
1	Orientation	Keeping informed through *Det danske bogmarked* (*The Danish Bookmarket*), reviews, books sent on approval, taking part in "Introduction to the Book Season," preparing and compiling proposals for presentation at book selection meetings.

2	Newspaper reviews	Clipping and filing book reviews.
3	Reviews within library	Preparation of reviews and annotations for books taken on approval and other books being considered for purchase.
4	Duplicate purchases	Control to prevent duplication of purchase orders.
5	Want lists	Preparation of desiderata lists, slips, card files, including checking catalogs and book lists against shelf lists.
6	Books on approval	Ordering, distributing to book selection committee, and, finally, returning of books received for approval.
7	Book selection decisions	Decision on book purchases (decision either by one person alone or at book selection meeting). Decision on allocation of the books to departments of the library even if this decision is not made simultaneously with book selection proper. Determining policies on gifts. Discussion and consideration of methods of book selection.
10	*Total book purchase*	
11	Verification	Verification of titles, dealers, etc.
12	Ordering	Ordering by telephone, preparing order lists, etc.
13	Receiving	Receiving books. Control of delivery against order lists. Checking in the continuations list. (Account control under 124). Return of unsatisfactory second-hand books, etc.
14	Collation	Collation of second-hand books.
20	*Total accessions, etc.*	
21	Book cards, etc.	Preparation of book cards, date slips, book pockets, and shelf list cards.
22	Accessions list	Preparation of accession list and lists of acquisitions for use within library.
23	Accessions stamping	Stamping accessions and noting acquisition in books.
24	Accessions statistics	Statistics of book purchases.

25	Filing shelf list cards	Arranging, filing, removing shelf list cards, accession slips, in-process slips or work slips of shelf lists and other lists.
29	Other	Preparation of joint shelf list cards. Providing book with copy number or revising this number (when this is done as an independent operation).
30	*Total binding, etc.*	
31	Books to bindery	Preparation of books for binding. Decision on kind of binding, bindery, etc.
32	Bindery list	Preparation of bindery list.
33	Books from bindery	Receiving books from bindery.
34	Binding control	Binding control.
35	Preparation of bound books	Final preparation of bound books. Includes adding book plates, series slips.
36	Reinforcing with plastic	Reinforcing books and pamphlets with plastic jackets.
37	Books not bound	Final preparation of books (including pamphlets, etc.) that are not to be bound. Adding classification number, date slip, book pocket, etc. Putting unbound periodicals in cardboard cases.
39	Other	Distribution of new books to departments of the library. Inserting pages in looseleaf volumes. Consideration of, discussion about, binding practices.
40	*Total cataloging*	
41	Classification	Classification of books for which printed cards are not available or not used, when classification is not done immediately in connection with cataloging (see 44).
42	Ordering printed cards	Ordering and receiving printed catalog cards.
43	Adapting printed cards	Completing or making changes on printed catalog cards.
44	Preparing manuscript slips	Cataloging (and possibly classification) without use of printed catalog cards, that is, preparing manuscript card copy.
45	Copying catalog cards	Copying catalog cards from manuscript copy.

46	Catalog cards without manuscript	Preparation of catalog cards directly, without use of printed cards or manuscript slips.
47	Filing	Sorting and alphabetizing printed catalog cards and slips; filing in catalogs or other files.
48	Corrections	Corrections, due to changes in catalog rules or cataloging practice. Includes making corresponding changes in classification numbers, changes on spines of books, book cards, etc.
49	Other	Distribution of catalog cards to various departments and catalogs. Additions and corrections to cards in catalogs because of purchase of new editions, new annual volumes, serials, continuations, etc. Preparation of analytics and "genre" cards for previously cataloged books. Preparation of new guide cards, new cross reference cards. Removal of outdated periodical analytics. Cataloging of pictures and photographs. Consideration, discussion of, and correspondence on cataloging practice. Work for the Committee on Revision of The Danish Decimal Classification System.
50	*Total book conservation*	
51	Examination of book stock	Examination of holdings for repair, rebinding, storage, discard.
52	Repairs	Repairs. Rewriting book cards, etc.
53	Rebinding	Rebinding (to the extent that this can be distinguished from 30-39).
54	Withdrawal	Withdrawal (weeding). Includes removing shelf list and catalog cards, stamping discards, etc.
55	Storage	Storage and other permanent removal from one department to another. Includes corrections in catalogs caused by such transfers.
59	Summer deposits	Selection of books coming from, or being placed on, summer deposit.

60	*Total registration of borrowers*	
61	Registration	Receiving applications, issuing borrower's cards, introduction to the library.
64	Preparing borrowers' registers	Preparing cards for alphabetical and numerical borrowers' registers.
65	Renewals	Renewals.
66	Filing in borrowers' registers	Filing cards in borrowers' registers.
67	Reissuing cards	Reissuing borrowers' cards.
68	Corrections	Correction of address, occupation, name, or the transfer of borrowers from one department or branch to another.
69	Other	Filing and withdrawing borrowers' cards "on deposit." Work with temporary borrowers' cards. Arranging new borrower serial numbers. Statistics. Correspondence (to borrowers who have had two overdue notices, for example).
70	*Total circulation control*	
71	Circulation	Charging, discharging, renewal of books. Includes stamping date cards.
72	Inserting book cards	Inserting book cards in returned books. Correction of mixed-up cards.
73	Shelving	Shelving and arranging books in circulation departments, reading rooms, stacks, summer deposits, and all special collections.
74	Shelf reading	Shelf reading.
75	Clearing counter	Clearing off circulation counter and rearranging circulation and reading rooms at closing.
76	"Statistics"	Keeping circulation statistics.
77	Overdues	Writing overdue notices.
78	Messenger slips	Writing messenger slips.

79	Other	Temporary circulation desk duty, giving directions at information desk and circulation counter. Individual reminders, replacement matters. Searching for missing books.
80	*Total assistance to readers*	
81	Assisting readers	Assisting readers, including providing all forms of information, receiving reserve and purchase requests, aid in preparing reading lists, help in using catalogs, assistance in selecting reading materials, and all forms of reference work. (However, see 91.)
84	Reserves	Making out reserve cards and clipping book cards. (Receiving reserve requests under 81.)
85	Verification	Bibliographic work in connection with obtaining material from other libraries. Verifying requests.
86	Interlibrary loan	Loan of material from and to other libraries, and single loans between the main library and branches. Includes preparing special forms, etc., and notices to libraries and readers concerning interlibrary loans.
88	Introduction to the library	Introducing the library to groups and school classes, including preparation for such sessions.
89.1	Work with deposits	Selection, assembling, transportation of deposits, including regular deposit collections, class sets, and "traveling libraries" to hospitals, nursing homes. Also includes making any special book cards for such books or lists of such collections.
90	*Total reading room work*	
91	Reading lists	Compiling bibliographies and reading lists as requested.
92	Charging periodicals and newspapers	Charging, stamping, setting out periodicals and newspapers.

93	Storage of older serials and newspapers	Sorting, withdrawal, storing, of older issues of periodicals and newspapers.
94	Special card indexes	Arranging and keeping up to date any special card files or catalogs in reading room, including essay file, magazine and newspaper indexes, etc.
95	Clipping collection	Preparation and maintenance of the clipping collection, including cutting, mounting, and arranging pictures and articles. (For book reviews, see 2.)
96	Reading room statistics	Totaling visits to reading room and keeping the "question and answer" book.
100	*Total public relations*	
101	Library exhibitions	Arranging exhibitions in the library.
102	Signs and posters	Preparation of signs and posters.
103	Catalogs	Compiling catalogs and book lists. Also includes writing, duplication, or work in connection with the printing of these catalogs.
104	Exhibitions outside the library	Arranging exhibitions outside the library.
105	Other events	Arranging other events inside or outside the library. Includes meetings, lectures, literary evenings, study circles.
106	Lists of recent acquisitions	Compiling lists of books recently purchased.
107	Story hours	Story hours, book talks, etc.
108	Articles and interviews	Preparing articles and interviews for newspapers and magazines.
109	Other	Correspondence. Sending notices, pamphlets, book lists, and catalogs to readers, or placing them in waiting rooms, etc. Preparing and sending pamphlets or other material to municipalities or parishes without libraries.
109.1	Children's book week	All preparation and work in connection with children's book week.

110 *Total county library work (work in surrounding area)*

111	Book proposals	Preparation of proposals for book purchases for part-time libraries.
112	Budgets	Preparation of budgets for part-time libraries.
113	Review of book proposals and budgets	Review of book proposals and budgets at meetings in the part-time libraries or at the county library.
114	Bookmobiles	Driving bookmobiles.
115	Bookmobile collections	Maintaining special bookmobile collections. Includes class set collections.
118	Technical advice	Advice and consultation on library technical services.
119	Other	Taking part in inspection trips. Survey and reorganization of part-time libraries and associated follow-up work.

120 *Total administration, etc.*

121	Board meetings	Attending board meetings.
122	Professional meetings, trips, courses	Attending professional meetings, courses; making trips. Includes preparation for and taking part in such meetings as the annual meeting of the DLA, county library meetings, contact meetings, board meetings of library associations and committees of the DLA, librarians' associations, Bibliotekscentralen, etc.
123	Budget	Budget preparation.
124	Accounts and auditing	Bookkeeping and auditing.
125	Personnel	Personnel. Scheduling staff, making appointments to staff, staff meetings, taking part in work of staff association.
126	Premises and furniture	Maintenance of premises and furniture.
127	Planning	Planning of new activities, new buildings, reorganization of work, etc. (General planning of current work is included under the work concerned.)
128	General office work, etc.	Office work and general administration, including correspondence. General in-

formation within the library ("shop talk," and preparing staff bulletin, for example). Telephone switchboard operation. Purchase of office material. Rental or loan of study rooms or other premises, film or slide projectors, and film or slides. Visits of colleagues. Answering questionnaires of general nature. Annual report, etc.

129.1	Danish authors' report	Report on library use of works by Danish authors.
129.2	Inventory	Taking stock of book collection.
130	*Total other*	
131	Work for investigation	Work for Work Simplification Committee or other investigation.
132	Vacation and time off	Vacation and time off, including compensatory time for overtime and sick leave.
133	Illness	Illness.
135	Orientation in recently acquired literature	Keeping up with recently acquired literature and professional reading. Book discussion meetings. (Does not include reading done outside of working hours or book selection work.)
136	Inducting trainees and new staff members	Inducting trainees and new staff members (over and above general daily instructions).
137	Personal time	Personal time. Private visits, telephone calls, use of restroom, coffee and tea breaks, etc.
139	Messenger service, transportation, etc.	Messenger service, packing, unpacking books. Transportation. "Stand-by time," that is, where presence is required without being able to carry out duties. Arranging and watering flowers. Work for local "friends of the library" association. Other types of non-private work.
139.1	Study time	Study time for library trainees and clerical (business school) trainees.
139.3	Janitorial work	Custodial and janitorial work. Includes sweeping walks and stoking furnace.

139.4 Cloakroom duty

140 *Total military library work*

Cloakroom duty.

(Includes all library work at defense installations which can be quantified, that is, circulation work in particular.)

8 Composition of library work: results of the investigation

COMPOSITION OF THE WORK LOAD IN 14 LIBRARIES

For our purposes, complete library operation includes work survey activities 1-129.2 + 135 + 136 + 139. Activities 131, 132, 133, 137, 139.1, 139.3 and 139.4, which include such things as vacation time, illness, study time, cloakroom duty, and time spent on the survey itself, do not concern library work as such, cannot be estimated with any reasonable degree of accuracy, and are not included in Table 20 which shows the composition of the work load during the four-week survey in the 14 libraries, both as a group, and by type. Activity 140 (library work at defense installations) had to be eliminated from the investigation as it was found to be impossible to accurately report on library work at individual military installations.

Table 20. Composition of the work load in terms of the proportion of total working hours spent on each activity during the four-week work survey in the 14 libraries, as a group, and by type (percent)

	Activity	All 14 libraries	6 county libraries	3 suburban libraries	5 "other" libraries
0	*Total book selection*	*5.70*	*5.44*	*5.17*	*7.55*
1	Orientation	2.57	2.15	2.26	4.75
2	Newspaper book reviews	0.49	0.49	0.46	0.53
3	Reviews within the library	0.05	0.06	0.02	0.01

	Activity	All 14 libraries	6 county libraries	3 suburban libraries	5 "other" libraries
4	Control to prevent duplicate orders	0.09	0.11	0.02	0.09
5	Want lists	0.21	0.31	0.01	0.24
6	Books on approval	0.15	0.17	0.15	0.07
7	Book selection meetings	2.14	2.15	2.25	1.86
10	*Total book purchase*	*1.19*	*1.16*	*1.01*	*1.56*
11	Verification	0.04	0.04	0.04	0.02
12	Ordering	0.58	0.55	0.54	0.73
13	Receiving	0.54	0.54	0.39	0.81
14	Collating	0.03	0.03	0.04	—
20	*Total accession, etc.*	*4.78*	*4.65*	*5.40*	*4.38*
21	Book cards, etc.	2.88	2.82	3.32	2.49
22	Accessions list	0.22	0.15	0.27	0.43
23	Accession stamping	0.84	0.80	1.06	0.68
24	Accessions statistics	0.08	0.08	0.11	—
25	Filing of shelf list cards	0.63	0.64	0.52	0.76
29	Other	0.13	0.16	0.12	0.02
30	*Total binding, etc.*	*2.74*	*2.90*	*3.01*	*1.67*
31	Books to bindery	0.35	0.42	0.30	0.17
32	Bindery list	0.21	0.21	0.24	0.22
33	Books from bindery	0.24	0.27	0.15	0.28
34	Binding control	0.57	0.32	1.47	0.21
35	Preparing bound books	0.86	1.03	0.52	0.58
36	Reinforcing with plastic	0.07	0.10	0.01	0.03
37	Books not bound	0.25	0.35	0.05	0.13
39	Other	0.19	0.20	0.27	0.05
40	*Total cataloging*	*10.45*	*9.62*	*16.38*	*4.87*
41	Classification	0.13	0.14	0.02	0.23
42	Ordering printed cards	0.56	0.68	0.34	0.43
43	Adapting printed cards	0.94	0.52	1.99	1.05
44	Preparing manuscript slips	0.96	0.92	1.38	0.54
45	Copying catalog cards	1.65	0.87	4.81	0.12
46	Catalog cards without manuscript	0.21	0.18	0.24	0.29
47	Filing in catalogs	1.92	2.02	2.02	1.38
48	Corrections	1.55	0.92	3.90	0.60
49	Other	2.53	3.37	1.68	0.23

	Activity	All 14 libraries	6 county libraries	3 suburban libraries	5 "other" libraries
50	*Total book conservation*	*2.74*	*2.89*	*2.01*	*3.26*
51	Examination of book stock	0.75	0.77	0.35	1.27
52	Repairs	0.71	0.82	0.64	0.33
53	Rebinding	0.06	0.10	—	—
54	Withdrawal	0.79	0.62	0.88	1.35
55	Storage	0.29	0.39	0.05	0.30
59	Summer deposits	0.14	0.19	0.09	0.01
60	*Total registration of borrowers*	*2.05*	*2.38*	*1.37*	*1.72*
61	Registration	0.44	0.43	0.39	0.57
64	Preparing borrowers' register	0.62	0.73	0.41	0.46
65	Renewals	0.07	0.05	0.09	0.12
66	Arranging borrowers' register	0.35	0.41	0.23	0.28
67	Reissuing borrowers' cards	0.10	0.08	0.11	0.14
68	Corrections	0.14	0.21	0.03	0.03
69	Other	0.33	0.47	0.11	0.12
70	*Total circulation control*	*28.32*	*27.13*	*27.96*	*33.94*
71	Charging	8.16	7.47	8.51	10.63
72	Inserting book cards	5.05	4.63	5.22	6.60
73	Shelving	6.84	6.80	6.65	7.15
74	Shelf reading	1.80	1.93	1.38	1.96
75	Clearing counter	1.60	1.88	0.90	1.48
76	"Statistics"	2.51	2.28	2.48	3.58
77	Overdues	1.77	1.52	2.18	2.20
78	Messenger slips	0.20	0.20	0.22	0.14
79	Other	0.39	0.42	0.42	0.20
80	*Total assistance to readers, etc.*	*17.04*	*17.26*	*16.26*	*17.48*
81	Advising readers	11.00	11.00	9.88	12.57
84	Reserves	1.88	2.11	1.67	1.24
85	Verification	0.68	0.62	0.97	0.59
86	Interlibrary loan	2.11	2.12	2.00	2.36
88	Introduction to library	0.44	0.39	0.84	0.08
89.1	Work with deposits	0.93	1.02	0.90	0.64
90	*Total reading room work*	*1.94*	*2.11*	*1.50*	*1.91*
91	Reading lists	0.17	0.13	0.35	—

	Activity	All 14 libraries	6 county libraries	3 suburban libraries	5 "other" libraries
92	Charging periodicals and newspapers	0.77	0.87	0.35	1.03
93	Storing back issues of periodicals and newspapers	0.27	0.28	0.25	0.26
94	Special card indexes or catalogs	0.19	0.15	0.39	0.09
95	Clipping collection	0.49	0.64	0.11	0.45
96	Reading room statistics	0.05	0.04	0.05	0.08
100	*Total public relations*	*3.19*	*2.14*	*5.84*	*3.58*
101	Exhibitions in library	0.29	0.22	0.37	0.45
102	Signs and posters	0.27	0.21	0.42	0.32
103	Catalogs	0.81	0.62	1.76	0.07
104	Exhibitions outside library	0.04	0.02	0.13	0.02
105	Other events	0.12	0.18	0.01	0.04
106	Lists of recent acquisitions	0.48	0.34	1.11	0.18
107	Story hours	0.09	0.13	0.03	—
108	Articles and interviews	0.04	0.02	0.09	0.06
109	Other	0.23	0.14	0.44	0.29
109.1	Children's book week	0.82	0.26	1.48	2.15
110	*Total county library work in surrounding area*	*3.48*	*5.55*	—	—
111	Book proposals	0.53	0.84	—	—
112	Budgets	0.14	0.21	—	—
113	Review of book proposals and budgets	0.18	0.27	—	—
114	Driving bookmobiles	1.56	2.51	—	—
115	Bookmobile collections	0.02	0.03	—	—
118	Advice on technical services	0.14	0.23	—	—
119	Other	0.91	1.46	—	—
120	*Total administration, etc.*	*10.28*	*10.11*	*9.21*	*12.60*
121	Board meetings	0.13	0.15	0.11	0.03
122	Professional meetings, trips, courses	2.16	1.86	1.44	4.59
123	Budget preparation	0.30	0.08	1.05	0.06
124	Accounts and auditing	1.72	1.78	1.37	2.06
125	Personnel	1.02	1.05	0.84	1.15
126	Premises and furniture	0.25	0.28	0.24	0.12
127	Planning	0.56	0.24	0.98	1.28

	Activity	All 14 libraries	6 county libraries	3 suburban libraries	5 "other" libraries
128	General office work, etc.	3.54	3.99	2.99	2.38
129.1	Report on library use of works of Danish authors	0.40	0.35	0.18	0.93
129.2	Inventory of book stock	0.20	0.33	0.01	—
135	Keeping up with recent acquisitions	0.75	0.46	1.00	1.51
136	Induction of trainees and new staff	0.28	0.21	0.62	0.04
139	Messenger service and transportation	5.07	5.99	3.26	3.93
	Total	*100.00*	*100.00*	*100.00*	*100.00*

Library work proper (activities 1-129.2 + 135 + 136 + 139) includes work in all of the departments of the 14 libraries (except sections at military posts), including departments for both children and adults, main libraries as well as branches, and departments at hospitals and old people's homes. However, circulation and other work done by school librarians at school libraries and school library departments are entirely outside the investigation. Technical library services and all other work for school libraries and children's departments at the schools are included in the investigation to the extent that such work is done by the regular staff of the libraries included in the survey.

The staff included in the survey included all personnel employed in the 14 libraries, excluding school librarians, such pages as might be employed at departments taken care of by school librarians, and janitorial staff. (See the instructions for the participants in Appendix 1.)

The figures in the table are given to two decimal places. This was done to allow comparisons of the individual activities to be made without the risk of inaccurate totals which would result from rounding off the decimals, and is not intended to indicate the actual degree of accuracy of the results.

The survey reveals that there are great fluctuations in the extent of the individual activities from library to library. In addition to a certain inevitable inaccuracy in reporting, these fluctuations may be due to differences in the size, the type, the extent of activity, the resources, or the working methods of the libraries involved. They may also be due to the fact that some library activities are performed only at varying intervals, and these activities may, therefore, be strongly over- or under-represented in any given period.

Examples of activities which occur only periodically are most often found in the area of book selection, and are apparently most prevalent in the smallest libraries. The differences in the final figures for activity group 0 (total book selection) between any two libraries may therefore be strongly influenced by the degree to which this activity takes place in those particular libraries during any given four-week period. Certain random fluctuations in almost all activities must be expected because of their intermittent occurrence or degree of intensity. These fluctuations will be greatest in those activities which take place at long intervals— once every year for example (such as preparing the budget, reporting on library use of works by Danish authors, and even, to some extent, renewing borrowers' cards)—and least in activities the extent of which is governed by fairly stable public usage during the year. Typical of the latter activities are 81 (advising readers) and 71-73 (circulation counter work and shelving books), and the reasons for variations in the extent of these activities among the 14 libraries are to be sought in differences in size and type of the libraries and, perhaps more particularly, in their operations, resources, and working methods. These differences are further discussed later on.

The figures gathered for individual activities reveal that differences in a library's working methods may affect the frequency of the occurrence of these activities. For example, the figures for activity 24 (accession statistics) show that 6 of the 14 libraries keep a running count of their accessions, or make such tallies at frequent intervals, while 8 libraries (in which, by the way, this activity did not take place during the period of the investigation) make such a count at longer intervals, perhaps only once a year.

An example of the effect of unusual circumstances on the statistics gathered during the survey is the high figure for some of the activities within group 40 (cataloging), which was influenced by the extensive changes that were being made in the catalog of one library (F1) during the time of the investigation.

The material from the investigation strongly confirms that the average figures for the composition of the work load in the 14 survey libraries are very close to the nationwide averages. However, the figures for any one library may, of course, differ greatly from these averages because of its own particular characteristics of size, type, extent of activities, resources, and working methods. This means that no other individual library can unqualifiedly accept the survey figures as indicating the composition of its own work.

The average figures for each of the three types of libraries investigated do not indicate the "typical" work composition for those types as a whole with complete accuracy. This is because the 14 libraries investigated were not selected in such a way that the 6 county libraries corresponded to the average of all county libraries, or the 3 suburban libraries to the average of all of the suburban libraries, or the 5 "other full-time libraries" to the average of all "other full-time libraries." The category of suburban library in particular contained too few libraries to ensure that the intermittent fluctuations in the amount of work were evened out, and that special circumstances at particular libraries did not affect the figures noticeably. In terms of staff, for example, library F1 is five times as large as libraries F2 and F3 combined, and from this it follows that the work of changing the catalogs which was being done during the period of investigation in library F1 strongly influenced the figures for certain activities in group 40 for the entire class of suburban libraries.

VARIATIONS IN COMPOSITION OF WORK
AT DIFFERENT TIMES OF THE YEAR

The purpose of the supplementary work survey made in two of the libraries in February was to reveal what differences may exist in the work load at different times of the year. Differences due to the time of year, however, can only be ascertained for activities which take place so frequently (daily, for example) that they will be properly representative for the time of year during any short period taken at random, such as those tasks concerned with public service (activities 61, 65, 71, 72, 73, 76, and 81, for example). The figures for these activities will reflect variations according to the time of the year with a considerable degree of accuracy.

THE ANNUAL LIBRARY WORK LOAD

Because of the large amount of material gathered and the number of libraries investigated, the extent of the library activities in the 14 libraries as a group as listed in Table 20 was probably relatively unaffected by the periodic nature of certain activities over the course of the year in individual libraries, at least for those which occurred at fairly frequent intervals. In addition, the period of investigation was selected so that most of the activities would probably take the same percentage of the total working time during that period as they would on the average during the entire year. Therefore the results of the four-week survey should really need to be corrected only for those tasks which are done at very infrequent intervals—once a year, for example.

Such a corrective measure was provided for through the year's estimate of the distribution of work made by 6 of the 14 libraries. (Instructions for preparing the year's estimate are included in Appendix 2.)

The yearly estimate was also considered desirable for those activities which, while they occurred frequently enough, or at short enough intervals, appeared, in the opinion of some of the participants in the work survey, to take up a different percentage of their working time when computed on the basis of an entire year, than during the relatively short period of the investigation.

The estimates of the yearly distribution of work by the staff of the six participating libraries may be considered sufficiently reliable so that the figures showing differences in the composition of their work loads can be taken as being fairly accurate. At the same time it should be noted that errors in the estimates of very minor tasks may be quite large when computed on the basis of an entire year, and also that it was quite difficult for the staff members to avoid being influenced by the four-week figures on which they partially based their estimates for the year.

Significance of resources for composition of the work load

We can take library F3 as an example of the effect that the available staff resources have upon the distribution of the work load. The large percentage of the total work load of F3 taken up by circulation control [51 percent as compared to 28 percent for all six libraries as a group] is not due to inefficient or time-consuming working methods, but to the size of its staff in proportion to circulation. Control of each volume circulated does not require more time in library F3 than in the other libraries, but even so, about 50 percent of its staff are involved in this work. It is therefore apparent that differences in available staff alone can bring about great differences in the composition of the work load. It is also apparent that a limited staff in proportion to the volume of circulation will result in poor reader's advisory service, and will also, given the present distribution of work in the libraries, result in very little time spent on book selection.

The work surveys and the year's estimate

A comparison of the estimate of the year's work load in the six participating libraries with that of the same libraries' work load during the four-week work survey, and a comparison of these figures with those obtained by all of the 14 libraries which took part in the four-week work survey shows that there is, in general, rather good agreement between the three figures. However, for certain activities the differences are large.

The work survey period may be considered, for most activities, to be representative for the year, and enough libraries are included so that the periodic fluctuations in the extent of the activities in the individual libraries will tend to cancel each other out.

The results of the four-week survey in the 14 libraries as a group may therefore be considered on the whole dependable for the majority of activities, and these results (shown in Table 20) are used in subsequent computations of the report as the average composition of the yearly work load in the full-time libraries as a group.

COMPARISON WITH THE RESULTS OF THE SWEDISH WORK SURVEY

In the work survey included in the Swedish work simplification study during 1958-60, library activities were not divided in the same way as in the Danish survey. Therefore, the results cannot be compared directly. However, there is strong agreement between the results of the two work surveys, and there is reason to believe that the differences were due more to actual differences between the working methods of Swedish and Danish full-time libraries than to inaccuracies of the investigations.

DISTRIBUTION OF THE PRINCIPAL LIBRARY TASKS

Library activities can be divided into seven principal groups of activities which the libraries, according to their objectives, are to carry out.

Group 1. Selection of material (book selection)—includes survey activities 1, 2, 3, 4, 5, 6, 7, and 51.

Group 2. Indexing, cataloging, etc. (making accessible the material selected)—includes activities 11, 12, 13, 14, 22, 23, 25, 29, 31, 32, 33, 34, 35, 36, 37, 39, 41, 42, 43, 44, 45, 46, 47, 48, 49, 52, 53, 54, 55, 59, 73, 74, 84, 85, 86, 89.1, 91, 92, 93, 94, 95, 115, and 129.2.

Group 3. Assisting readers—includes activities 81 and 135.

Group 4. Circulation control—includes activities 61, 64, 65, 66, 67, 68, 69, 71, 72, 75, 76, 77, 78, and 79.

Group 5. Publicity and public relations—includes activities 88, 101, 102, 103, 104, 105, 106, 107, 108, 109, and 109.1.

Group 6. Administration—includes activities 24, 96, 121, 122, 123, 124, 125, 126, 127, 128, 129.1, 136, and 139.

Group 7. County library work—includes activities 111, 112, 113, 114, 118, and 119.

(Note that activities 131, 132, 133, 137, 139.1, 139.3, 139.4, and 140 are not included.)

This division of the activities among the seven principal groups involves certain minor errors because some activities contain component tasks which do not come under the same main heading, and while certain activities are intended primarily to accomplish one task, they are also relevant in accomplishing one or more of the others. However, these possible errors appear to have little influence in determining the relative proportions of these groups of activities. The proportionate size of these groups, based on the results of the four-week work survey of all 14 libraries, and on the results of the four-week work survey and the year's estimate of the six libraries which took part in the yearly estimate are shown in Table 21.

Table 21. **Proportion of total working hours for the principal groups of library activities (percent)**

Group	14 libraries during 4-week work survey	6 libraries during 4-week work survey	Year's estimate of same 6 libraries
1. Book selection	6.45	9.03	8.73
2. Indexing, cataloging, etc.	37.42	35.60	37.89
3. Assisting readers	11.75	11.14	11.91
4. Circulation control	21.73	20.28	22.00
5. Public relations and publicity	3.63	3.13	2.81
6. Administration	15.56	14.72	13.51
7. County library work	3.46	6.10	3.15
Total	100.00	100.00	100.00

9 Distribution of work load by category of staff: results of the investigation

COMPOSITION OF STAFF IN THE LIBRARIES STUDIED AND IN ALL FULL-TIME LIBRARIES

The average composition of the staffs of the 14 libraries which took part in the work survey was not identical with that of the full-time libraries as a group; the most significant difference being the former's relatively large percentage of library trainees [14.2 percent as against 6.7 percent for all full-time libraries], and a somewhat smaller percentage of clerical (business school) trainees [2.6 percent as against 6.7 percent].

However, the differences in the percentage of other staff groups (librarians, trained clerical staff, and assistants without professional training) were quite modest, and the distribution of staff in the work survey libraries, except for the difference in the proportion of trainees, corresponds quite closely to that of the full-time libraries as a group.

COMPOSITION OF WORK OF THE VARIOUS CATEGORIES OF STAFF

Table 22 shows how large a part of the total working time of each staff group was taken up by each activity during the four-week work survey. For example, the table shows that librarians spent 10.25 percent of their time on total book selection, while library trainees spent 3.18 percent, clerical staff 0.83 percent, etc. Total book selection (0) is then further broken down into its separate components—orientation, newspaper book reviews, etc. (subactivities 1-7).

Table 22. Percentage of time spent on individual activities by the various categories of staff during the four-week work survey.

Activity	Librarians	Library trainees	Clerical staff	Clerical trainees	Assistants	Other staff
0 *Total book selection*	*10.25*	*3.18*	*0.83*	*1.31*	*0.87*	*1.02*
1 Orientation	4.95	1.05	0.12	—	0.18	—
2 Newspaper book reviews	0.61	0.57	—	1.31	0.42	1.02
3 Reviews within the library	0.09	—	0.01	—	—	—
4 Control to prevent duplicate orders	0.15	0.03	0.05	—	—	—
5 Want lists	0.29	0.28	0.16	—	0.02	—
6 Books on approval	0.17	0.01	0.32	—	0.05	—
7 Book selection meetings	3.99	1.24	0.17	—	0.20	—
10 *Total book purchase*	*1.42*	*0.35*	*2.32*	*0.20*	*0.12*	—
11 Verification	0.06	0.04	0.01	—	—	—
12 Ordering	0.71	0.19	1.12	—	0.02	—
13 Receiving	0.62	0.12	1.14	0.20	0.10	—
14 Collating	0.03	—	0.05	—	—	—
20 *Total accession, etc.*	*2.25*	*1.92*	*15.13*	*11.00*	*2.41*	—
21 Book cards, etc.	0.96	1.42	9.95	7.00	1.41	—
22 Accessions list	0.16	0.02	0.65	0.45	0.04	—
23 Accession stamping	0.59	0.10	2.61	0.98	0.25	—
24 Accessions statistics	0.10	—	0.12	—	—	—
25 Filing of shelf list cards	0.35	0.38	1.32	2.57	0.71	—
29 Other	0.09	—	0.48	—	—	—

Table 22. *Continued*

Activity	Librarians	Library trainees	Clerical staff	Clerical trainees	Assistants	Other staff
30 *Total binding, etc.*	*2.52*	*1.23*	*5.02*	*5.30*	*1.28*	*5.04*
31 Books to bindery	0.42	0.06	0.76	—	0.01	—
32 Bindery list	0.17	0.09	0.51	0.87	0.05	—
33 Books from bindery	0.26	0.20	0.38	0.31	0.11	—
34 Binding control	0.55	0.18	1.45	—	—	—
35 Preparing bound books	0.68	0.55	1.29	0.97	0.74	3.25
36 Reinforcing with plastic	0.03	0.06	0.01	0.44	—	1.46
37 Books not bound	0.19	0.07	0.27	2.50	0.25	0.33
39 Other	0.22	0.02	0.35	0.21	0.12	—
40 *Total cataloging*	*11.19*	*12.89*	*14.24*	*8.28*	*2.90*	—
41 Classification	0.24	0.08	0.01	—	—	—
42 Ordering printed cards	0.68	0.14	1.06	0.18	0.13	—
43 Adapting printed cards	0.72	0.95	2.17	2.21	—	—
44 Preparing manuscript slips	1.49	1.75	0.02	0.07	0.07	—
45 Copying catalog cards	0.28	1.40	5.65	3.83	1.19	—
46 Catalog cards without manuscript	0.37	0.14	0.06	0.04	—	—
47 Filing in catalogs	2.21	3.70	1.08	0.72	0.87	—
48 Corrections	1.95	1.61	2.01	0.23	0.04	—
49 Other	3.25	3.12	2.18	1.00	0.60	—
50 *Total book conservation*	*3.01*	*1.09*	*3.48*	*2.34*	*2.14*	*5.60*
51 Examination of book stock	1.51	—	0.07	—	0.05	—
52 Repairs	0.11	0.67	1.28	1.39	1.16	5.60

53	Rebinding	0.06	—	0.13	0.39	—	—
54	Withdrawal	0.81	0.31	1.45	0.23	0.49	—
55	Storage	0.27	0.11	0.49	0.24	0.37	—
59	Summer deposits	0.25	—	0.06	0.09	0.07	—
60	*Total registration of borrowers*	*1.09*	*2.00*	*5.00*	*4.04*	*1.51*	*1.74*
61	Registration	0.63	0.44	0.16	0.40	0.27	—
64	Preparing borrowers' register	0.09	0.63	2.01	1.55	0.48	—
65	Renewals	0.06	0.10	0.05	0.12	0.11	—
66	Arranging borrowers' register	0.13	0.30	0.99	1.04	0.26	—
67	Reissuing borrowers' cards	0.08	0.07	0.17	0.01	0.12	—
68	Corrections	0.03	0.13	0.51	0.24	0.05	—
69	Other	0.07	0.33	1.11	0.68	0.22	—
70	*Total circulation control*	*14.19*	*46.47*	*20.13*	*34.23*	*69.83*	*1.74*
71	Charging	6.25	15.86	3.66	8.77	13.93	—
72	Inserting book cards	1.99	9.72	2.27	5.32	14.75	—
73	Shelving	1.85	8.89	2.52	8.07	26.94	—
74	Shelf reading	0.94	4.09	1.52	2.96	2.89	—
75	Clearing counter	1.55	2.38	0.83	2.02	1.88	1.74
76	"Statistics"	0.87	3.14	3.96	4.16	5.50	—
77	Overdues	0.29	2.12	4.31	2.24	3.14	—
78	Messenger slips	0.02	—	0.38	0.58	0.69	—
79	Other	0.43	0.27	0.68	0.11	0.11	—
80	*Total assistance to readers, etc.*	*26.20*	*17.89*	*5.69*	*4.16*	*5.40*	*2.28*
81	Advising readers	19.07	9.37	0.79	1.25	2.24	—
84	Reserves	1.56	3.85	0.87	2.20	2.59	—

Table 22. *Continued*

Activity	Librarians	Library trainees	Clerical staff	Clerical trainees	Assistants	Other staff
85 Verification	1.33	0.39	—	—	—	—
86 Interlibrary loan	2.41	3.88	1.82	0.52	0.28	2.28
88 Introduction to library	0.80	0.15	0.12	—	0.09	—
89.1 Work with deposits	1.03	0.25	2.09	0.19	0.20	—
90 Total reading room work	*2.06*	*1.42*	*1.54*	*2.24*	*1.35*	*9.96*
91 Reading lists	0.24	0.23	0.10	—	—	—
92 Charging periodicals and newspapers	0.84	0.61	1.03	1.03	0.50	—
93 Storing back issues of periodicals and newspapers	0.19	0.13	0.16	0.31	0.48	2.25
94 Special card indexes or catalogs	0.36	0.13	—	—	0.01	—
95 Clipping collections	0.37	0.25	0.25	0.60	0.36	7.71
96 Reading room statistics	0.06	0.07	—	0.30	—	—
100 Total public relations	*4.19*	*1.63*	*2.89*	*3.36*	*1.82*	*3.10*
101 Exhibitions in library	0.48	0.37	0.06	—	—	—
102 Signs and posters	0.28	0.77	—	—	0.18	—
103 Catalogs	0.67	0.21	1.56	0.19	0.74	1.93
104 Exhibitions outside library	0.03	—	—	—	0.18	—
105 Other events	0.25	—	—	—	—	—
106 Lists of recent acquisitions	0.33	0.10	0.94	1.72	0.69	—
107 Story hours	0.19	—	—	—	—	—
108 Articles and interviews	0.08	—	—	—	—	—
109 Other	0.29	0.18	0.09	0.97	0.02	1.17
109.1 Children's book week	1.59	—	0.24	0.48	0.01	—

110 *Total county library work in surrounding area*	*4.73*	*2.80*	*3.47*	*5.94*	*0.25*	—
111 Book proposals	0.67	0.21	0.85	0.35	0.01	—
112 Budgets	0.21	0.01	0.13	—	—	—
113 Review of book proposals and budgets	0.35	0.05	—	2.34	0.23	—
114 Driving bookmobiles	2.04	2.39	0.94	—	—	—
115 Bookmobile collection	0.04	0.02	—	—	—	—
118 Advice on technical services	0.06	—	0.63	—	—	—
119 Other	1.36	0.12	0.92	3.25	0.01	—
120 *Total administration, etc.*	*12.52*	*1.84*	*17.88*	*11.93*	*1.83*	*5.85*
121 Board meetings	0.19	—	0.19	—	—	—
122 Professional meetings, trips, courses	4.22	0.21	0.55	0.78	—	—
123 Budget preparation	0.46	—	0.43	—	—	—
124 Accounts and auditing	1.13	0.05	5.69	3.48	0.23	0.09
125 Personnel	1.50	0.56	0.86	1.23	0.17	—
126 Premises and furniture	0.35	0.05	0.02	—	0.08	2.67
127 Planning	1.13	—	0.07	—	0.03	—
128 General office work, etc.	3.22	0.82	8.21	3.24	1.20	3.09
129.1 Report on library use of works of Danish authors	0.31	0.08	0.83	3.20	0.12	—
129.2 Inventory of book stock	0.01	0.07	1.03	—	—	—
135 Keeping up with recent acquisitions	1.35	0.36	0.09	—	0.17	—
136 Induction of trainees and new staff	0.27	0.90	0.04	0.11	0.07	—
139 Messenger service and transportation	2.76	4.03	2.25	5.56	8.05	65.41
Total	*100.00*	*100.00*	*100.00*	*100.00*	*100.00*	*100.00*

As might be expected, 0 (book selection), and 80 (advising readers, etc.) took up a significantly greater amount of the working time of the librarians than of the staff as a whole, while 10 (book purchase), 20 (accession, etc.), 30 (binding, etc.), 40 (cataloging), and 120 (administration) took up a greater part of the working time of the clerical staff than of the staff as a whole. More than two-thirds of the working time of the assistants was occupied with 70 (circulation control), while this work formed less than one-third of the working time of the library staff as a whole.

DISTRIBUTION OF ACTIVITIES AMONG THE CATEGORIES OF STAFF

The percentage of the work done by the various types of staff for each activity during the 1961 survey is shown in Table 23. The table shows, for example, that librarians did 89.2 percent of the work of classifying books (activity 41), while library trainees did 9.3 percent, and the clerical staff the remaining 1.5 percent.

Because of the difference between the percentage of the staff made up by the library and clerical trainees in the 14 survey libraries and the full-time libraries as a whole, the figures throughout the table for the share of the work done by library trainees are undoubtedly greater than the national average, while the corresponding figures for clerical trainees are smaller.

Table 23 should be compared with the full descriptions of the activities given in Chapter 7. These descriptions will explain, for example, why activity 81 (advising readers) is partly done by staff other than librarians or library trainees. The full description of this activity shows that it also includes answering all kinds of queries from users, including, for example, telephone calls about hours of opening and closing. The answering of many of these queries requires little, if any, professional competence or training.

Variations between libraries

Distribution of the activities among the types of staff varies widely from library to library. One factor that affects this distribution is, of course, the composition of the staff of the individual library. If the staff consists of librarians only, for example, then it must, of course, follow that 100 percent of all activities carried out in that library will be performed by librarians. If, on the other hand, there is a shortage of librarians on a particular staff, and an unusually large proportion of say, clerical personnel, then much of the work ordinarily handled by librarians will, in this library, have to be distributed among the clerical staff.

Table 23. Percentage of the work done by the various categories of staff for each individual activity during the four-week work survey

Activity	Librarians	Library trainees	Clerical staff	Clerical trainees	Clerical Assistants	Other staff
1 Orientation	92.5	5.6	0.9	—	1.0	—
2 Newspaper book reviews	60.3	16.2	—	5.8	13.3	4.4
3 Reviews within the library	96.4	—	3.6	—	—	—
4 Control to prevent duplicate orders	82.9	5.5	11.6	—	—	—
5 Want lists	65.9	18.6	14.2	—	1.3	—
6 Books on approval	54.7	1.1	39.6	—	4.6	—
7 Book selection meetings	89.1	8.0	1.5	—	1.4	—
11 Verification	80.0	15.5	4.5	—	—	—
12 Ordering	58.6	4.6	36.4	—	0.4	—
13 Receiving	54.2	3.1	39.2	0.8	2.7	—
14 Collating	62.5	—	37.5	—	—	—
21 Book cards, etc.	15.8	6.9	64.7	5.3	7.3	—
22 Accessions list	36.1	1.1	55.6	4.4	2.8	—
23 Accession stamping	33.1	1.6	58.3	2.5	4.5	—
24 Accessions statistics	67.7	—	32.3	—	—	—
25 Filing of shelf list cards	26.6	8.3	39.0	9.0	17.1	—
29 Other	32.0	—	68.0	—	—	—
31 Books to bindery	57.6	2.3	39.7	—	0.4	—
32 Bindery list	37.4	6.0	44.4	9.0	3.2	—
33 Books from bindery	50.9	11.0	28.4	2.8	6.9	—
34 Binding control	46.8	4.5	48.7	—	—	—
35 Preparing bound books	38.4	9.0	28.6	2.5	13.3	8.2
36 Reinforcing with plastic	23.4	12.2	2.1	14.6	—	47.7

Table 23. *Continued*

	Librarians	Library trainees	Clerical staff	Clerical trainees	Clerical Assistants	Other staff
37 Books not bound	36.4	3.9	20.1	22.0	14.8	2.8
39 Other	53.3	1.5	33.9	2.4	8.9	—
41 Classification	89.2	9.3	1.5	—	—	—
42 Ordering printed cards	57.4	3.4	35.0	0.7	3.5	—
43 Adapting printed cards	37.0	14.1	43.7	5.2	—	—
44 Preparing manuscript slips	73.4	25.1	0.3	0.2	1.0	—
45 Copying catalog cards	8.2	11.7	64.2	5.1	10.8	—
46 Catalog cards without manuscript	84.2	9.6	5.8	0.4	—	—
47 Filing in catalogs	55.2	26.8	10.4	0.8	6.8	—
48 Corrections	60.6	14.4	24.3	0.3	0.4	—
49 Other	62.0	17.3	16.3	0.9	3.5	—
51 Examination of book stock	97.2	—	1.7	—	1.1	—
52 Repairs	7.6	12.9	33.8	4.3	24.4	17.0
53 Rebinding	47.6	—	39.2	13.2	—	—
54 Withdrawal	49.7	5.6	34.6	0.6	9.5	—
55 Storage	43.1	5.2	30.9	1.8	19.0	—
59 Summer deposits	83.8	0.4	7.5	1.3	7.0	—
61 Registration	68.5	13.8	6.9	2.0	8.8	—
64 Preparing borrowers' register	7.4	14.1	61.1	5.5	11.9	—
65 Renewals	39.2	20.3	12.8	3.7	24.0	—
66 Arranging borrowers' register	17.8	11.7	52.6	6.5	11.4	—
67 Reissuing borrowers' cards	39.9	10.3	31.9	0.3	17.6	—
68 Corrections	9.1	13.3	69.0	3.7	4.9	—
69 Other	9.6	13.9	62.0	4.5	10.0	—

71	Charging	36.7	26.9	8.4	2.4	25.6	—
72	Inserting book cards	18.8	26.7	8.4	2.3	43.8	—
73	Shelving	13.0	18.1	6.9	2.6	59.4	—
74	Shelf reading	25.1	31.5	15.8	3.6	24.0	—
75	Clearing counter	46.7	20.7	9.8	2.8	17.7	2.3
76	"Statistics"	16.6	17.4	29.5	3.6	32.9	—
77	Overdues	7.9	16.8	45.8	2.8	26.7	—
78	Messenger slips	5.3	—	35.5	6.4	52.8	—
79	Other	52.8	9.8	32.4	0.6	4.4	—
81	Advising readers	83.4	11.9	1.4	0.2	3.1	—
84	Reserves	39.8	28.3	8.7	2.6	20.6	—
85	Verification	92.3	7.7	—	—	—	—
86	Interlibrary loan	53.9	25.3	16.0	0.5	2.0	2.3
88	Introduction to library	86.9	4.8	5.1	—	3.2	—
89.1	Work with deposits	51.8	3.7	40.9	0.4	3.2	—
91	Reading lists	69.8	18.6	11.5	—	—	—
92	Charging periodicals and newspapers	51.7	10.9	24.7	2.9	9.8	—
93	Storing back issues of periodicals and newspapers	34.4	6.9	11.3	2.6	26.7	18.1
94	Special card indexes or catalogs	89.8	9.3	—	—	0.9	—
95	Clipping collection	36.1	7.2	9.5	2.6	11.0	33.6
96	Reading room statistics	65.4	21.3	—	13.3	—	—
101	Exhibitions in library	78.4	17.7	3.9	—	—	—
102	Signs and posters	50.1	39.8	—	—	10.1	—
103	Catalogs	40.3	3.6	36.6	0.5	13.8	5.2
104	Exhibitions outside library	33.6	—	—	—	66.4	—
105	Other events	100.0	—	—	—	—	—
106	Lists of recent acquisitions	32.4	2.8	35.9	7.7	21.2	—

Table 23. *Continued*

Activity	Librarians	Library trainees	Clerical staff	Clerical trainees	Clerical Assistants	Other staff
107 Story hours	100.0	—	—	—	—	—
108 Articles and interviews	100.0	—	—	—	—	—
109 Other	60.5	10.6	7.6	9.1	1.3	10.9
109.1 Children's book week	92.9	0.1	5.5	1.3	0.2	—
111 Book Proposals	62.4	5.6	30.1	1.5	0.4	—
112 Budgets	81.1	0.7	18.2	—	—	—
113 Review of book proposals and budgets	96.2	3.8	—	—	—	—
114 Driving bookmobiles	62.1	21.2	11.2	3.3	2.2	—
115 Bookmobile collection	87.3	12.7	—	—	—	—
118 Advice on technical services	18.3	—	81.7	—	—	—
119 Other	71.4	1.8	18.9	7.8	0.1	—
121 Board meetings	71.6	—	28.4	—	—	—
122 Professional meetings, trips, courses	93.1	1.3	4.8	0.8	—	—
123 Budget preparation	73.0	—	27.0	—	—	—
124 Accounts and auditing	31.5	0.4	61.6	4.4	2.0	0.1
125 Personnel	71.1	7.7	15.9	2.7	2.6	—
126 Premises and furniture	67.4	3.0	1.2	—	5.2	23.2
127 Planning	96.7	—	2.4	—	0.9	—
128 General office work, etc.	44.0	3.3	43.7	2.0	5.1	1.9
129.1 Report on library use of works of Danish authors	36.8	2.6	38.7	17.5	4.4	—
129.2 Inventory of book stock	1.2	4.7	94.1	—	—	—
135 Keeping up with recent acquisitions	87.4	6.8	2.3	—	3.5	—
136 Induction of trainees and new staff	47.3	45.8	2.4	0.8	3.7	—
139 Messenger service and transportation	26.3	11.1	8.3	2.4	24.0	27.9

10 Procedures, working methods, use of time, and salary costs in the processing work of the full-time libraries: methods of investigation

The total "processing" activity by which is meant the associated activities of book selection, purchasing, accession, binding, and cataloging, makes up 24.86 percent of all work done in the libraries. Because of the extent of these processes, a closer investigation of them offers the prospect of significant findings.

The component parts of these work processes are carried out in different ways and in different sequences in the various libraries. This made the investigations more difficult and necessitated the use of several other methods in addition to the work surveys. The methods used in investigating processing work therefore also included: questionnaires, work flow analyses, time counts, calculations, and other counts.

In most of the investigations, a distinction was made between processing of (1) books for adult departments of the libraries, (2) books for children's departments of the libraries, and (3) the processing work done by the county library departments of the county libraries for the part-time libraries.

In the smaller full-time libraries, the processing work for both the adult and children's departments is done entirely or in part by the same staff. As a rule, in the larger full-time libraries, however, there is a separate catalog department in which processing for the adult departments is done. In fact, in some of the largest full-time libraries, processing work for the adult departments is separated into several subdepartments. There may be separate accession departments, catalog departments, and binding departments, for example. In most of the children's libraries, the processing work is done as a part of the general office work of the library, or department, and only in the largest of these (whether they are formally independent institutions or are departments of a consolidated library), is this work separated into a proper "catalog department." In the county departments of the county libraries, the processing work for the part-time libraries is not a separate or independent part of the department, even though it constitutes the largest part of the work done by those departments. Regardless of the organizational structure of the various libraries, however, those places where the processing work is done are here referred to as the *catalog* departments of (1) the public library, (2) the children's library, and (3) the county department, respectively.

WORK SURVEYS

The work surveys carried out in the 14 libraries during the autumn of 1961, in two of the libraries during February, 1962, and the estimate of the year's work load for 1961-62 in six of these libraries, all included the processing work of the public libraries as well as the processing work of the children's libraries and of the county departments, and the results are not separately specified for each of these three catalog departments.

In addition to information on the extent of the activity and its distribution among the various types of workers, the surveys also gave data on the number of units processed in some of the activities. For example, in activity 23, the number of volumes stamped with the accessions number; in activity 44, the number of titles for which catalog manuscript copy was prepared; in activity 72, how many volumes had book cards inserted; and in activity 76, how many volumes were circulated. For those activities for which the number of units processed can be counted, the working time per unit processed can, of course, also be calculated.

The year's estimate made during the investigation allowed a more extensive calculation of working time per unit processed, at least for those activities for which yearly statistics were compiled. By means of the circulation statistics for the year (from departments included in the work survey—that is, excluding school libraries and departments at military installations), it is possible to determine the time used to charge out one book in activity 71, and the average time for advising readers per circulated volume in activity 81. In the same way, the average working time per volume for total processing can be calculated by means of the accessions statistics.

Determining the time used per unit (by volume or by title) by the methods of the work survey has the advantage over time counts in that such factors as waste time, all preparation time, and cleaning up time are included, as well as the actual performance time. Time measurements made by this method therefore agree more closely with the performance of the work in actual practice. The difference between the two methods will be discussed further in Chapter 12.

QUESTIONNAIRES

In January, 1962, a questionnaire was sent to all full-time public libraries, children's libraries, and the county departments of the county libraries. It included questions concerned with processing work, and covered such topics as the organization of, and the sources used for, book selection, methods of accession, registering of shelf lists, use of standard forms, arrangement of catalogs and card files, etc. The questionnaire was answered by 95 of the 96 full-time libraries then in existence. The information for 1962 in Chapter 11 was taken from this questionnaire.

In May, 1963, a questionnaire was sent to all full-time libraries in Sweden. The purpose of this questionnaire was to find out to what extent the recommendations made in the report on the Swedish work simplification study of 1958-60 (*Organisation och arbetsmetoder vid kommunala bibliotek*), had been carried out. This questionnaire was answered by 114 of the 132 Swedish full-time libraries then in operation. The answers made possible a comparison on individual points between the working methods of Swedish and Danish full-time libraries.

In December, 1963, a questionnaire was sent to all the Danish full-time libraries on binding matters, including their opinion of the cooperative binding regulations of Indbindingscentralen. This questionnaire was addressed to both public and children's libraries. Answers were received from all the 103 full-time libraries then in operation. The information for 1964 in Chapter 11 was obtained from the response to this questionnaire.

The high percentage of responses to these questionnaires has made it possible to obtain a good overall view of the working methods of libraries for certain parts of the processing work. From among these responses, individual libraries with various working methods may be selected for further investigation.

WORK FLOW ANALYSES

The flow of work was investigated in 13 catalog departments which were using various working procedures. Of these departments, eight were in public libraries, three in children's libraries, and two in county departments. Thorough analyses, including diagramming the flow of work, were carried out in 10 of the 13 catalog departments. Of these, two were public library departments in county libraries, three public library departments in "other full-time libraries," two children's library departments in county libraries, one a children's library department in an "other full-time library," and two were county departments in county libraries.

Work flow analyses were carried out by means of interviews with the workers in the catalog departments who actually did the work from day to day. The procedures were recorded in work flow diagrams and these were then verified by a review of the diagrams with the staff members who had been interviewed.

The work flow diagrams indicate which operations were involved in the work and the sequence in which they were carried out. In addition, they show which forms and other aids were used in the various operations. They also show the category of staff which performed the individual operations. They are not, however, very dependable as far as this latter information is concerned, since only a few libraries have carried out a well-defined division of the activities among the various categories of staff. The libraries investigated could only report which staff category performed the operation most frequently. In most of the libraries, moreover, almost all tasks are in practice done at various times by staff members belonging to different categories.

TIME COUNTS

During the winter of 1962-63, time counts were made in the public and children's library catalog departments of 17 libraries, of which five were in county libraries, four were in suburban libraries, and eight were in "other full-time libraries."

The time counts included the following operations:

1. Writing work slips
2. Writing order lists for book dealers
3. Ordering printed cards
4. Adapting printed cards
5. Writing manuscript slips for catalog cards
6. Copying catalog cards from manuscript
7. Writing catalog cards without manuscript
8. Writing book cards
9. Writing date slips, book pockets, or pocket labels
10. Writing series slips
11. Writing shelf list cards

12.   Writing bindery lists
13.   Receiving books from bindery
14.   Writing accessions lists
15.   Stamping and noting accessions information in books
16.1 Sorting printed cards by alphabet
16.2 Sorting typed and printed cards by alphabet and number
16.3 Sorting handwritten cards by alphabet
16.4 Sorting typed two-part slips by alphabet
16.5 Filing cards by alphabet
16.6 Filing cards by class divisions
16.7 Checking of the alphabetical filing
16.8 Checking of the classified filing
16.9 Sorting printed slips in numerical order of printed cards
16.10 Sorting printed cards by class divisions

The time counts were made by the workers themselves following written and oral instruction given at each library, and were carried out over relatively brief periods for each activity measured.

The instructions included a description of each operation as it was done at the library concerned, with carefully written rules about which component operations should be included in the measurements. An attempt was made to avoid altering the operations as carried out in daily practice due to the taking of the measurements, and to have the tasks done at the usual pace as far as possible. The time counts covered certain preparations for carrying out the operation, including setting out the materials (books, cards, etc.), carrying out the actual operation, such control or revision of the completed operation as might be necessary, and the correction of any errors. The instructions included practical details for making the time counts and keeping records.

Time counts were not successfully carried out for operations 6, 7, 10, 13, and 16.3 because the variations in working methods in the 17 libraries were too extensive, and because it was not possible to do time counts for a sufficient number of the units (volumes, titles, or cards) involved in those operations to get reliable results.

During the autumn of 1963, further time counts were made of operation 5 (writing manuscript slips for catalog cards) and operation 6 (copying catalog cards from manuscript) in ten libraries, of which seven were county libraries, and three were "other full-time libraries." Of these ten libraries, seven had not taken part in the previous time counts made during the winter of 1962-63. As with the first time counts, these supplementary counts were made by the staff members of each library, following written and oral instructions.

An additional time count of operation 5 was made at the public library catalog department of one of the largest of the county libraries during the winter of 1963-64 for such a large number of units (titles) that the result probably corresponds quite closely to the actual average time and salary cost for this operation in this library.

Although every one of the operations measured was carried out by different methods in different libraries, the number of cooperating libraries included in the counts ensured the collection of a large enough body of data so that the results probably correspond closely to the time actually required to perform the operations in the libraries. The proportion of beginning and experienced staff and fast and slow workers may also be taken to correspond closely to the average for all the full-time libraries.

For each operation, the results of the time counts were given in minutes *per work unit,* that is, the number of volumes, titles, or cards processed. Salary cost per unit was calculated for each operation on the basis of salaries paid to the worker plus the pension contributions of the libraries. Salary cost per minute was calculated from the annual salary plus the total annual pension contribution for each individual worker, taking into consideration holidays, vacation, sick leave, and study time for library trainees. Waste time was accounted for in the results by adding an increment of 15 percent.

The working time and costs arrived at in the time counts will not, of course, correspond exactly to the actual time and costs for each of the operations measured. In measuring the performance of the operations, attempts were made to include both preparation and follow-up time. However, some of the component elements of work which link the individual operations in the total work processes will always defy measurement; and some work involving time-consuming or difficult units (which because of snags in procedure or special handling required, were not processed along with those units they would ordinarily precede or follow in the normal processing sequence) was not measured in the time counts. In addition, it is almost impossible to work at a normal rate when measuring one's own work, and operations must be considered as usually being done more quickly during time counts than they normally are.

The percentage by which the time count costs should be incremented in order to make them correspond to the actual costs will vary with the complexity of the operations (including the amount and extent of those parts which cannot be measured), and with the number of work units which must be carried out separately, as time counts can include only work that falls within the normal work flow.

The results of the time counts should, however, after certain corrections, approximately indicate the libraries' average time and salary costs per work unit. The general administrative expenses of the libraries, for example, such as rent, interest on office equipment, etc., are not included. These expenses are, however, sufficiently uniform so that an average increment will make an individual library's estimated costs correspond fairly closely to its actual costs. This administrative increment can be computed at 17.5 percent.

For certain operations, the results can be checked against the results obtained from the work surveys. Operation 5 (writing manuscript slips for catalog cards) may be compared with work survey activity 44, for example, and operation 15 (stamping and noting accessions information in books) may be compared with the results of work survey activity 23.

CALCULATIONS

To supplement the results of the time counts, one of the largest county libraries (the same one which carried out the time counts for operation 5 during the winter of 1963-64) calculated the time and salary costs per title cataloged in its public library catalog department and also the time and costs for the entire processing sequence, including purchasing, accession, binding, and cataloging, but excluding book selection. The salary costs were based on the results of the time counts and also on the actual use of the various categories of staff for the individual work processes. This allowed for great reliability in the estimate.

OTHER COUNTS

In addition to the methods mentioned above, individual tallies and smaller investigations were carried out. In one of the larger "other full-time libraries," and in one suburban library with only one librarian on the staff, the annual accessions were divided into the number of titles and volumes which (1) could be obtained through the cooperative binding of Indbindingscentralen; (2) for which printed cards were available from Bibliotekscentralen; and (3) for which printed cards were not available. These were then further broken down into non-fiction and fiction, periodicals, and yearbooks, and into newly published, or older titles.

Finally, statistics available in *Biblioteksårbog* and the State Library Inspection were used.

11 Procedures and methods of processing work: results of the investigation

Processing work in the more than 100 full-time libraries is done separately for those books acquired for adult departments and for those acquired for children's departments. Books which the county libraries acquire for the part-time libraries are processed separately from their own. There are, however, as far as can be determined, no instances where the work is done separately for a main library and its branches. Apart from the independent children's libraries which are managed by part-time librarians, there are more than 200 "catalog departments" in the slightly more than 100 libraries which do processing work. In all of them the work consists of book selection, purchasing, accession, binding, and cataloging, but the detailed operations are not done in the same way or in the same sequence in any two catalog departments.

Even within an individual catalog department there may be several parallel but different procedures and working methods. Processing of the books varies according to whether:

1. The books are recent publications or older books being acquired through supplementary or replacement purchases.

2. The books are bought through trade booksellers or through second-hand booksellers.

3. The books are delivered through cooperative binding.

4. Printed catalog cards are available.

5. The books are in paper covers or in publisher's bindings.

6. The books are for main library circulation, for reading room use, for departments, or for branches.

Of most importance for the processing procedure is whether the books are bought through the cooperative binding service of Bibliotekscentralen and whether printed cards are obtained from that agency. Three main types of procedures can be established:

1. Procedures for books procured through cooperative binding and for which printed catalog cards are available.

2. Procedures for books not procured through cooperative binding, but for which printed cards are available.

3. Procedures for books not procured through cooperative binding, and for which printed catalog cards are not available.

Appendix 4 shows an example of the flow of processing work in the public library catalog department of a medium-size county library (code designation CF2). The district served by this library has a population of between 15,000 and 25,000, and the annual accession for the adult departments of the library is about 3,000 volumes. The diagram shows the processing sequence for all titles new to the library, that is, both newly published titles, and older (but in-print) titles which were not previously held by the library, bought for the adult circulation departments. Variations in the work flow for smaller categories of purchased books, such as those that have usable publisher's bindings and are therefore not to be given library bindings, for example, are not included in the diagram. Moreover, the diagram is normalized (all corrections of errors are omitted, for example—and no regard was taken of the effect on the flow of work of new staff members or trainees being brought into the department).

The work flow analysis in Appendix 4 was made about six months before the rearrangement of Indbindingscentralen's cooperative binding procedure. Consequently no use is shown in the diagram of the new cooperative binding service. The main emphasis during the analysis was on procedures for titles for which printed cards were available from Bibliotekscentralen, as this included the largest part of the accessions of the library. Procedures for titles for which printed cards were not available were, however, also analyzed, so that the diagram therefore includes procedures for titles for which printed cards were available, as well as for titles for which they were not.

A code of symbols and a list of abbreviations used in the diagram is given in Appendix 3. Appendix 4A shows what information was contained on the forms used in the processing work.

BOOK SELECTION

By 1962 almost all library boards had delegated the authority for book selection to the chief librarians. Only in nine full-time libraries had this authority not been delegated for the adult departments, and in seven full-time libraries for the children's departments. The libraries in which the boards took part in book selection were almost all "other full-time libraries" having only one librarian on the staff.

In 1962 there was no full-time library in which all book selection decisions were delegated by the chief librarian to other staff members. In 26 full-time libraries, however, the chief librarian had delegated all book selection decisions for the children's departments, either to the supervising children's librarian, or to a committee consisting of children's and school librarians. In 31 libraries the chief librarian had authorized one or more staff members to make some book selection decisions for the adult departments. Of these, in 21 libraries one or more staff members were authorized to make decisions on book selection for certain sub-departments only—for the reading room or for the hospital collection, for example. In 12 libraries the authorization to make the final decision concerned the number of copies and in 12 libraries replacement purchases. In eight libraries this authorization concerned the placement of books in the departments of the library, and in six libraries the authorization was for selection within certain subject fields, such as technology, for example.

Thus, while book selection is determined principally by the chief librarians, there are a good many instances where final decisions on selection, to a larger or smaller degree, are delegated to other staff members.

Even the librarians who do not have the right of final decision in book selection are generally not without some influence in this respect. Their expert knowledge may be utilized through advisory book selection meetings. In 41 libraries which had more than one librarian on the staff in 1962, book selection meetings were held in which all the librarians took part, and in 13, book selection meetings were held in which at least some of the librarians took part. No book selection meetings, however, were held in 21 libraries.

In 24 of the total of 34 libraries which either did not hold book selection meetings, or which held meetings in which not all of the librarians took part, the librarians who did not participate were able to suggest books for purchase in other ways. Written proposals could be made in 16 of these libraries. In 8 of these 16 libraries written proposals were of such quantity and quality that they were of practical significance in the selection process. In the other eight libraries, however, such written proposals were of no practical significance.

Sources of book selection
The book selection sources used by the full-time libraries for Danish books for their adult departments during 1962 are shown in Table 24.

Table 24. Book selection sources used in the selection of Danish books for the adult departments of 95 full-time libraries

Sources	Number of libraries
Semiannual list, annual list from Bibliotekscentralen	90
Regular review of *Det danske bogmarked*	85
Clipped newspaper reviews	64
Regular review of certain periodicals, excluding *Bogens Verden*	53
Regular receipt of books on approval without special order	27
Reading and reporting on books ordered on approval	26
Advice from subject specialists (not including subject specialists on library staffs)	30

The libraries were not questioned on the use of the reviews in *Bogens Verden,* published by the Danish Library Association, as it may be taken for granted that all full-time libraries are guided to some extent by these reviews in selecting books for both adult and children's departments.

During 1964, 17 libraries clipped reviews from one to three newspapers, 21 libraries clipped reviews from four to eight newspapers, and nine libraries clipped reviews from more than eight newspapers. Forty libraries did not clip any newspaper reviews. Standing orders for book reviews from a clipping service were maintained by seven libraries.

During 1964, the adult departments of 45 libraries received books on approval, after specifying individual titles to the dealer, for use in selecting books. Current books sent on approval without order were received by 21 libraries. Four libraries bought approval examples during the first order period of the cooperative binding procedure of Indbindingscentralen [see page 112 for an explanation of Indbindingscentralen's "order periods"]. Twenty-six libraries took no books on approval.

In book selection for the children's departments in 1962, the semiannual cumulations of the "Weekly List," the "Annual List," and the regular reviews of *Det danske bogmarked,* [the journal of the Association of Danish Publishers, which also contains the "Weekly Lists"], were used in practically all places. Regular checking of the reviews in journals (*Bogens Verden* excepted) was done in about two-thirds of the libraries, and reviews clipped from newspapers were used by about half the libraries.

In 1964, the children's departments of 41 libraries made use of consignments sent on approval. In these consignments, the titles had been ordered by the libraries. In 26 libraries, current approval consignments were sent without a library order by the booksellers. The first order period of the collective binding service was used for approval by three libraries. Twenty-one libraries made no use of approval consignments for selection for the children's departments. All of these 21 libraries were in areas of less than 15,000 inhabitants; 18 of them were in districts of less than 10,000.

Registration of book selection
Several methods are used to record book purchase decisions. These methods include marking copies of *Det danske bogmarked* or the lists used during selection meetings, writing out selection slips during the meeting, or marking selection slips prepared before the meeting.

In 1962, printed or duplicated selection forms (work slips) prepared before, during, or after the selection were used for the adult departments of 56 libraries, of which 21 used the standard library forms. While 38 libraries used no special printed or duplicated form for selection, several of these libraries used special typed or handwritten form slips.

In 1961, one library introduced the use of multiple-copy forms interleaved with carbon. After Bibliotekscentralen began to supply order forms in sets in 1962, several libraries adopted this type of form.

Use of printed multiple-copy forms means that the work slip, the order slip for the bookseller, the accession slip, and the slip for the "in-process file" kept at the circulation desk are all prepared at the same time.

New arrangement of cooperative binding
The new collective binding arrangement of Indbindingscentralen in 1963 has had a noticeable effect on book selection in those libraries which use this service. In January, 1964, information from 90 libraries indicated that 78 of these used the cooperative binding. For the purchase of books for adult departments, 41 libraries used Indbindingscentralen's first and second order periods [see page 112] while 35 libraries used only the first order period. For the purchase of books for children's departments, 36 libraries used the first and second order periods, while 17 libraries used only the first order period. Use of the first order period of the cooperative binding service means that the libraries have made quick decisions, based, as a rule, entirely on the annotations printed on Indbindingscentralen's order slips.

The county departments
During the past ten years, advice and consultation on book selection

by the county library departments of the county libraries to the part-time libraries in their districts has grown to include most, if not all, of the book selection for those libraries. In recent years this consultation generally has comprised: holding one or two joint meetings each year with all the part-time libraries in the district for the purpose of reviewing new books, issuing duplicated book proposals, sending individual proposals, and participating in local book selection meetings at those libraries. Even before the new arrangement of the cooperative binding service, the county library in Roskilde (and, later, other county libraries) had introduced advisory book selection meetings for the part-time libraries in the district at about monthly intervals during the winter months. It now also holds meetings in connection with the second order period of the collective binding service.

PURCHASE

The majority of the library book purchases are made through local booksellers. Purchases are also made, however, through second-hand booksellers and by using dealer's catalogs and search lists. In addition, special purchases are made of subscription works, and periodicals and yearbooks are purchased directly from publishers. Book salesmen are also used.

Generally, purchase through booksellers is made by written order. Orders are also placed by telephone or by visit to the bookstore, however, and in certain libraries a great part of the buying is done in this way. The most common method is to prepare order lists from the work slips which are written before, during, or after the selection is made. In 1962, 36 libraries used special forms for ordering from booksellers. Of these, 19 libraries used order lists and 17 used individual order slips.

Library book purchases, however, have been strongly influenced by the new arrangement Indbindingscentralen established in 1963 for cooperative binding.

ACCESSION

Accessioning includes entering acquisitions data in the books and keeping accessions lists. It also includes maintaining shelf lists, preparing book cards, date slips, book pockets or labels, and keeping statistics of library material acquired.

The extent of the accessions data entered in the books processed during 1962 in the public library catalog departments is shown in Table 25. Table 26 shows how many libraries used the various forms of accession lists in the catalog departments of the public libraries in 1962. The extent of the information contained in the accessions lists is shown in Table 27.

Table 25. **Accessions data entered in books processed in the catalog departments of 95 public libraries**

Information entered	Number of libraries
Name of library	91
Location of book in library (reading room, etc.)	85
Classification number	89
Volume number (for multi-volume works)	87
Copy number	83
Accession number	61
Price of book	7
Bookseller	3
Bookbinder	1
Accessions date	12
Other information	6

Table 26. **Forms of accessions lists in catalog departments of 95 public libraries**

Forms of accessions lists	Number of libraries
Handwritten accessions book	18
Copies of order lists	20
Copies of statements from dealers	9
Accessions lists, typed specifically for purpose	33
Copies of orders (order slips)	5
Accessions slips, specially prepared	7
No accessions list or slips (only general shelf list)	9
Other form for recording accessions	6

Table 27. **Information on accessions list over and above author, title, number of copies, and dealer, in the catalog departments of the same 95 public libraries**

Information	Number of libraries
Classification number	41
Lot book price	35
Net book price	11
Accession number	60
Accession date	45
Distribution to departments of library	49
Number of copies	34
Other information	25

Shelf list

Shelf lists are kept in a number of different ways. In some libraries the shelf list corresponds exactly to the distribution of the books in the departments of the library; that is, it is divided into sections corresponding to the various departments. Other libraries arrange the shelf list in classified order with cards for the books in all departments in one sequence. However, the shelf list in all libraries is divided into (1) a list for adult departments, and (2) a list for children's departments.

Some libraries have a central shelf list divided by departments plus a union shelf list (with the cards for all departments in one sequence) located in the main library, and have, in addition, separate shelf lists for each department which are located in the departments themselves.

In 1962, standardized shelf list cards (library standard forms 38, 39, or 40) were used by 27 libraries, and printed catalog cards were used by 41 libraries. Besides these standard forms, some libraries made their own shelf list cards, and some used several different forms for the shelf list. The total number of different shelf list cards (or forms) used in the catalog departments of the public libraries, children's libraries, and county departments was about 200. The extent of the information on the shelf list cards is shown in Table 28.

Table 28. **Information entered on shelf list cards in the catalog departments of 95 public libraries. (In addition to the departmental location, classification number, author, title, edition, and volume number.)**

Information	Number of libraries
Number of copies	86
Accession number	62
Accession date	28
Dealer	32
Price	32
Binder	26
Binding price	9
Entry date	27
Other information	30

Note: Other items occurring most frequently were publisher and year of publication.

Inventory

The extent of inventorying the book stock—that is, checking the shelf list against the existing book stock in the adult departments of the libraries—is shown in Table 29. For comparison, the extent of inventorying the book stock in the adult departments of the Swedish full-time libraries is shown in Table 30.

Table 29. **Extent of inventory taking in adult departments
of 95 Danish full-time libraries during a two-year period
from April 1, 1959 to March 13, 1961**

Inventory taken	Number of libraries
Entire book stock more than once	5
Entire book stock once	21
Part of book stock more than once	6
Part of book stock once	30
No inventory	37

Note: In 3 libraries the entire book stock was inventoried once and part of the stock more than once; and in one library part of the book stock was inventoried more than once and part of the stock once.

Table 30. **Extent of inventory taking in adult and children's departments
of 114 Swedish full-time libraries during a four-year period
from January 1, 1959 to December 31, 1962**

Inventory taken	Number of libraries
Entire book stock more than once	0
Entire book stock once	10
Part of book stock more than once	13
Part of book stock once	29
No inventory	65

Book card

In 1964, book cards were written in about half the libraries according to the rules in *Vejledning ved ordningen af biblioteker, der ikke anvender Cutternumre (Guide for the Arrangement of Libraries Not Using Cutter Numbers)*. In some libraries, books for certain departments were provided with two book cards. This was most prevalent in some of the special collections of the county libraries used for circulation to the part-time libraries (bookmobile collections, for example). One of the two cards served to record the loan of the book from one department to another or from the county library to a part-time library, while the other card served to record the loan of the book to an individual reader. With the introduction of photocharging in some libraries in recent years, most of those libraries have discontinued using book cards.

Date slip

In January, 1962, 72 libraries used pasted-in date slips, 19 used loose date cards, and 4 used transaction cards (photocharging). In most of the 72 libraries which used pasted-in date slips, information about the book (classification number, author, title, volume number, and copy

110

number) was only entered on the slip itself, but in some libraries, notations were also made on the book pocket. The 19 libraries which used loose date cards noted information about the book either on the pocket or above it. Purchase through cooperative binding has reduced the work of writing book cards and pockets since Indbindingscentralen's new collective binding arrangement includes the delivery of books with printed book cards and pockets.

Accessions statistics

In the full-time libraries, accessions statistics are kept concurrently with preparation of the acquisitions lists, either monthly or at the end of the fiscal year. Accessions statistics usually are reported from the accessions lists, but also by using running notations on special cards for each separate author (also used for the author's report). Also used are accessions slips (a copy of the multiple order form, for example) which are now replacing the accessions lists. These slips are filed and stored until the accessions count at the end of the fiscal year, and the author's report about a half a year later, are completed.

BINDING

Use of the collective binding facilities of Indbindingscentralen, both under the old arrangement used until February, 1963, and the new arrangement used after that date, has had a noticeable effect on the binding work of the libraries.

Old cooperative binding arrangement

Under the old cooperative binding arrangement, Indbindingscentralen sent out lists of titles which had been selected for collective binding. Books were then ordered either by returning a copy of the lists with an indication of the number of copies of each title wanted, or by sending in a typewritten order list. At the same time, a copy of the order to Indbindingscentralen was usually sent to the bookseller through whom delivery of the books was desired. There was no time limit on placing the order, and the individual libraries were free to select the position of the classification number on the spine and even to specify the style and placement of the lettering for author and title. The type and color of binding, however, were determined by Indbindingscentralen. All copies of the same title in the same lot were bound in uniform color and style, and most lots were done in whole niger. The bound books were delivered with date slips attached and included book pockets without the classification number, author, title, or volume number. Delivery was made from Indbindingscentralen to the bookseller specified by the libraries, then from the bookstores to the libraries. The billing for the books was made by the bookseller from whom the books were received, and by Indbindingscentralen for the binding.

Because the orders by Indbindingscentralen to the publishers for unbound books were based only on anticipated demand, at intervals Indbindingscentralen was forced to send out remainder lists of library bound books at reduced prices.

New cooperative binding arrangement

Under the new cooperative binding arrangement, Indbindingscentralen sends out two-part order slips for each title to be included in the collective binding service. Brief annotations about the books are given on the verso of the order slips. The order is placed by returning one part of the slip to Indbindingscentralen giving the desired number of copies. The slips are to be returned within a time limit which is stated on the slip. The first order period expires on, or shortly after, the publication date of the book, and the second order period expires seven to nine weeks after the first period. In connection with publication by Bibliotekscentralen of the semiannual cumulations of the "Weekly List" of new books (which appears in *Det danske bogmarked*), Indbindingscentralen has established a third order period for which ordering is done by returning a checked copy of the semiannual list indicating which titles and how many copies are wanted. Finally, in connection with publication of Bibliotekscentralen's annual list (subtitled *Årskatalog*), Indbindingscentralen sends out quotation lists of titles included in that list which were not previously offered.

After a short transition period, the new collective binding introduced standardized printing on the spine in conformance with the catalog cards of Bibliotekscentralen, including classification numbers for nonfiction. Under this arrangement, the books are not supplied with author and title marks or other special lettering on the spine. The type and color of binding are still determined entirely by Indbindingscentralen, and most titles are still bound in full niger. The books are delivered with book card and pocket, both printed with classification number, author, title, and volume number.

Delivery is from Indbindingscentralen to the Danish Booksellers' Association distribution organization (Danske Boghandleres Kommissionsanstalt), which forwards the books to the libraries via the bookseller. Billing for both books and binding is made to the distribution organization. The bookseller specified on the order slip receives his commission from the distribution organization even though he merely acts as a forwarding agent.

The introduction of order periods means that Indbindingscentralen need not buy more copies of each title than the number of orders on hand at the end of each order period, and remainder sales of bound books are thus avoided.

Use of the new cooperative binding arrangement saves the libraries the preparation of both order lists for the bookseller and bindery lists. In addition, sending new books from the library to the bindery is avoided, as are the preparation of book cards and pockets (which now need only to be given a copy number), and the details of specifying the type, color, and lettering of the binding. Billing is simplified by the use of a single statement for both purchase and binding.

Use of cooperative binding
In 1964, of 90 full-time libraries, 78 used the new cooperative binding arrangement, while only 63 had used the old.

Other binderies
In 1962, binderies were located in the districts of 75 Danish full-time libraries. These local binderies were used by 65 libraries. Sixty-two of these also used non-local binders other than Indbindingscentralen.

In 1964, of 90 full-time libraries from which information was received, 68 used local binderies, while 45 also used non-local binderies other than Indbindingscentralen.

Delivery time
In January, 1964, the delivery time for books ordered through Indbindingscentralen's cooperative binding service was about three months because of the great use of the new arrangement. However, because of the elements of work simplification involved in the cooperative binding system, considerably less time can normally be expected in the processing work of the libraries using it than in the libraries using other binderies, or which use the individual, or non-collective, binding service of Indbindingscentralen.

Binding prices
The average binding prices per bound volume for local binderies are shown in Table 31, and for non-local binderies in Table 32.

Table 31. Average prices of local binderies (not including sales tax) in January, 1964

Price per volume in kroner	Number of libraries
7.00— 7.99	12
8.00— 8.99	38
9.00— 9.99	7
10.00—10.99	3
12.00—12.99	2

Table 32. Average prices of non-local binderies (not including sales tax) in January, 1964

Price per volume in kroner	Number of libraries
6.00—6.99	3
7.00—7.99	13
8.00—8.99	30
9.00—9.99	7

In January, 1964, the average binding price per volume in whole niger delivered through the cooperative service of Indbindingscentralen, including book card and pocket with printed classification number, author, title, and volume number was 8.00 kroner (sales tax included).

Bindery list

Table 33 shows the usage in 1962 of various forms of bindery lists. Most of the 23 libraries which didn't use any of the forms listed may be assumed to have used a general list without printed headings. Some libraries used combinations of several forms for binding lists. The most common were combinations of bindery lists with printed headings and book cards, date slips, or book pockets.

Table 33. Forms of bindery lists used in catalog departments of 95 public libraries

Bindery lists	Number of libraries
Bindery list with printed heading	33
Bindery slip (one slip per volume)	6
Book card, date slip, or book pocket	40
None of these	23

Use of books without library bindings

In recent years, the use by the full-time libraries of paperbound books and books with the original publisher's bindings (sometimes with plastic jackets added in the library) has increased noticeably. This development may be presumed to be due principally to the better quality (especially the durability) of the publisher's bindings and to the desire of the libraries for a more attractive book stock. Table 34 shows the percentage of the books acquired during 1963 which were not given library bindings.

114

Table 34. **Books without library bindings shown as a percentage of accessions in adult and children's departments**

Percent of accessions not given library bindings	Adult departments	Children's departments
0— 10	54	42
11— 20	24	12
21— 40	5	9
41— 60	0	4
61— 80	0	2
81—100	0	0

Note: According to estimates made by the libraries in January, 1964.

The county departments

The greatest reorganization of work due to the new cooperative binding arrangement has been in the county departments of the county libraries. In those districts where a significant number of part-time libraries use the cooperative binding extensively, the work of the county departments, such as preparing orders for bookstores, making binding lists, book cards and date slips, book pockets or labels, and the delivery of shipments to binderies, has been greatly reduced. However, the new cooperative binding arrangement is not yet used in any county library district to the fullest possible extent.

CATALOGING

The establishment of the cataloging operation of Biblioteckscentralen and the use of the printed catalog card have, of course, been of tremendous importance in easing the cataloging work of the libraries.

Printed catalog cards

In recent years, Biblioteckscentralen has cataloged more than 2,000 Danish books annually. The cataloging is first offered by distributing printed slips on a subscription basis. These slips are used for ordering the printed catalog cards. The printed cards from Biblioteckscentralen are main entry unit cards without a classification number or added entry headings. Suggestions for classification numbers and added entries, are made, however, on the bottom of the printed catalog card. These suggestions were also made on the order slips until April 1, 1964, after which they were discontinued, and are now printed only on the cards. Libraries order the desired number of cards by the card serial number and then adapt them by adding classification numbers and headings.

In 1962, 91 Danish full-time libraries used the printed cards from Bibliotekscentralen, while four full-time libraries did not. (However, three of these libraries used the printed order slips as manuscript for their own catalog cards.) These four libraries printed all of their own catalog cards on office offset printing equipment. Four other libraries printed at least some of their own cards.

The public catalog departments of 23 libraries used the printed cards (or slips) from Bibliotekscentralen without changing the suggested classification numbers and added entries, while changes were made by 71 libraries. Classification numbers were changed in 32 libraries, added entries were changed in 67 libraries, and other changes were made in 6 libraries. The majority of libraries which did not follow the proposed added entries made fewer author and title cards than suggested, but the author and title cards prepared were selected from among the entries proposed by Bibliotekscentralen. In 23 libraries, more subject cards were made than were suggested, 12 libraries made fewer subject cards, and 21 libraries made subject cards different from those proposed.

Arrangement of catalogs

The organization of the catalog apparatus in the full-time libraries varies widely. This applies to the public as well as to the official catalogs. In addition to card catalogs, some libraries, particularly the larger, publish their own printed accessions catalogs.

The public catalogs may consist of:

1. A dictionary catalog with author, title, and subject cards in one list.

2. An author and title catalog, either combined or separate, supplemented with an alphabetical subject catalog.

3. An author and title catalog either combined or separate, supplemented with a classified catalog with a subject index either separate or interfiled in the author and title catalog.

In addition to these three principal forms of the public catalogs, there are, particularly in branch libraries, various forms of incomplete catalogs. An example might be a title catalog supplemented with an author catalog for nonfiction only.

Despite the general use of the same classification and cataloging rules, the standardization necessary for the complete utilization of centralized processing facilities is not yet prevalent in Danish full-time libraries. However, in recent years, development in this area has increased, and this has occurred without any stimulation from the central organizations other than the reorganization of the collective binding service of Indbindingscentralen in 1963.

FINAL PROCESSING

In most of the catalog departments of the full-time libraries, the binding and cataloging work are carried on more or less at the same time. In the majority of these departments, final preparations of varying extent still remain after this work is completed. These preparations include the stamping of the bound books, the distribution of the volumes to the various departments of the library, and the filing of catalog, shelf list, and other cards or slips in the catalogs and other files. If not already done in connection with earlier processing, this stage of the work in many libraries also includes preparing and inserting series slips and book plates, and possibly such minor tasks as packaging volumes of periodicals which are not to be bound and inserting new pages in looseleaf volumes.

12 Amount of work, time, and costs of processing activities: results of the investigation

THE ENTIRE PROCESSING SEQUENCE

According to the four-week survey of 1961, the processing sequence (activities 1-49) made up 24.86 percent of the total work load of the 14 participating libraries. This percentage includes the processing done by by county libraries for the part-time libraries in their areas. In four of the six libraries which made an estimate of their work load on a yearly basis (the four non-county libraries), the processing sequence made up 24.12 percent of the total.

The average time spent on processing an accessioned volume varies significantly from library to library. Working methods as well as the percentage of accessions for which printed cards from Bibliotekscentralen are used have a bearing on processing time. In the eight non-county libraries which took part in the work survey, the shortest time for processing was 34.27 minutes per volume, the longest time was 78.83 minutes, and the average was 50.65 minutes. In the four non-county year's estimate libraries, which were, on the average, considerably smaller than the non-county libraries which took part in the four-week survey, processing time took an average of 41.31 minutes per volume. This difference can probably be largely accounted for by the fact that these four libraries made greater use of the printed catalog cards from Bibliotekscentralen.

The more high-salaried members of the library work force (librarians and trained clerical staff) are usually much more strongly represented in processing activities than in library work on the whole. However, if the salary cost per working minute is computed on the same basis for processing activities as that which applies to library work on the whole, the 50.65 minutes per accessioned volume in the eight non-county survey libraries corresponds to a salary cost of 8.33 kroner. In the four non-county libraries which took part in the yearly estimate, the corresponding salary cost would be 7.41 kroner per volume.

According to the work survey, about 15 percent of the total working time of the full-time libraries is taken up with general administrative tasks. Consequently the cost for carrying out the various operations should be increased by a corresponding administrative increment.

The average acquisition cost per accessioned volume in the eight non-county survey libraries is shown in Table 35. This cost does not, however, include the amount which would have to be added to cover the proportionate share of the library's costs for such things as rent, janitorial service, depreciation on office equipment, etc. This amount would be extremely difficult to estimate since it varies widely from library to library depending on many factors, including, for example, the age and condition of the building. The book price shown in the table is the average for the adult and children's departments combined, and is very close to the average for all full-time libraries as a whole, which in 1961-62 was 18.34 kroner.

Table 35. Average cost of acquisition per accessioned volume (in kroner)

Components of acquisitions price	Average cost per volume
Price of book (including binding)	18.60
Materials:	
work slips	
catalog cards	
book cards and pockets	
shelf list cards	(approx.) 0.50
Salary cost	8.33
Increment for administration	1.46
Total	28.89

Salary costs are further broken down and the distribution of working time for various phases of the processing work is shown in Table 36. The difference in time and costs between the two groups of libraries can be largely accounted for by the fact that the libraries which made the yearly estimate were on the average smaller than the four-week work survey libraries (therefore their salary scales tended to be smaller), plus the fact that they made greater use of printed cards.

Table 36. **Average distribution of processing work among the separate procedures according to working time and salary costs per volume accessioned**

Process	According to work survey in 8 non-county libraries		According to year's estimate in 4 non-county libraries	
	minutes	kroner	minutes	kroner
Book selection	11.62	1.91	15.69	2.82
Book purchasing	2.34	0.39	3.46	0.62
Accessioning	9.50	1.56	6.88	1.23
Binding	4.71	0.77	4.92	0.88
Cataloging	22.48	3.70	10.36	1.86
	50.65	8.33	41.31	7.41
Administrative increment, 17.5%	—	1.46	—	1.30
Total per volume	50.65	9.79	41.31	8.71

Working time and salary costs in processing activities depend not only on the working methods of the libraries, and what percentage of the cataloging is done by the use of printed cards from Bibliotekscentralen, but also upon how large a part of the accessions is purchased through the cooperative binding service of Indbindingscentralen.

No statistics are available for the country as a whole. However, in two libraries, a special count of one year's accessions were made. One library (A) was a small library with only one librarian on the staff; the other (B) was a non-county library in a district with just under 20,000 inhabitants. The count included only the acquisitions for the adult departments. Library A acquired 745 titles (863 volumes) during the year and library B, 1,843 titles (2,998 volumes).

In library A, 41.2 percent of the titles acquired were obtainable through the cooperative binding service; in library B, 31.7 percent. It should be noted that under the present arrangement, the percentage of a library's accessions that are available through the cooperative binding service depends to a considerable extent upon how recently the books desired were published and whether or not they were published in Denmark. In general, Danish publications and those purchased within a year of publication are more often available than foreign or older publications.

In library A, printed catalog cards were used for 95.6 percent of all titles; in library B, 82.8 percent.

BOOK SELECTION

The processes of book selection, which include reading annotations, reviews, etc., attending book selection meetings, making decisions as to purchase, and preparing purchase proposals, are reported inadequately, at best, by the results of the work survey. The year's estimate figures are more dependable for these activities. The working time used by librarians in book selection activities in the six libraries which made annual estimates is shown in Table 37.

Table 37. Working time of librarians in book selection activities

| Library | Approx-imate annual accession in volumes | Percentage of total working time of librarians | Annual working time of librarians in hours | | Working minutes of librarians per volume selected |
			Total	Per librarian	
C4	4,600	4.68	1,060	133	13.86
C5	3,200	6.72	1,212	242	22.47
F2	3,600	9.56	844	236	13.89
F3	1,800	2.56	115	58	3.77
K1	5,700	8.18	1,491	240	15.58
K5	500	7.07	180	180	20.91

Note: Includes book selection for both adult and children's departments (activities 1 and 7 of the work survey).

There is a fairly good correspondence among the libraries listed in the table in the amount of time spent per librarian on book selection except for library F3. As was pointed out earlier, this library had insufficient staff, and consequently the amount of time which the librarians in this particular library were able to spend on book selection was considerably less than for the other libraries. The staff shortage in this library also affected some of its other activities in the same way.

The time available to a library for book selection and the quality of the selection depend on a number of factors. Among them are the number of librarians actively involved in selection, the number of titles selected, and also the number of titles which have to be considered in making the selections.

Table 37 does not, of course, indicate anything about the quality of selection in the libraries involved. It should be said, however, that because of the importance of book selection for the entire operation of the library, the factors affecting the quality of selection must be as carefully considered by a library as the time and cost factors.

121

Registration of book selection

In most libraries either before, during, or after book selection meetings, selection or work slips are prepared. Time counts were taken for preparing these work slips in 17 libraries. These counts included only the initial preparation of the slips and not later additions, stamps of approval, or sorting and filing. The average time per slip (title) was 1.30 minutes, and the average salary cost was 27.89 øre.[1]

PURCHASE

Time counts were taken in 15 libraries of the work of preparing order slips or lists for the booksellers. Most frequently these lists were prepared from the book selection work slips, but several other methods were used in various libraries. Again, the counts measured only the actual preparation of the lists and did not include any time used for sorting or filing. This work took 0.82 minutes per title at a salary cost of 16.30 øre.

ACCESSION

Recording accessions

Time counts for recording and stamping in accessions were made by 18 libraries. The operation comprised entering or stamping on the verso of the title page of the book some or all of the following information: name and department of the library, classification number, copy number, volume number, year of accession, accession number, accession date, and size. Some libraries also stamp the name of the library in other parts of the book at the same time.

In the time count, the time required was 0.98 minutes per volume; the salary cost was 18.80 øre per volume.

The time used for recording accessions can also be determined from the figures for activity 23 of the work survey as this activity is identical with the operation for which these time counts were made. During the four-week work survey, the time amounted to 1.48 minutes per volume. In the four non-county libraries that estimated their annual work loads, the time estimated for this activity was almost identical— 1.47 minutes per volume.

For such a simple operation, the differences between the results of the time counts and that of the work survey and annual estimate are considerable. The reasons for such disagreements were mentioned previously. It was also pointed out that the results of the work survey should be accepted as indicating more closely the actual use of time, while the time counts include significant sources of error which mean that the time and salary costs as calculated by this method are less than

[1] [The øre is one-hundreth part of the Danish krone, or about one-seventh of a U.S. cent.]

the actual time and salary costs in the average day-to-day work of the library.

Accessions lists

Time counts for preparing special accessions lists or accessions slips were taken in seven libraries. In five of the libraries, lists were typed, in one library slips were handwritten, and in one library a handwritten accessions book was kept. The average working time per volume was 0.67 minutes, and the salary cost per volume was 7.50 øre per volume.

This time and cost agrees quite well with the figures obtained by the non-county libraries for work survey activity 22. However, it should be pointed out that the practice of preparing accessions lists from other lists already made up for other purposes is quite widespread, and if the work survey figures were restricted to those libraries preparing special lists, they would undoubtedly be higher than those obtained in the time count.

Book cards

Time counts for writing book cards were carried out in 10 libraries. In all 10 libraries, preparation included writing on both sides of the cards some or all of the following information: classification or call number, author, title, volume number, copy number, location or shelving symbol, and (occasionally) the edition.

The time required was 1.17 minutes per card, and the salary cost was 13.34 øre.

Date slips

Time counts were taken in 21 libraries for preparing date slips, book pockets, or labels to be pasted on the pockets. In most instances, the date slips were prepared from the book cards, but books, work slips, shelf list cards, or printed slips were also used. The information shown was the same as that on the book cards. The time counts did not include any sorting or filing of the cards or slips used as manuscript copy.

In eight libraries, the date slips, book pockets, or labels were typed. In these libraries, the time used was 1.12 minutes per volume, and the salary cost was 11.34 øre per volume.

In six libraries, the information was written directly by hand on the pockets pasted in the books. The average time and salary cost per volume were 0.83 minutes and 14.18 øre, respectively.

In seven libraries, the work included typing and pasting in the date slips, book pockets, or pocket labels. The average time and salary costs per volume were 0.99 minutes and 10.98 øre, respectively.

The differences between the results of these three groups of libraries are due more to the different representation of the various categories of staff in the operation than upon differences in method. In the eight libraries cited first, two-thirds of the date slips (or pockets or pocket labels) were typed by comparatively low-salaried but slow workers, that is, by library trainees. In the six libraries that made entries by hand directly on the book pockets, comparatively high-salaried staff was used. In the third group of libraries where the operation included typing as well as pasting in date slips, pockets, or labels, trained clerical staff was used to the greatest extent (for half of the work).

Shelf list cards

Time counts for making shelf list cards were made by eight libraries. Several forms of shelf lists were used in these libraries. Some were made up with one card per title, some with one card per copy, and some with one card per volume. None of these libraries used printed catalog cards as shelf list cards. The cards contained a varying number of the following items: call number, author, title, edition, year of publication, volume number, publisher, copy number, accession year or date, dealer, delivery date, and price.

The average time required was 1.69 minutes per volume and the salary cost was 24.20 øre per volume.

Book cards, date slips, and shelf list cards

According to the time counts, the combined work of preparing book cards, date slips, pockets or pocket labels, and shelf list cards cost a total of 48.41 øre per volume in salary corresponding to a working time of 3.85 minutes per volume.

The same time and costs can also be calculated from the figures for activity 21 of the four-week work survey. The eight non-county libraries that participated in the survey used 5.69 minutes per volume accessioned at a cost (using the same salary rate) of 71.52 øre per volume.

The results from the work survey and the time count cannot, however, be compared directly. In the work survey libraries, some volumes received more processing than in the time count libraries, and some less; some of the work survey libraries used printed catalog cards for shelf lists, while none of the libraries included in the time count did. In general, the figures obtained from the work survey libraries would probably be closer to the actual figures for time and salary costs than those obtained from the time count.

BINDING

Time counts for preparing bindery lists and slips were made in 12 libraries. In these libraries, the lists were made from (a) work slips, (b) book cards, or (c) the books themselves. In almost all of the libraries, the binding list contained the classification number, author, title, volume number, and number of copies. Sometimes the size, library department, or year of publication were included. The time taken to prepare the list was 0.90 minutes per volume, and the salary cost was 19.03 øre.

It is not possible to compare these figures with those obtained from the work survey. The work survey figures would include activities 31 (preparing books for binding), 33 (receiving books from the bindery), and 34 (binding control). The time requirements for these activities were 1.26, 1.72, and 1.72 minutes, respectively.

CATALOGING

Ordering of printed cards
The ordering of printed catalog cards is done in a number of different ways. The results were calculated from time counts in nine libraries which used the following procedure:

1. Noting the number of printed cards desired on printed slips or work slips.
2. Sorting the printed slips or work slips in serial number order of the catalog cards.
3. Preparing the order list for Bibliotekscentralen.
4. Rearranging printed slips or work slips in alphabetical order.
5. Filing printed slips in the cards on order file.

With such a procedure, the operation required 1.34 minutes and cost 23.91 øre in salary per title. Less operations 4 and 5, the working time becomes 0.81 minutes, and the salary cost 16.53 øre, per title.

Adapting printed cards
In 14 libraries, time counts were made for adapting the printed catalog cards for use in the individual libraries. This operation included adding classification number and headings and (sometimes) the tracings on the back of the main entry card. No distinction was made between libraries with alphabetical and classified subject catalogs, nor between libraries which prepare comparatively few cards per title and those that catalog very thoroughly with many cards per title.

In five libraries, the time count included adapting the printed cards for catalogs with author, title, and subject cards, but not for special catalogs. In these libraries the time and salary costs per title and catalog were 1.37 minutes and 22.95 øre, respectively.

In nine libraries, adapting the printed cards for the author, subject, and title catalogs also included preparing cards for special indexes and catalogs such as poetry indexes or local history or hospital collections.

125

In these nine libraries, 3.40 minutes of working time were used for each title and catalog, including the special catalogs, and the salary cost was 49.80 øre per title.

In all 14 libraries which did time counts of this operation, the average time per title and catalog was 2.67 minutes and the salary cost was 40.01 øre.

As in the other time counts, it was not possible to include all the relevant elements of work in the count. It must be taken for granted that such elements as keeping the official catalog up to date, establishing new subject headings, and preparing reference cards elude proper time measurement.

Catalog card manuscript
In 18 libraries, time counts were made for the work of preparing catalog card copy for titles for which printed cards were not available. In one library, the manuscript prepared was a typed shelf list card with added entries included, in two libraries the manuscript was a main entry card with added entries, and in almost all the other libraries, the manuscript was a handwritten slip, but manuscript worksheets or forms were also used.

The average working time in these 18 libraries was 10.69 minutes, and the salary costs were 205.03 øre per title.

Activity 44 of the 1961 four-week work survey consisted of preparing manuscript slips, and for this activity the time required was 17.42 minutes per title. Using the same salary rate per minute as in the 18 libraries that made the time counts, this corresponds to a salary cost of 334.12 øre per title.

Copying of catalog cards from manuscript
Time counts for copying catalog cards from manuscript were made in 10 libraries. These counts included only preparing cards for the public catalog and not for the shelf list (which in some libraries is done together with copying catalog cards). The counts also did not include preparing cards for the special or incomplete catalogs, but only those catalogs which included author, title, and subject cards.

Per title and per catalog, the time required was 10.23 minutes at a salary cost of 138.18 øre.

Complete cataloging
Preparing the manuscript and copying catalog cards from the manuscript constitute only a part of the cataloging work libraries must do for those books for which printed cards are not available from Bibliotekscentralen. Therefore, total time and salary cost figures for the entire cataloging process were sought in the public library catalog department of one of

the largest of the county libraries. This catalog department did not use printed cards from Bibliotekscentralen, and the distribution of manpower among the different tasks in the department made it possible to distinguish the time and salary costs required to catalog new titles from the other work of the department quite accurately.

The cataloging in this library included preparing manuscript for cards, copying the cards by typewriter for up to six copies, and by offset printing for seven or more copies, preparing the cards by adding the heading, keeping the subject headings and reference authority file (for an alphabetical subject catalog) up to date, and filing cards in the public catalog of the main library and the official catalog in the departments. The work did not include the other technical processing activities such as book selection, purchase, accession (which subsumes preparing shelf list cards, book cards, and pockets), and preparation for binding, nor did it include filing in the branch catalogs. It did include the preparation of cards for the public catalog in the main library, for three branches, for three hospital departments, an old people's home, a department at a military installation, and the catalog department's copy of the public catalog, but it also excluded preparing cards for the children's libraries and the county department.

For the total work, the average time came to 2 hours and 50 minutes per title corresponding to a salary cost (including pension contribution, but excluding the increment for administration) of 33.71 kroner.

The average time and salary costs of the department for the other technical processing activities (excluding book selection) were calculated to be 36 minutes and 7.09 kroner per accessioned volume. Thus the total cost of processing (excluding book selection) a single volume work in one copy purchased for this library was about 40.80 kroner. Preparation of catalog cards for departments other than the main library should really be omitted. However, it was not feasible to calculate the size of this deduction.

FINAL PROCESSING

In the four-week work survey, the final preparation of books accessioned for the public departments of the libraries was divided into the final preparation of library bound books (activity 35) and the final preparation of books and items that are not library bound (activity 37).

Final preparation of library bound books includes the adding of book plates or series slips, inserting book cards if this has not been done in connection with earlier processes, distributing books to the different library departments, and distributing shelf list and catalog cards and possibly other cards for filing in catalogs and indexes; but it does not include the transport of the books, or the filing of the cards and slips in the catalogs and files. The time required for this activity during the work survey was 1.67 minutes per volume.

The final preparation of books that are not library bound comprises adding the classification on the spine, inserting date slips and book pockets, and sometimes also book plates, series slips, and book cards, putting protective covers on runs of periodicals that are not to be bound, and distributing books and cards to departments, catalogs, and other files. The time for this activity during the work survey was 3.12 minutes per volume.

Sorting and filing cards and slips in catalogs and other files

Time counts were taken in 22 libraries of various sorting and filing activities with the following results: Sorting printed catalog cards by alphabet took 0.16 minutes per card at a salary cost of 2.10 øre. Sorting printed catalog cards in classified order took 0.14 minutes per card at a salary cost of 1.94 øre. Sorting typed and printed catalog cards by alphabetical and classified order took 0.13 minutes per card at a salary cost of 1.85 øre. Sorting typed two-part slips alphabetically took 0.21 minutes per slip at a salary cost of 3.82 øre. Sorting printed slips in catalog card serial number order took 0.20 minutes per slip at a salary cost of 2.50 øre. Alphabetical filing of cards in catalogs and indexes took 0.37 minutes per card at a salary cost of 5.28 øre. Filing cards by classified order in catalogs and indexes took 0.37 minutes per card at a salary cost of 5.20 øre. Revision of alphabetical filing in catalogs and indexes took 0.22 minutes per card at a salary cost of 5.08 øre. Revision of filing in classified catalogs and indexes took 0.13 minutes per card at a salary cost of 3.44 øre.

EVALUATION OF THE RESULTS OF THE TIME COUNTS

As was mentioned earlier, the sources of error in the time counts are the following:

1. It is not always possible to include all of the component operations that are necessary for carrying out a complete operation during the time it is being measured.

2. Time counts are made only for those books which are processed in the normal sequence of operations, and the processing of particularly time-consuming books which, either because of special operations or error, are not included in the general flow of books are not normally included.

3. Counting the time of one's own work often causes a faster rate of

performance; thus it must be assumed that the pace of work during time counts generally exceeds the normal rate.

These sources of error combine to cause the results, both in time and in salary costs, to fall short of the actual time and salary costs for carrying out the operations measured, and this is not necessarily counteracted by other sources of error which might affect the result of the time counts in the opposite direction. It must be assumed, therefore, that all time counts result in time and salary costs that are less than the actual costs.

Certain results of the time counts may be compared with the results of the four-week work survey. Since the work survey recorded all work carried out during a four-week period, the results may be considered to include all parts of the operations investigated and thus be in better agreement with the actual distribution of time for the different activities or operations in the libraries than the results of the time counts.

The tallies of the number of units processed under some of the activities in the work survey may perhaps be assumed to contain errors because too few units were counted. It was, however, possible to verify the unit count of activity 76 (keeping circulation statistics) and activity 23 (accessions stamping, etc.), and this verification revealed no incorrect counts for these activities. It does not seem highly probable, therefore, that appreciable errors in counting units were made in other activities.

As stated earlier, the difference between the result of the time count of the operation of accession checking and stamping and the result of the work survey for the same activity (23) was about 50 percent; the difference for the operation of preparing catalog card copy was over 60 percent; and for the operation of preparing book cards, date slips, book pockets or labels, and shelf list cards, just under 50 percent.

These comparisons appear to indicate that the results of the time counts should be increased by an increment of varying size—at least 45 to 50 percent even for the most simple operations—in order to make them correspond with the actual time and salary costs of the libraries.

PART III

Proposals of the
Work Simplification Committee

Part III contains the recommendations of the Work Simplification
Committee based on the objectives of the public libraries and the most
recent developments in the full-time libraries as described in Part I, and
on the results of the investigations of the Work Simplification Committee as
described in Part II.

Part III may be read independently of Parts I and II.

Appendices 5, 6, and 7 pertain to Part III. They show in diagram form
the Committee's proposals for new work procedures for processing activities.
Appendix 3 contains the symbol code and list of abbreviations for the
diagrams. Appendices 5A, 6A, and 7A list the information which is to be
shown on the forms, etc., under the new recommended procedures.

131

13 Proposals concerning Main Task 1: book selection

The working methods used in libraries must be judged according to the effectiveness with which they contribute to the fulfillment of library objectives.

The purpose of book selection as it relates to the main tasks of public libraries was described in Chapter 1, Part I, as follows:

"1. Literature is to be selected in accordance with library objectives. That is, a general book collection must be assembled from that part of the available literature which meets the requirements of the objectives clause of the Public Libraries Act regarding the diffusion of knowledge, information, and general cultural values."

Book selection forms the basis for the ability of the libraries to fulfill their obligations to the community and the individual patron and to promote informational, educational, and cultural activities. High quality of book selection is therefore essential to the effectiveness of libraries.

For the greatest possible effectiveness, the choice of the form and method of book selection should be on the basis of selecting the one that will best ensure the quality of book selection rather than the one that will simply result in the least expense per volume. However, among those forms and methods which do ensure a sufficiently high quality of book selection, economic factors must also be considered.

BOOK SELECTION AUTHORITY

Book selection for adult and children's departments is today, more often than not, carried out separately. Authority and responsibility for selection for the adult departments usually are entrusted to the director of the library, while the authority and responsibility for selection for the children's departments are delegated to the children's librarian, or the head of the children's department. There are also instances where the authority for book selection is delegated to specialists in certain departments or subject areas.

According to the provisions of the Public Libraries Act of 1964, book selection for children's departments of public libraries and for school libraries must be done by two different persons. The librarian in charge will, as a rule, have authority for the decision in book selection for the children's departments of the public library, while the chief school librarian will have authority for the decision for the school library.

Whenever book selection authority is divided among (a) a person who selects books for the adult departments, (b) a person who selects books for the children's departments, and (c) a person who selects books for the school libraries, the book budget must be divided into separate accounts so that each of the persons responsible can be held accountable for his own share of the book budget. If the selection authority is further divided, the book budget must be correspondingly divided so that those individuals responsible for special subject fields or for special departments know in exact detail the economic resources at their disposal.

COOPERATION IN BOOK SELECTION

For the highest possible quality of book selection, all librarians ought to take some part in this activity, either orally or in writing. The knowledge and special interests of each librarian should be used to the best advantage.

In the smaller libraries, participation in book selection can probably be organized most suitably by holding book selection meetings in which all librarians take part. However, the expense of holding book selection meetings will rise with the increasing number of participants. In addition, the effectiveness and significance of the meetings for achieving the highest possible quality of selection will not rise in direct proportion to the increasing number of participants. On the contrary, it may be assumed that the ideal number of participants in book selection meetings, as in other forms of working groups, is between three and seven. With a larger number, active cooperation on the part of individuals becomes limited. It is hardly possible, even during a well-conducted meeting, to achieve enough active cooperation from all who take part to justify the large expense incurred when the number attending exceeds 10 or 12 persons at the most.

In libraries with more than seven or eight librarians, consideration must therefore be given to achieving the cooperation of these librarians by book selection meetings in which some librarians personally participate while others merely submit written proposals. In libraries with more than 12 librarians, a combination of book selection meetings and written cooperation must be considered an absolute necessity.

The number of participants in the book selection meetings should not be increased over the number needed to attain high quality selection merely in the interest of using the meetings as a means of informing the largest possible number of librarians about recently acquired literature. Keeping up with new acquisitions and maintaining knowledge of the older stock is better achieved by individual browsing among the holdings, supplemented possibly by orientation meetings at which the professional staff members inform each other about material they have read or examined, thus making possible a common use of their special knowledge and interests. Such meetings are already being held at some libraries.

It is important, however, that possibilities for some kind of active participation in book selection be made available to all librarians, either by working together in selection meetings, or by written cooperation. Therefore, all librarians must have access to reviews and other book selection tools. Where books received on approval are used for selection, they must be made available to all librarians. Written cooperation in book selection may be organized in several ways, but reviews written by staff members are so expensive to prepare that this procedure should probably be excluded in all but the largest libraries. Even in those libraries, the expense of the preparation of written reviews is justified for only a small number of titles. The internal reviews of the largest libraries should be prepared only for titles for which other reviews are not available, or do not exist either in sufficient quantity or quality.

BOOK SELECTION AIDS

In choosing Danish books, the most important selection aids are the "Weekly Lists" of *Det danske bogmarked*; the reviews, particularly those by librarians, in *Bogens Verden*; the annotated order lists of the cooperative binding service; and reviews by professionally qualified reveiwers in the daily newspapers.

While the reviews in *Det danske bogmarked* and the library periodicals are easily accessible, extensive use of newspaper reviews is fairly expensive. Some libraries subscribe to clipping bureaus for newspaper reviews, but the general procedure is to clip and file them at each individual library. It is likely that Bibliotekscentralen will soon be able to establish a subscription service for copies of newspaper reviews at a price which is below the cost to individual libraries of clipping them. Bibliotekscentralen ought to offer a subscription service to reviews analogous to that provided by Bibliotekstjänst in Sweden. However, to the extent that it is economically feasible, these reviews should be reproduced separately on single sheets (with author and title imprinted as a heading) in order to facilitate their use. It is also important that the reviews be sent to the libraries at frequent intervals and as soon as possible after their publication.

BOOK SELECTION DECISIONS

In selecting books for the libraries, a distinction must be made between making the final decision and merely cooperating in selection. The final responsibility for selection rests solely on the librarians who have the authority to make decisions, while the cooperation of other librarians is only advisory.

Selection decisions with respect to quality must be made on the firmest possible basis. This can only be achieved by the cooperation of all librarians and by the use of reviews written by librarians as well as by newspaper critics.

With the present order periods of the cooperative binding service, sufficient information for making a decision is often not available during the first order period. Therefore, this order period should be changed so that not only the reviews provided through Indbindingscentralen, but also a reasonable number of newspaper and other reviews are available before the selection decisions must be made. The time limit for the first order period of the collective binding service therefore ought to be postponed until from three to five weeks after publication of the issue of *Det danske bogmarked* in which the titles appear.

For reasons of economy, all copies of the title purchased should be bought, whenever possible, at one time. If the final number of copies of titles purchased through the collective binding service cannot be determined before the expiration of the first order period, the decision to purchase should be postponed so that all delivery is made during the second order period. For titles which are not bought through the cooperative binding service, purchase of all copies of a title should, if possible, also be made at the same time.

With the present working methods, purchase of copies of the same title on two or more occasions results in the following additional work:

1. Book selection becomes more complicated and requires more time.
2. The order list to the bookseller costs twice or more as much.
3. Control of invoices from booksellers cost twice or more as much.
4. With the most customary method used for this work, the task of keeping the accessions list costs twice or more as much.

136

5. Numbering the copies of the title becomes more complicated.

6. Work connected with binding normally costs twice or more as much.

7. Cataloging becomes more complicated because of the necessity to check the cataloging done at the first purchase, and because of the possible necessity for the making of additional notes on the catalog cards.

The additional expense of buying the same title more than once cannot be exactly calculated on the basis of the investigations of the Work Simplification Committee, but it is clearly not insignificant.

Avoiding the additional expenses of purchasing the same title more than once would also stimulate the entire purchase of all copies of that title within the same financial year, thus simplifying the accounting system.

In making the initial selection, the library should therefore try to determine the number of copies which would result in the fewest possible supplementary purchases within the years following the publication of a title. An investigation of the accessions of two libraries in the period 1961-63 seems to indicate that supplementary purchases by libraries in the course of the year immediately after publication of the titles can be decreased significantly if a serious attempt is made to do so. Supplementary purchases made long after the publication of a title result not only in more expensive technical processing, but also in increased book costs, because generally these purchases cannot be made through the cooperative binding service.

FOREIGN LITERATURE

Today, only the largest libraries are in a position to carry on thorough book selection work for both foreign nonfiction and fiction. At the same time, however, the need for foreign literature is increasing in all full-time libraries.

The Coordinating Committee of the Public and Research and Special Libraries (which was appointed in 1963 following the round table conference concerned with revision of the library law) ought to appoint a subcommittee to deal with the public library book selection problems in this area. This subcommittee should consider the appointment of a standing group of experts to prepare periodic lists of suggested purchases of fiction in Swedish, English, German, and French, and also of foreign nonfiction in the fields of technology, art, science, etc.

The work of such a group would result in the better selection of foreign literature in full-time libraries, and would at the same time allow Bibliotekscentralen to catalog those books included in the subcommittee's lists of recommended purchases. It would also allow Indbindingscentralen to offer through its cooperative binding service those foreign titles not available in publisher's bindings of sufficient quality. Bibliotekscentralen and Indbindingscentralen are not now able to offer cataloging and binding service for foreign literature.

BOOK SELECTION IN CHILDREN'S DEPARTMENTS AND SCHOOL LIBRARIES

In book selection for children's departments of public libraries and for school libraries, special circumstances prevail in that the selection is done by library and education experts together, and in that selection from books sent on approval must be regarded as more necessary than in adult departments.

Gradually, as effective cooperation in book selection becomes established in all full-time libraries, and as selection from books sent on approval becomes more widespread, the time limit for the first order period for children's books may very well become inadequate for full-time as well as for part-time libraries. Therefore, Indbindingscentralen should consider offering books for children with a time limit corresponding to the present second order period, supplemented with the offer made in connection with publication of Bibliotekscentralen's lists of new books issued during the year.

BOOK SELECTION ADVICE OF THE COUNTY DEPARTMENTS

The substantial increase during recent years in the book budgets of the part-time libraries has enabled an increasingly large number of these libraries to acquire book stocks which meet the prevailing standards, so that their former book selection procedures and practices have become outdated. The achievement of standards established for book stock in part-time libraries, as well as the consolidation of rural parishes and the contracting of local library associations with these parishes, have made it necessary for an increasing number of part-time libraries to adopt the selection practices of full-time libraries.

As a consequence, book selection activities of county departments ought to include monthly selection meetings for the part-time librarians (and possibly interested board members) during the period from September through May. These meetings should be supplemented by selection meetings held in the part-time libraries once or twice a year for the purpose of giving part-time librarians the guidance necessary to achieve a well-rounded book stock. The book selection meetings in part-time libraries ought to result in new methods for the purchase of books through the annual lists of the cooperative binding service, for replacement and supplementary purchases, and for discarding. With the changes in book selection practices, the current practice of inventorying and updating the book stock of part-time libraries only every five to ten years has become obsolete.

The number of full-time libraries with only one or two librarian staff members is increasing, and this development may be expected to accelerate. At the same time, the rising need for more and more specialized literature necessitates an increasingly diversified book stock even in the smallest full-time libraries. Needless to say, this means that more and more of the smaller full-time libraries are unable to handle their book selection without outside help.

It has always been difficult for one person to acquire an adequate understanding of the entire book market, and the continually increasing diversity of the acquisitions of even the smallest full-time libraries, together with the better quality of selection which is demanded, constantly increases the need for consultation on book selection. Gradually, as the number of smaller full-time libraries in the county library districts justifies it, the county departments should arrange regular selection meetings, possibly each week, for the heads of the smaller full-time libraries in their districts. Such selection meetings would not only make advice on book selection from the county departments more readily available, but would also enable the heads of these libraries to exchange experiences among themselves and to utilize the knowledge of their colleagues in special subject fields or interests. At the same time, such meetings would allow the heads of the small full-time libraries to keep informed about the acquisitions of the county library that are too specialized to be added to their own collections.

PROPOSALS CONCERNING BOOK SELECTION

The Work Simplification Committee, therefore, recommends:

1. That the methods of book selection be investigated and reorganized to ensure the performance of high-quality book selection; that each division of authority for selection be attended by a clearly defined corresponding economic responsibility; and that all librarians be guaranteed the necessary instruction and the opportunity for contributing in one way or another to the book selection activity.

2. That the number of participants in the selection meetings be decided solely on the basis of the effectiveness of book selection procedures, and for no other purpose.

3. That keeping informed about the new acquisitions and maintaining knowledge of the older stock by the librarians be separated from book selection activities.

4. That staff-written (internal) reviews be prepared only in the

largest libraries, and then only for titles for which other reviews are not available in sufficient quantity or quality.

5. That reviews of titles offered through the cooperative binding service in Indbindingscentralen continue to be distributed regardless of changes in the time limit for ordering books during the first order period.

6. That Bibliotekscentralen investigate the possibilities of distributing copies of newspaper reviews by subscription as soon as possible after the publication of such reviews, with each review reproduced on a separate sheet.

7. That Indbindingscentralen change the time period for books supplied through the first order period of the cooperative binding service so that most newspaper reviews will normally appear within that period.

8. That, as a rule, all copies of one title be bought at one time, and that the number of copies ordered be sufficient to avoid, as much as possible, the necessity for making supplementary purchases.

9. That the Coordinating Committee of the Public and Research and Special Libraries appoint a subcommittee to deal with the needs of the public libraries for increased purchases of foreign literature.

10. That Indbindingscentralen consider the possibilities of offering books for children through the cooperative binding service only after an order period corresponding to the present second order period.

11. That the county departments arrange advisory book selection meetings for the part-time libraries monthly and in conjunction with the second order period of the cooperative binding service during the months from September through May, and that these general book selection meetings be supplemented by consultation on book selection in the individual part-time libraries once or twice a year.

12. That the county departments, as soon as the number of smaller full-time libraries justify it, arrange book selection meetings for the chiefs of these libraries, perhaps as often as weekly.

14 Proposals Concerning Main Task 2: technical processing

Technical processing and book selection together constitute the total processing work of the libraries. The role of technical processing in the fulfillment of the overall objectives of the public libraries was given in Part I, Chapter 1, as follows:

"2. The literature selected must be made available for use through, among other things, the processes of indexing and arranging library materials in such a way that library patrons can find, or be helped to find, the specific material they desire."

In fulfilling this task, the library should attempt to organize and carry out the work of technical processing in such a way that these library materials are made as easily and quickly available to the library patron as possible, and at the least possible cost.

Technical processing includes purchasing, accessioning, and all of the tasks connected with binding and cataloging. In the full-time libraries as a group, these processes are carried out by widely varying methods. Even within the individual library, different methods are used—not only are there differences between the methods used in the public catalog departments, the children's departments, and the county departments—there are also different methods used even within the same department.

STANDARD PROCEDURES

It is not possible to completely avoid differences in the processing of books within the same catalog department. Certain variations may be in order depending, for example, on whether the books are received from the dealers in paper covers or in usable publisher's bindings; or perhaps the department of the library in which the books are to be used may have special requirements of its own. However, the main differences in processing depend upon which of the three following basic methods are used:

1. The books are supplied through the cooperative binding service of Indbindingscentralen, and printed catalog cards are bought from Bibliotekscentralen (method 1).

2. The books are not supplied through the cooperative binding service, but printed catalog cards are bought from Bibliotekscentralen (method 2).

3. The books are not supplied through the cooperative binding service and printed catalog cards are not bought from Bibliotekscentralen (method 3).[1]

In principle there need be no difference in the degree to which the objectives of processing are fulfilled no matter which of these three basic methods is used. On the other hand, the differences in the cost of processing by the three methods are rather considerable.

Savings result from using method 1 rather than method 3 (assuming the use of current work routines), because in method 1:

(a) A special order slip does not need to be written for books supplied through the cooperative binding service, but is available as a copy of the cooperative binding order slip.

(b) An order list for the bookseller does not need to be prepared.

(c) A bindery list is not necessary.

(d) An invoice is received for both books and binding together, and accounting procedures are thereby simplified.

(e) Book cards (where photocharging is not used) and book pockets do not need to be prepared, but are received with the bound book, and require only the addition of the copy number.

(f) Manuscript copy for catalog cards does not need to be prepared.

(g) Catalog cards do not need to be copied, but can be bought from Bibliotekscentralen at less cost (including the expense of ordering the cards) than that of copying.

To these savings, lesser economies may be added depending upon the library's own working methods.

Savings result from using method 2 rather than method 3 (assuming the use of current work routines), because in method 2:

[1][Theoretically, there would be a fourth alternative: that books would be supplied through the cooperative binding service, but that printed cards from Bibliotekscentralen would either not be available, or not used. In practice, however, printed cards are available for all titles furnished through the cooperative binding service, and one of the recommendations of the Work Simplification Committee is that these printed cards be used by all public libraries to the fullest extent possible.]

(a) Manuscript copy for catalog cards need not be prepared.

(b) Catalog cards do not need to be copied, but can be bought from Bibliotekscentralen at less cost (including the expense of ordering the cards) than that of copying.

A study of the results of the processing of books by the three basic methods show that although the quality of the work is highest when method 1 is used and lowest when method 3 is used, the differences in quality are not as significant as the differences in cost.

The exact savings cannot be calculated for all of the elements of technical processing, because they will vary according to the differences in the present methods and procedures followed in each library. If consideration is made only of those savings that can be calculated on the basis of the investigations carried out so far, however, it can be shown that there are considerable savings to be effected by the use of method 1 compared to the use of method 2, and somewhat lesser, but still substantial, savings in the use of method 2 instead of method 3.

It follows, then, that libraries ought to make the fullest possible use of the cooperative binding service of Indbindingscentralen and of the printed catalog cards from Bibliotekscentralen. Further, Indbindingscentralen should expand its cooperative binding service by making available through that service all titles for which there seems to be any reasonable commercial basis, and Bibliotekscentralen should prepare printed catalog cards for as many titles as possible.

It should be added that since the share of a library's acquisitions which can be processed by method 1 depends to a large extent on how large a part of the acquisitions consists of new books, a sufficient number of copies should, if possible, be specified in the initial purchase to avoid the need for making supplementary purchases at a later date.

It is not possible, on the basis of the investigations undertaken, to report precisely what proportion of the accessions of the full-time libraries can be processed by methods 1 and 2 at the present time. However, carrying out the Committee's proposals concerning the limitation of supplementary purchases, and increasing the number of titles offered through the cooperative binding service, would increase significantly the number of accessions that can be processed by the least expensive method (method 1).

No investigations were made of how large a part of the accessions for the children's departments and for the school libraries may now be processed by method 1, but it may be considered quite possible to increase the number of titles offered through the cooperative binding service so that practically 100 percent of their new book accessions may be processed by that method. It is now possible to process 100 percent of their accessions of older titles by method 2.

As far as the part-time libraries are concerned, they should now be able to process 100 percent of their new titles by method 1, and 100 percent of their older titles by method 2.

It is possible for public libraries to process many more books by method 1 than are now actually being processed by that method. In the fiscal year 1963-64, that part of the total accessions for both the children's and adult departments of full-time, part-time, and school libraries processed according to method 1, was less than 15 percent.

The full-time libraries can achieve substantial economies in technical processing not only by transferring accessions now processed by the more expensive methods to the less costly methods, but also by changing the flow of work within their basic routines.

As mentioned earlier, processing procedures in the individual full-time libraries vary widely from one catalog department to another. Therefore, it is not possible to describe existing procedures within each of the three basic methods, let alone estimate the total savings that could be made in all full-time libraries. However, for certain elements of the work, it is possible to calculate average savings in relation to existing methods.

In the work flow diagrams in Appendices 5, 6, and 7, proposals are shown for new basic work methods or standard procedures. Appendices 5A, 6A, and 7A show what information is to be entered on the forms, etc., used with these standard procedures.

New standard procedure I (Appendix 5) is recommended for use in processing all titles and copies that can be supplied through the cooperative binding service of Indbindingscentralen.

New standard procedure II (Appendix 6) is recommended for use in processing all titles and copies for which printed catalog cards can be supplied by Bibliotekscentralen, but which cannot be supplied through Indbindingscentralen.

New standard procedure III (Appendix 7) is recommended for use in processing all titles and copies that cannot be processed according to new standard procedures I and II.

It is intended that the main features of all three standard procedures ought to apply in all full-time libraries. It may be advantageous, however, for individual libraries to make changes in certain details to fit their own circumstances. In other words, the proposals may be adapted to the needs of the individual library.

FORMS FOR TECHNICAL PROCESSING
AND THE SOURCES OF BOOK SELECTION

Sets of forms

It is proposed that Bibliotekscentralen provide a set of four-part work slips for all new titles for which it prints catalog cards, and sell these sets in two subscription series — one series for titles that can be supplied through the cooperative binding service, and the other series for titles that cannot. According to estimates of Bibliotekscentralen as of April, 1964, this set of forms (referred to as B1-4) can be sold for an annual price of 38 kroner for the smaller series (titles available through cooperative binding) and 146 kroner for the larger series (titles not available through cooperative binding). The cost for both series would thus be 184 kroner.

The production of the form sets should be so scheduled that they will be available in the libraries at the same time as the issue of *Det danske bogmarked* in which the titles involved are listed.

In the form proposed, the slips would be without carbon. The sets cannot be supplied to the libraries at a profitable price if interleaved with one-time carbon or printed on no-carbon-required (NCR) paper. However, the carbon is of little consequence as the notations which the libraries must make on the slips include stamping on only two of the forms and adding single figures which do not always come through on carbon anyway.

The printed text recommended for the set of forms would correspond to the entry of the individual title in the "Weekly List" in *Det danske bogmarked,* plus information and headings shown in the flow chart diagrams for new procedures I and II (Appendices 5 and 6). The individual slips of the set would be separated by a perforated strip. The set would consist of the following forms:

B1—In-process slip and slip for the books-on-order file.

B2—Order slip for the cooperative binding service of Indbindings-centralen (or for the bookseller).

B3—Order slip for cards from Bibliotekscentralen.

B4—Work slip for the processing department.

(See following page for a sample set of forms.)

Simultaneously with the production and sale of these printed forms, it is recommended that the present work slips or lists be discontinued.

By using the B1-4 printed set of forms instead of the present forms, libraries can effect considerable savings. Libraries that can avoid preparing only 275 of the old work slips by using the printed sets can recover the entire cost of the subscriptions by the savings from this alone. Additional savings can be made in the work of ordering printed catalog cards and books through the cooperative binding service.

The total savings to be made by the introduction of the printed work slip forms would, of course, be greatest in those libraries with the largest accessions, but even the smallest libraries would save substantial sums.

It is also recommended that Bibliotekscentralen prepare a special set of forms (hereafter referred to as F1-3) with interleaved carbon or chemical carbon for titles for which printed catalog cards are not

Bk description from DdB   cc no.   B1

In-process slip

Bk description from DdB   cc no.   B2
                                                    Ibc o.p.
                                                                    Order slip for
                                                                    Indbindingscentralen
(Space for   or bookseller
stamping
name of lib
& bkseller)   (No. of copies
                            ordered)

                                                    cc no.   B3

                                                                    Order slip for
                                                                    Bibliotekscentralen
(Space for   slc
stamping
name of   b-c-p-s
lib)
                cc set

Bk description from DdB   cc no.   B4
                                                    Ibc o.p.
                                                    bk price   Work slip

(Spaces for checking off progress
of bks & cards thru processing routine)

available. The headings of these forms would correspond to those on forms B1, B2, and B4.

It is further recommended that another set of forms with interleaved or chemical carbon (hereafter referred to as set A1-4) be prepared for titles for which, despite all efforts to reduce the number of supplementary purchases, copies must be purchased more than once. The headings on this set of forms would correspond exactly to those of the B1-4 set.

When the B1-4 set is used for the initial purchase, the A1-4 set for supplementary or replacement copies may be prepared from the B1 slip in the library's file. Recommended standard procedure II should then be used, and the A1-4 slips would be used throughout in place of the B1-4 slips.

After the production of form sets F1-3 and A1-4 has begun, it is recommended that the production of the present set of work slip forms be discontinued. It is expected that the substitution of these new forms for the present forms would result in further savings to the libraries.

Reviews

As was mentioned in Chapter 13, it is recommended that Indbindings-centralen print a review (or "lector's evaluation") of all titles which are offered through its collective binding service. It is not always possible, however, to obtain an advance copy of the book from the publisher in time to review it before Indbindingscentralen's list comes out. Since, according to the proposed standard procedure I, a title must be listed before the B1-4 slips are produced, some titles must therefore be listed before a review has been made. In that case, the inclusion of a title in the list cannot, of course, constitute any guarantee as to its quality. This should not, however, exclude it from being listed. In fact, admission to the list should be determined solely on the basis of a realistic estimate of whether a title can be sold to the libraries in a sufficient number of copies to make it profitable to Indbindingscentralen.

At the same time as the proposal for producing and distributing the set of B1-4 forms on subscription is carried out, it is recommended that the present two-leaf order set of Indbindingscentralen be replaced by a single-leaf review notice sent out as the reviews become available. However, these notices must be distributed before the expiration date of the cooperative binding order period The adoption of this proposal implies that the libraries would, as a rule, receive a review in a professional journal and also be able to see copies of newspaper reviews within the order period. As just mentioned, Indbindingscentralen reviews will not always be available, and this may be taken by the libraries as an indication that the quality of the titles should possibly be questioned, and that selection should be postponed until the second order period, particularly if newspaper reviews do not give a sufficient basis for decision.

Replacement of the two-leaf order slip with a single-leaf review slip will result in a savings for Indbindingscentralen. The saving will be relatively slight, but it will contribute its part to keeping prices for cooperative binding attractive.

In principle, it should be possible to order books through the cooperative binding service either on a B2 form or on an A2 form filled in from a B2 form.

The proposal concerning the establishment of a subscription service of copies of newspaper reviews by Bibliotekscentralen was discussed in Chapter 13 (see proposal 6 at the end of that chapter).

ACCESSION

Accessioning in the full-time libraries, as this work sequence was defined in the Work Simplification Committee's survey, consists of noting and stamping accessions data in the books, preparing accessions lists, keeping statistics of accessions, writing book cards and date slips, writing and pasting in book pockets or pocket labels, and preparing shelf list cards.

Stamping and noting accessions data

Stamping and noting accessions data on the verso of the title page of the books, as is done in the libraries today, serves neither the main purpose of the libraries nor any secondary purpose, and should be discontinued.

The stamp identifying a book as the property of the individual library now appears (or ought to appear) on the inside back cover, which is examined by library personnel at the circulation counter when the book is charged out and when it is returned for the purpose of determining whether the book being serviced belongs to their own or to some other library. This should be sufficient identification.

The significance of noting accessions data for the audit of financial records is discussed below under the subject of the accessions list.

The financial savings in discontinuing the accessions notation would be considerable.

Accessions list

Accessions lists in their present form, that is, as specially typed lists or slips, should be eliminated.

Accessions lists are kept today presumably to make a thorough inventory of the book stock possible. This can now be achieved, if it is considered necessary, by less expensive means.

By the methods recommended in the diagrams of new procedures

I-III (Appendices 5, 6, and 7), a complete inventory can be carried out to the same extent as with the present procedures.

Books listed on dealers' invoices can be checked off as appearing in the accessions file and the shelf list when the invoice date is stamped on the B4 slip (or the F3 or A4 slip) and on the shelf list cards (see Appendix 5, symbol 42; Appendix 6, symbol 40; and Appendix 7, symbols 23 and 40). The physical presence of the books can be determined from the copy number of the volume on the shelf list to the same extent as now. However, the value of such an examination of the stock, even on a sample basis, may be questioned. Therefore, stamping the invoice date on the B4 slip (or F3 or A4) as well as the shelf list cards should not be done solely for the purposes of inventory control.

In some libraries, however, stamping the date or year of accession may be considered helpful in making a decision on possible supplementary purchases. In deciding on supplementary purchases (perhaps in connection with the publication of a new edition or a new impression of a work already in the library), it may be of benefit to be able to see on the shelf list how old the library's copies are. However, for this purpose, stamping the year of accession on the shelf list card alone suffices.

In libraries whose accounting procedures do not expressly demand the ability to make a complete inventory of books purchased, or in libraries whose boards reject such a requirement, stamping the invoice date on the B4, F3, and A4 slips should be deleted from the diagrams of the proposed new procedures.

This step should also be deleted from the diagram of the proposed new procedures in libraries where facilitating selection in supplementary purchases by stamping the accessions date or year on the shelf list cards is not felt to compensate for the additional work involved.

The savings in discontinuing the preparation of accessions lists in those libraries where they are specially typed would amount, with the present distribution of this work among the different categories of staff in the full-time libraries, to a large yearly savings in salaries and pension contributions.

Book cards, book pockets, and shelf list cards

The books now supplied through the collective binding service are furnished with printed book cards and pockets, but they should also be furnished with one shelf list card per volume. The shelf list card ought to have the same text as the B4 slip and include a place for adding (or stamping) the copy number and the accounting department voucher date.

Indbindingscentralen should therefore furnish the bound books from its collective binding service with a printed book card, a printed book

pocket, and a shelf list card. It would obtain these items from Bibliotekscentralen.

According to cost estimates as of April, 1964, it would be possible
for Bibliotekscentralen to produce and sell sets of printed book cards,
book pockets, and shelf list cards (for titles for which it prints catalog
cards) at a price which is only a fraction of the cost of preparing these
items in the library. To this price, only a slight expense for ordering
the items needs to be added, as they can be ordered at the same time
as the printed catalog cards by means of the printed card order slip
(B3 or A3). Before production of printed book cards, pockets, and shelf
list cards in sets is started by Bibliotekscentralen, however, additional
estimates ought to be made to determine what effect a limitation of the
number of titles for which these items are to be supplied would have.
If it appears that the greatest overall economic advantages for the
libraries can be attained by the production by Bibliotekscentralen of
printed book cards, pockets, and shelf list cards for a number of titles
less than the total number of titles which it catalogs, it should produce
these items only for that lesser number of titles. In that case, each card
order slip in the B1-4 set should indicate whether these items are available
for that title. If, on the other hand, the total economic advantage for the
libraries appears to be greatest in the production of sets of these items
for all titles that it catalogs, then Bibliotekscentralen ought to produce
and sell such sets for all cataloged titles.

The economies in buying printed sets of book cards, book pockets,
and shelf list cards from Bibliotekscentralen (or Indbindingscentralen)
will be significantly less for libraries which use photocharging, and thus
do not use book cards, than in libraries which use charging systems where
book cards are required. Libraries which use photocharging can most
advantageously buy only the printed shelf list cards together with the
printed catalog cards from Bibliotekscentralen and then write out their
own pocket labels for pasting on the book pockets in the libraries.

Printed book cards, book pockets, and shelf list cards for titles for
which Bibliotekscentralen does not print catalog cards (it should be
noted that catalog cards are printed for all books available through the
cooperative binding service) cannot be produced at a central installation
at a price which is advantageous to the libraries. Book cards, book
pockets, and shelf list cards for such titles must be prepared in the libraries.
They should be made, however, so as to conform with those produced by
Bibliotekscentralen.

Carrying out the proposals for supplying printed book cards, book
pockets, and shelf list cards with the books provided through the
cooperative binding service, and the sale by Bibliotekscentralen of sets
of printed book cards, book pockets, and shelf list cards (and of separate

150

shelf list cards) for all titles for which it produces printed catalog cards, will result in considerable savings to the libraries.

Shelf list

Shelf lists are inventory records of the book stock of the libraries, and are used as such in determining how many copies the library has of various titles in different departments, particularly in connection with reserving books and the selection of books for purchase. The shelf lists are not only important for supplementary book selection, but also for the selection of new titles, since in deciding whether a title should be bought (and how many copies), consideration must be given to what kind and how many other books the library has on the same subject.

It is not possible, on the basis of the material available from the investigation, to determine whether the least expensive form of the shelf list is:

1. One shelf list card per title, containing a record of all volumes and copies of that title.

2. One card per each volume and copy.

3. One card per title, but with perhaps continuations of the card when it is not possible to record all volumes and copies of the book on one card.

The actual preparation time per volume accessioned is longer when one shelf list card per volume and copy is used than when the shelf list card contains a record of several volumes or copies. However, in using the latter, adding supplemental purchases of volumes and copies and crossing off discarded volumes sometimes becomes more difficult and time-consuming than when one card per copy is used. The total costs for writing shelf list cards, and making changes for copies bought later, or copies withdrawn, apparently vary only slightly for the three forms of the shelf list card.

In the future most shelf list cards will probably be produced centrally either by Indbindingscentralen or Bibliotekscentralen and will be supplied with one card per volume.

Thus the shelf lists ought to be consistently made with one shelf list card per volume, at any rate in libraries where photocharging is not used.

It is possible to arrange the shelf list in one single classified order, or to divide it among the various departments. The advantages and disadvantages of these two arrangements could not be evaluated on the basis of the present investigations. It is possible, however, to make a few observations on the subject based on general experience.

The rapid survey of the book stock of a single department, in connection with book selection, for example, is done most easily by using a shelf list divided by departments, while a survey of the total resources of the library is achieved most easily by means of one classified listing of the entire collection. As the book stock of the library must in principle be considered as a unit, the entire shelf list in one classified order ought presumably to be preferred in most instances. The form of arrangement must, however, be determined by the individual library on the basis of local needs. It should be noted, for example, that because of the different ways in which book selection is done in adult and children's departments, shelf lists for at least these two kinds of departments should probably be separated.

In some libraries the same books are now registered in several different shelf lists at the same time. In principle, every book ought to be entered in only one shelf list. Making additional copies of the shelf list is everywhere an expensive measure, and the advantages achieved in such duplication ought to be weighed carefully against the costs.

In some libraries with many departments and branches, cogent arguments may be advanced for keeping an additional shelf list, particularly in the children's departments of large libraries. The facilitation of cooperation between children's librarians and school librarians in book selection may perhaps make it desirable that besides a collective shelf list of the book stock in all children's and school library departments of the main library, there also be available a shelf list in the individual school libraries, and perhaps also in each individual children's department of the books in those libraries or departments. Where such a solution is chosen, the cards of the individual departmental shelf list ought to have one card per each volume and copy, while the collective shelf list ought to be a "union shelf list" with all volumes and copies of the same title entered either on one card or as few cards as possible. The cards for the departmental shelf lists can be supplied through the cooperative binding service or from Bibliotekscentralen for practically 100 percent of the titles. On the other hand, union shelf list cards cannot be produced by a central institution at a price that is advantageous to the libraries due to the fact that they would have to be of a special format to fit the requirements of each individual library.

Numbering copies

In libraries with a limited number of departments and branches, the departmental location of the book (and the shelf list card, if the shelf list is divided) may be indicated by the copy number. Each separate department and branch would be assigned regular, fixed blocks of copy numbers, the numbers assigned being determined by the highest possible number of copies of the same title that a department or branch may be likely to hold.

In a similar manner, children's departments may be allocated fixed copy numbers. Where a union shelf list is used, this number would indicate only in which branch or at which school the titles are located and in how many copies, while the location within the individual branch or school library would appear from the shelf list cards in the branch or school library concerned. The current extensive decentralization of the book stock of the school libraries into circulation collections, classroom reading collections, class reference books, free reading sets, class sets, etc., will often make such a numbering system necessary. It is hardly possible to adequately register all of these locations on union shelf list cards.

The assignment of fixed copy numbers to the departments and branches of the library has the advantage that all other marks indicating the location may be omitted except those which indicate whether the book is for the adult or the children's department, and this may be worked into the library stamp that is placed on the inside back cover of the books.

BINDING

Objective of bindings; types of bindings

The purpose of a library binding is in part protective, in part aesthetic, and in part what one might call advertisement, or public relations. In most libraries up until now, the greatest emphasis has been given to the protective qualities of the binding. If protection is the exclusive consideration, a library binding should be sought which protects the book as well as possible for the lowest possible cost (there is no value in having a binding that will outlast the text of the volume itself). The present library binding completely satisfies the consideration of durability, and the aesthetic aspect is fulfilled today by the most widely used type of binding, the simple and clean appearance of full niger. The present public relations value of the library binding must be considered, however, as slight.

Apparently because of the widespread impact of advertising on consumer packaging, and the desire to create a lively and casual atmosphere in libraries, many of them are using books with publishers' bindings to an increasing extent, and in many instances are trying to preserve the decorative dust jackets by placing plastic covers over them. It is to be expected in the future that increasing consideration will be given to preserving the varied, colorful, and lively appearance of trade books.

Despite their increasing durability in recent years, however, publisher's bindings as a rule still do not have sufficiently protective properties. Indbindingscentralen ought therefore to try to develop new types of bindings that, while they would still satisfy the requirements of durability, would at the same time have decorative or "public relations" value, and can thus increase the use of library books in exhibitions inside and

153

outside of the libraries, and such bindings ought in due course to be made available through the cooperative binding service.

Prices and work simplification

The individual bindings of Indbindingscentralen and those of some other trade binders are of a protective quality that is completely satisfactory, and some of these other binderies can compete with the prices and delivery schedules of the cooperative binding service. However, the paperwork saved in connection with the use of cooperative binding is so great that the price per volume of other binderies must be well below the cooperative binding price in order to make up for the extra work required on the part of the libraries when they use those other binderies.

Work flow and delivery time

The present delivery schedules of the cooperative binding service, and therefore the pressure of work in library catalog departments, is strongly influenced by book trade publishing schedules. That is, the pressure of work is concentrated to a very high degree in the winter months (during which, incidentally, public demands upon the libraries are also the greatest). This has a detrimental effect on the delivery time required for books obtained through the collective binding service during these months.

In the interest of achieving a more even distribution of the work load in the catalog departments, and a more reasonable delivery time from the cooperative binding service during the winter months, supplementary and replacement purchases by the libraries should be confined as much as possible to other times of the year when few books are being published and the demands on the cooperative binding service are less. Indbindings-centralen ought to contribute toward a stabilization of its own work load (1) by pricing policies which encourage the purchase of individual bindings in the summer months, (2) by giving priority to collective binding over individual binding orders during the winter months, and finally (3) by offering new printings, certain new editions, books at reduced prices, and older titles through the collective binding service during the spring and summer months. Also, the offerings of foreign titles in connection with the lists of the proposed subcommittee discussed in Chapter 13 should appear, if possible, during the spring and summer months.

Distribution

As indicated in the description of the present cooperative binding arrangement in Chapter 11, the service rendered by the bookseller in delivering books through cooperative binding is modest in proportion to the agent's commission he receives, which is generally 15 percent of the retail price. Indbindingscentralen ought therefore to try to change the form of this distribution to make it more advantageous to the libraries.

Standard procedures II and III
With the present low standard of durability of publisher's bindings, at least part of the accessions of the libraries which cannot be supplied through the cooperative binding service ought to be bought in paper covers and then be given library bindings. However, reference works in heavy publisher's bindings can frequently be used to good advantage as is. The same applies to books and pamphlets with limited interest, since the infrequent use made of such items may justify their purchase in less substantial bindings, with the possible addition in the library of a plastic jacket.

In the interest of work simplification, as few types of bindings as possible ought to be used.

In order to attain as uniform a procedure as possible for all books that are processed in library catalog departments, the four-part set of forms, B1-4, ought to be used for those purchases which are made through bookstores as well as those which are made through the cooperative binding service. When cooperative binding is not used, the B2 slip would become the order slip for the bookseller, and a book pocket (to be printed in new standard procedure II, and typed in new standard procedure III) would be sent with the book to the bindery. The text on the book pocket should give the lettering for the spine of the book. Other than the book pocket, no bindery list or slip would need to be used. In the catalog department, the book cards would serve as bindery control slips and they would be filed behind guide cards indicating the bindery and the dates sent. The book cards may also be divided according to the type of binding desired.

The savings to the libraries which would result from carrying out the recommendations of the Work Simplification Committee concerning the binding processes cannot be given in detail. Carrying them out, however, would definitely result in savings with all three proposed standard procedures. By far the greatest savings would, however, be attained by processing a greater part of the accessions of the libraries according to new standard procedure I. Discontinuing the preparation of binding lists alone would result in a large savings each year for the full-time libraries.

CATALOGING

The greatest savings in the processing work of the catalog departments, using both the present and the new proposed working methods, can be made by using the central cataloging of Bibliotekscentralen for the majority of the Danish titles that are in the libraries.

The time counts show that cataloging and preparing catalog cards for one catalog currently costs about 4.80 kroner per title in salaries when this work is done by the individual libraries. When printed cards are bought from Bibliotekscentralen and adapted in the libraries, the total cost is only about 1.20 kroner. With the new recommended ordering procedures, using the printed set of forms, the cost would become even less.

Sets of catalog cards

According to cost estimates in April, 1964, Bibliotekscentralen can produce and sell catalog cards in prepared sets for a unit price of 65 øre per set, irrespective of the number of cards in the individual set. This price assumes that the sets average three cards, and that the libraries take sets with less as well as more cards than the average. The cards would be completely ready for filing in catalogs consisting of alphabetical author and title entries, and in classified subject catalogs.

Use of the sets of catalog cards without changes would mean giving up all local variations from the official DDC classification system and from the official catalog rules, and that the catalog apparatus of the libraries would always include a classified subject catalog.

Card sets that would include subject cards for *alphabetical* subject catalogs cannot be centrally produced, as the subject headings which would be used in the individual library depend upon the size and extent of the book stock in that library and on fixed subject heading lists and cross reference systems that vary from library to library.

The relative value to library patrons of alphabetical and classified subject catalogs has not yet been thoroughly investigated. Much may be said for both types. Therefore, the decisive factor in the choice between the alphabetical and the classified subject catalog should be that the cards for the classified subject catalog may be produced centrally. A classified subject catalog of satisfactory quality is therefore considerably less expensive to maintain than an alphabetical subject catalog. Accordingly, a change to a classified subject catalog is advised for all libraries that do not now have one.

At the same time that production of prepared sets of catalog cards is begun, it is recommended that Bibliotekscentralen's catalog service be enlarged to offer the following items for the classified catalog:

1. Complete sets of guide cards.
2. Standard alphabetical subject indexes on cards, with new additions to these obtainable on a subscription basis.

156

Libraries that may not want to change to a classified catalog can use the classified subject cards as alphabetical subject cards by adding typed subject headings to the cards, but due to the necessity for keeping up the cross reference apparatus of the alphabetical subject catalog, this obviously entails more expense than maintaining a classified catalog.

Incomplete catalogs

Some libraries, including probably more than half of all the full-time libraries, today maintain various forms of incomplete or special catalogs. The maintenance of incomplete catalogs is not recommended. The existence of many incomplete catalogs today is presumably due to the fact that until now printed cards have been available as unit cards without classification numbers and headings, and that therefore it has been cheaper to maintain an incomplete rather than a complete catalog. These incomplete catalogs vary widely in form, and it is not feasible to produce complete sets of cards for these different forms at reasonable prices. With the implementation of the proposal for the production and sale of prepared sets of cards by Bibliotekscentralen, maintenance of incomplete catalogs with more than $1\frac{1}{2}$ cards per title for which the cards must be prepared in the libraries will be more expensive than ordering sets of cards from Bibliotekscentralen for making up complete catalogs.

Incomplete catalogs are most often found today in smaller branches, departments at hospitals, old people's homes, and the like. After prepared sets of cards are introduced, a distinction must be made between those branches and departments which are so limited that they can be controlled with a shelf list only and those which have such extensive book stocks that card catalogs are required. The latter should have complete catalogs.

Special lists

The appropriateness of maintaining special lists, indexes, or catalogs over and above the regular catalog should be considered very carefully in all instances. Bibliotekscentralen cannot produce and sell unit cards for use in special catalogs at a reasonable price because of the probable slight sales volume. Special catalogs can therefore be maintained only by copying cards in the catalog departments of the libraries. This copying, and the addition of the heading, would probably cost very nearly as much as it costs today to copy catalog cards from manuscript. The value of special card catalogs, lists, or indexes must always be weighed against the costs of their production and maintenance, and also the possibilities for obtaining the same amount of information through the use of printed bibliographies or other source material.

The savings which would be achieved by the purchase of complete sets

157

of catalog cards for catalogs by the full-time libraries, as opposed to the present practice of adapting unit cards, would be quite large.

FINAL PREPARATION

In the diagrams of the proposed new standard procedures (Appendices 5, 6, and 7), adding book plates and preparing and inserting series slips are omitted.

Book plates

The provision of books with book plates is not necessary for the fulfillment of the purpose of technical processing, which is to make the book stock quickly and easily available to library patrons. It must be judged solely on the basis of its aesthetic value versus its cost. The Work Simplification Committee did not carry out investigations on the costs of providing books with book plates; they would obviously, however, be fairly large.

Series slips

The costs of adding slips that give the place of each individual title and volume in a series include the costs of purchasing the slips, typing them, obtaining earlier volumes of the series from the stacks (or reserving them if they are charged out), typing corrected slips if necessary, and pasting the slips in the volumes. Attempts to make time counts of the work of writing and inserting series slips did not succeed because of the complexity of the work and its performance at frequent, but very brief, intervals. The costs must, however, be considerable.

If it is considered necessary to give all the titles of a series in each separate volume, the series statement can be placed on the bottom part of the book pocket and simply stated as follows: "(2nd, 3rd, etc.) part of a series of which the first title is. . . ."

This form of a series statement would result in considerable savings in the processing work of the libraries, but at the same time would, of course, result in a reduction in service. Neither all the titles in the series nor their sequence could be determined by examining one of the individual volumes in the series. To do this would require searching for the other titles by the same author on the shelves or checking the card catalog or other reference sources.

Because of this reduction in service, the Work Simplification Committee cannot fully recommend carrying out this change in all libraries, but it would be desirable to have the practical experience of some libraries as to the amount of work saved and also the extent of the possible reduction of service involved.

AUTHORS' REPORT

After being used in the count of the accession statistics and possibly in the annual financial audit, the work slips may be used for the yearly count and report for the Danish Authors' Fund.[3] The number of volumes by the authors concerned purchased during the year may be added to the previous year's count by means of these work slips, while the number of volumes by the same author withdrawn during the year may be deducted by means of a file of the shelf list cards of books discarded. With the introduction of one shelf list card per volume and copy, a shelf list card file of books withdrawn can be arranged immediately. After that the very time-consuming searches in the catalog and shelf list hitherto associated with the authors' report will be confined to those authors appearing in the yearly list for the first time.

CHILDREN'S DEPARTMENTS AND SCHOOL LIBRARIES

The technical processing work of the children's departments and the school libraries follows more or less the same pattern as that of the catalog departments of the public libraries in general, and the work flow diagrams of the three recommended new standard procedures can, in all essential respects, also be followed in the catalog departments of the children's departments and school libraries.

Processing books by method 3 [books not supplied through cooperative binding, and printed catalog cards not available] may be eliminated completely, or almost completely, in the children's departments and school libraries since, presumably, printed catalog cards are available for all, or practically all, of the titles they would be likely to purchase.

In addition, the portion of the accessions that can be bought through the cooperative binding service will be significantly larger in the children's departments and the school libraries than in the adult departments. Indbindingscentralen ought to carefully consider the possibility of supplying the entire part of the acquisitions of the children's departments and school libraries which is made up of the special nonfiction material for use in the work of the schools.

Indbindingscentralen should also offer to the greatest extent possible delivery through cooperative binding of new editions and new impressions of titles purchased by the children's departments and school libraries.

The need for union shelf lists must be considered greatest in the children's departments of the large libraries and those school libraries with which these libraries cooperate. Since the local shelf lists are usually

3[This is a fund set up to compensate Danish authors for the use of their books in public libraries. The compensation is based on the number of volumes of an author's book which are in use on the shelves of the libraries, and not upon the number of times they are circulated.]

159

divided up among the separate departments of the children's and school libraries, a union shelf list in the main children's library is necessary for use in coordinating book selection.

In libraries with comparatively few children's departments or which cooperate with relatively few school libraries, fixed copy numbers may be used advantageously in showing the location of the books.

COUNTY LIBRARY DEPARTMENTS

The steadily increasing growth of the part-time libraries, and in fact of the entire public library system, makes certain changes necessary in the work done by the county departments for the part-time libraries.

For example, the monthly advisory book selection meetings for part-time librarians and board members that were first introduced by the county library in Roskilde, and were later taken up by other county libraries, should be introduced into all county library districts. Book selection meetings held only once or twice a year in the part-time libraries are now inadequate because of the steadily increasing acquisitions necessary to build their stock up to prevailing standards and also because of the consolidation of the rural parishes, and the fact that many of these parishes are now making agreements to operate libraries in common. Monthly book selection meetings would also allow a simplification of the processing work done by the county departments for the part-time libraries.

The inventorying and updating of book stocks in part-time libraries only every fifth or tenth year has also now become outdated and inefficient. Consultation between county departments and part-time libraries on the weeding out of their stock and making supplementary and replacement purchases must be made more effective and must take place at more frequent intervals, probably once or twice each year.

The increasing size of the part-time libraries also means that the county department's copies of their shelf lists are becoming steadily larger in size and of constantly less value for the consultative work of the department. On-the-spot consultation on book purchase, using the shelf list of the part-time library concerned, together with such aids as standard catalogs of titles recommended for libraries of various sizes, should produce decidedly better results than proposals made out at the office of the county departments solely by means of the departmental copy of the shelf list.

Finally, the growth of the part-time libraries means that often their shelf lists, even when supplemented with incomplete catalogs, are no longer sufficient as the catalog apparatus. However, because of the production and sale of the printed catalog card as a single unit card requiring adaptation in the libraries, it has not been possible for the county departments to make out complete catalogs for the part-time libraries. With the carrying out of the recommendation for the production and sale of complete sets of catalog cards by Bibliotekscentralen, however, it would become fairly easy to provide these libraries with complete catalogs.

The procedures for the processing work of the part-time libraries must in the future be arranged so that these libraries would decide upon their current book selection at monthly selection meetings. The part-time librarians would then fill in the work slip set B1-4 (in the small series for titles offered through the cooperative binding service), and send the B2 slip to Indbindingscentralen and the B3 slip to Bibliotekscentralen. The books and cards could then be delivered by Indbindingscentralen and Bibliotekscentralen directly to the part-time libraries. (Under the present arrangement, distribution must be made via the Danish Booksellers' Association distribution organization and the local booksellers.) When received in the part-time libraries, the books would be ready for the shelves complete with book pockets and cards, and the shelf list and catalog cards would be ready for filing. Before being put in their proper places, the book pockets, book cards, and shelf list cards would only need to be given the copy number of the book. These are all simple processes in which the county departments need not be involved. If in some county library districts it should be desirable for purchases made through the cooperative binding service for all or some of the part-time libraries to go through the county departments, this can also be done. In this case, the librarians of the part-time libraries concerned could indicate their decisions on the B4 slips at the monthly selection meetings and then turn over the work slip sets to the county department, which would then complete the B2 and B3 slips and send them to Indbindings-centralen and Bibliotekscentralen with a rubber stamp notice that delivery should be made to the county department. The county department would then forward the cards and books received to the part-time libraries.

County departments wishing to maintain copies of the shelf lists of the smaller part-time library collections in the district could order an extra shelf list card on the B3 slips of those libraries. The extra shelf list cards would be delivered together with the cooperative binding books to the part-time libraries via the county department, and would cause no complications other than bookkeeping if the county library would pay for these cards from its county library grants. The bookkeeping could probably be handled most easily by having the county library make payment to the part-time library concerned, which would then in turn pay Bibliotekscentralen.

161

Consultation of the county departments on supplementary and replacement purchases ought to be coordinated with Indbindingscentralen's yearly list or with its offers of new editions and printings, and also possibly with its reduced price offers and notices of older titles available as publisher's remainders.

The clerical staff of the country department ought to handle the revisions of the shelf lists and catalogs and other technical work, while its trained librarians should advise on matters concerned with discarding, and with supplementary and replacement purchases.

In the future, part-time libraries should be able to process nearly all of their new books by method 1. However, part of the accessions of older titles will always have to be processed by method 2, and this part should continue to be processed in the catalog departments of the county departments. With the implementation of the Work Simplification Committee's proposals, the technical processing work of the county departments for the part-time libraries can be reduced considerably—but it cannot be eliminated entirely.

In the interest of obtaining the most effective and economical work possible, the part-time libraries should be required to pay the county libraries themselves for the processing work done for them. At the same time, they should be given the choice of having the work done by Bibliotekscentralen if they should find it cheaper to do so.

The savings to the part-time libraries and the catalog departments of the county libraries which would result from carrying out the proposals of the Committee concerning the new procedures to be used in processing work cannot be specified in detail because of the other changes that must take place in this work at the same time as a result of the recent developments in the part-time libraries. The Committee's proposals should, however, make it feasible to adapt the cataloging and book selection practices of the part-time libraries to the rapid growth and development of these libraries, and would result in considerable savings in the long run.

COLLECTIVE PROCESSING WORK

The question of carrying out the technical processing work of an individual library in one collective catalog department has not so far been considered in the Committee's proposals.

With the exception of book selection, the processing sequence outlined in the three proposed standard procedures applies uniformly to all of the catalog departments of the public libraries, children's libraries, and the county departments. This work can therefore be done by a single group of staff members in many libraries. This would have a number of advantages. It would result in an easier adjustment of the work load of the processing staff during vacation periods and sick leave. Also, the varying work loads for adult departments, children's departments, and county departments could be equalized to some extent, so that periodic peak loads in the processing duties of the three types of departments would not result in unduly long delays in processing. (However, in the largest libraries with very large separate catalog departments, the advantages in carrying out the processing work collectively are probably minimal.)

An attempt to coordinate the processing of books for the adult and children's departments and for the part-time library departments of the county libraries in such a way that the same title would also be *purchased* for all three departments at the same time is not practical, however, because it would often result in long delays due to the different book selection procedures necessary for each of these departments.

Establishment of a collective catalog department in each library with processing of books for departments for adults, departments for children, and possibly for part-time libraries by the same staff may therefore be recommended in all libraries except the largest, while an attempt to establish an integrated program for both purchasing and processing copies of a title is not to be recommended.

TOTAL SAVINGS

The total savings to the full-time libraries after carrying out the recommendations of the Work Simplification Committee concerning technical processing cannot be estimated with complete accuracy. It is possible, however, to estimate at least a part of the savings.

The savings are principally in working time, that is, in staff salaries.

The average savings per title and volume are summarized in Table 38. The costs shown in the table are calculated for a hypothetical library that buys 500 titles annually, enters the titles purchased in one catalog only, and does not use photocharging.

The additional costs for the purchase of prepared catalog card sets and prepared book card-pocket-shelf list card sets are included in the table, but the material costs saved are not included, which means that the actual savings would be somewhat greater than those shown. Over and above these savings, a whole series of other economies can be achieved as a result of carrying out the recommendations, but a reasonable estimate of these cannot be made here.

Table 38. Estimated savings in technical processing work after carrying out the recommendations of the Work Simplification Committee (in øre)

	Method 1		Method 2		Method 3	
	per title	per volume	per title	per volume	per title	per volume
Work slip	39.05	—	39.05	—	—	—
Order list for bookseller	22.82	—	22.82	—	22.82	—
Ordering of catalog cards (minus filing)	30.00	—	30.00	—	—	—
Noting accessions data	—	26.32	—	26.32	—	26.32
Accessions list	—	10.50	—	10.50	—	10.50
Book card-book pocket-shelf list card (minus purchase price)	—	67.77	—	29.77	—	—
Bindery list	—	26.64	—	26.64	—	26.64
Catalog card set (minus purchase price)	10.00	—	10.00	—	—	—
	91.87	131.23	91.87	93.23	22.82	63.46
Minus additional outlay for B1-4 and F1-3 form sets	22.00	—	22.00	—	11.33	—
Total Savings	79.87	131.23	79.87	93.23	11.49	63.46

PROPOSALS CONCERNING TECHNICAL PROCESSING WORK

The Work Simplification Committee further recommends:

13. That the procedures and methods of technical processing work be reorganized on the basis of the three new standard procedures proposed by the Committee.

14. That as many titles and copies as possible be purchased through the cooperative binding service unless prices can be obtained at other binderies that would more than offset the savings to be made in obtaining delivery through that service.

15. That Indbindingscentralen offer through the cooperative binding service all those titles for which a commercial basis may reasonably be assumed to exist.

16. That Bibliotekscentralen produce sets of catalog cards for as many titles as possible.

17. That sets of printed catalog cards from Bibliotekscentralen be obtained for all titles for which they are available, and that a set be obtained for each complete catalog in which the titles are to be entered.

18. That Bibliotekscentralen produce and sell four-leaf sets of work slips (B1-4) according to the guidelines given in the recommendations in this chapter of this report, and that at the same time, production and sale of the present work slips be discontinued.

19. That the subscription series be shown on the sets of work slips that Bibliotekscentralen produces and sells.

20. That Bibliotekscentralen produce and sell the special work slip sets, F1-3 and A1-4 as proposed on pages 144-47, and at the same time cease production of the present set of work forms.

21. That the printed set of work slips be used at all times and that individual work slips no longer be prepared.

22. That the order slip (B2) from the set of work slip forms always be used for ordering through both the cooperative binding service and through booksellers, and that the present order lists be discontinued.

23. That the catalog card order slip (B3) from the set of work slip forms always be used for ordering cards from Bibliotekscentralen, and that the present card order lists be discontinued.

24. That the in-process slip of the set of work slip forms (B1) be used, and that the use of specially prepared slips be discontinued.

25. That reviews from the cooperative binding service be issued on one-leaf slips and that the savings resulting from discontinuing the present two-leaf order-review slips be applied to reducing the price of this service.

26. That the recording and stamping of accessions be discontinued.

27. That accessions lists be abolished and replaced by files of work slips for compiling accessions statistics for the financial audit if necessary, and for the authors' report.

28. That Bibliotekscentralen produce and sell sets consisting of book cards, book pockets, and shelf list cards, and also sell separate shelf list cards.

29. That books supplied through the cooperative binding service be provided with printed book cards and pockets as well as with shelf list cards, and that the furnishing of these items be included in the binding price.

30. That the book card-pocket-shelf list card set from Biblioteks-centralen be bought for all books processed by new standard procedure II in those libraries that do not use photocharging.

31. That the printed shelf list card from Bibliotekscentralen be bought for all books processed by new standard procedure II in those libraries that use photocharging.

32. That shelf lists be made with one shelf list card per volume and copy.

33. That every book accessioned be recorded as far as is possible in only one shelf list, and never in more than two shelf lists.

34. That union shelf lists be established or maintained only after careful consideration of both the advantages and the costs.

35. That the possibility of indicating the location of the books in departments and branches by means of regularly assigned copy numbers be considered.

36. That Indbindingscentralen seek to develop new types of bindings which, while satisfying demands of durability, have more decorative and public relations value than the present types (this to be done possibly through the use of new materials, or by keeping the publisher's dust jackets on the books), and that such bindings be included in the collective binding service.

37. That efforts be made to ease the pressure of work in the catalog departments by scheduling supplementary and replacement purchases for periods when deliveries through the cooperative binding service are normally low.

38. That Indbindingscentralen contribute towards attaining a uniform work load throughout the year by its pricing policy, and try to reduce the time for delivery through the cooperative binding service by giving cooperative binding priority over individual binding during the most active months.

39. That Indbindingscentralen carefully consider the possibilities of offering new printings and new editions through collective binding during those periods when new titles do not take up the entire capacity of the cooperative binding service.

40. That Indbindingscentralen seek to change the delivery arrange- ment of the cooperative binding service so that a more effective form of distribution than that presently in effect will work to the financial benefit of the libraries.

41. That as few types of binding as possible be used; that full niger, or some satisfactory replacement for it, be used for as large a part of the accessions as possible; and that more expensive types of bindings be used only in exceptional circumstances. (See, however, recommendation 36 above.)

42. That books and pamphlets with an anticipated limited demand remain in publisher's bindings or unbound.

43. That the bindery list be abolished.

44. That the official DDC classification scheme and the official catalog rules be used without changes.

45. That the classified subject catalog be introduced and that alphabetical subject catalogs eventually be discontinued.

46. That Bibliotekscentralen produce and sell printed guide cards for the classified catalog.

47. That Bibliotekscentralen produce and sell standard alphabetical subject card indexes for the classified catalog, together with a subscription service for keeping them up to date.

48. That incomplete catalogs be discontinued or enlarged to complete catalogs.

49. That the value of special lists, catalogs, or indexes be considered carefully in comparison to the costs of maintenance and the possibilities of obtaining the information by other means.

50. That the authors' report be made by means of the accession work slip file and the shelf list file of discarded books.

51. That the shelf location of the book stock in the individual school library not be recorded in any union shelf list, but only in the shelf list of that library.

52. That the present systems of inventorying and updating of the book stock of the part-time libraries be replaced by annual or semi-annual advisory visits.

53. That the county department copies of the shelf lists of the part-time libraries be discontinued as these libraries expand and more frequent advisory visits are established.

54. That delivery direct from the cooperative binding service to the part-time libraries be carried out to the greatest possible extent.

55. That supplementary purchases and replacement buying in the part-time libraries be coordinated as far as possible with the year's list offering and other offers of new printings and editions from the cooperative binding service.

56. That payment be made directly from the part-time libraries for processing work in the county departments.

57. That processing work, except in the largest full-time libraries, be united in one department, but that an integrated technical services program comprising simultaneous purchasing and processing of the same title for adult departments, children's departments, and part-time libraries not be attempted.

15 Proposals concerning Main Tasks 3 and 4: assisting readers and circulation control

The Work Simplification Committee did not conduct special investigations into the working methods of the main tasks of assisting or advising readers, circulation control, publicity and public relations, administration and organization, or county library work. Some conclusions concerning the essential problems of assisting readers may, however, be deduced from the Committee's investigations of the library work load and its distribution among the categories of staff. For the main task of circulation control, the results of recent foreign investigations of circulation charging systems are available which, with appropriate modifications, are relevant to the Danish full-time libraries.

The Committee has set forth some preliminary proposals concerning assistance to readers and circulation control. The Committee also recommends that the work simplification section which it proposes be established in the State Library Inspection (see Chapter 17) undertake investigations of the main tasks of advising readers, circulation control, publicity and public relations, administration and organization, and county library work.

ASSISTING READERS

The purpose of assisting readers in relation to the main purpose of the public libraries was defined in Chapter 1, Part I, as follows:

"3. The library patrons, if they so wish, must also be guided to the desired literature where their interests are vague or not clearly defined. The purpose of this advisory service is to further extend the services made available by technical library processing."

Advising readers thus comprises all forms of providing information for readers, handling requests for reserving or purchasing books, preparing book lists, helping the library patron in the use of catalogs, selecting reading material, and all forms of reference work—in other words, all assistance to readers in both circulation and reference departments. For librarians, this includes keeping informed about new acquisitions and bringing their knowledge of the book stock up to date.

Separation of assisting readers and circulation control

In 1962, only a little more than one-third of the full-time libraries had separated the work of assisting readers from that of circulation control in the adult departments of the main library. (The two functions were considered by the libraries to be separated if a special reader's advisory counter [a "librarian's desk"] was provided in the public service area of the library, but only in part of the libraries did this constitute a really effective separation of these functions).

The results of the work surveys in 1961 and 1962 show that, in practice, circulation control will usually take precedence over assisting readers, particularly during rush periods, if these basically different duties are performed by the same staff at the same time.

These functions are both services to the public. The amount of time and effort spent in performing them, therefore, depends upon the size of the public to be served and, as far as advising readers is concerned, upon the desires and needs for assistance indicated by the patrons. They are therefore subject to wide variations during the hours libraries are open. In a small library with limited personnel this will mean that assisting readers must often be neglected in favor of circulation control.

The two functions require entirely different training and qualifications on the part of staff members. Taking charge of circulation functions does not require professional education, and only a relatively short period of training. Reader's advisory work, however, requires considerable professional library training and a thorough knowledge of the book stock of the library. Together with the quality of book selection, the quality of this service to the patrons determines to a large extent the effectiveness of the libraries and their ability to fulfill their main objectives.

Because of the great difference in the demands these two functions make upon the training and qualifications of the workers, they ought not, if only for economic reasons, to be performed by the same staff members. The most expensive manpower of the libraries—the librarians —should not be used for work that can be done by staff without professional training if this can be avoided. However, the most essential reason for the separation of assistance to readers and circulation control is qualitative. Library work should be so organized that the highest quality of service is always ensured for those functions that have the greatest significance for fulfilling the main purposes of the libraries, and the attention of the staff members carrying out these functions should not be distracted by subordinate tasks.

Thus advising readers and circulation control work ought to be fully separated in all full-time libraries and should each be attended to by staff members whose qualifications meet the demands required (and only those demands). In all full-time libraries there ought, therefore, to be at least two staff members on duty in the public service areas during the hours these areas are open to the public. Any time not taken up with assisting readers and circulation work by these staff members may be used for doing other work that is appropriate to their qualifications, is not dependent on the presence or absence of the public, and can be carried out with constant interruptions if necessary. For the professional staff, for example, certain preparatory book selection duties and the task of keeping acquainted with the book stock of the library can be performed as fill-in work while working in the public service areas, and certain kinds of sorting and filing can be done by nonprofessional staff assistants.

Orientation

A high quality of assistance to readers is not ensured simply by assigning professionally trained staff to this work. The skills required for reader's advisory work must be constantly brought up to date by orientation (keeping abreast of recently acquired literature and the literature in specific subject areas). The responsible staff members should also be aware of the various ways of dealing with this literature and its suitability for readers with varying backgrounds and needs.

The results of the work survey in September-October, 1961, show that the time used for orientation (activity 135) averaged about 27 minutes per week per librarian. It must be assumed that a considerable additional amount of time is spent by librarians on this activity outside of working hours.

It was not possible to calculate how much time should be spent on keeping up with the literature in order to attain a desired quality of service on the basis of the Committee's investigations. It can, however, be stated that a high standard of service in the libraries depends directly on the amount of this kind of activity by the staff. Therefore, the amount of time spent on it should be carefully considered from the viewpoint of attaining a desirable quality of reader's advisory service.

CONTROL

The purpose of control in relation to the main purpose of the public libraries was defined in Chapter 1, Part I, as follows:

"4. Provisions must also be made to protect books and other library materials, and to ensure that circulated literature is returned. Rules for use of the library are to be laid down in such a way that the individual borrower may have the most favorable conditions possible for using circulated material, while at the same time the maximum number of borrowers may have access to this material."

As the task of "control" is defined above, it comprises all work connected with the care and use of the book stock and all other materials of the libraries. From the aspect of working time involved, the various elements of circulation control make up the most important part of this task.

The Work Simplification Committee did not carry out direct investigations of the methods used in this task, but during the Swedish work simplification study of 1958-60 various methods of circulation control were thoroughly investigated, and a very detailed comparative study was made of a series of charging systems. The results of the Swedish study are given in the committee report *Organisation och arbetsmetoder vid kommunala bibliotek,* and Chapters 5 and 6 of that report should be used as the basis for a consideration of the methods and procedures for circulation control in the Danish full-time libraries. (The Swedish recommendation to discontinue the reservation of nonfiction, however, should not be followed as the Danish Work Simplification Committee feels that this would result in a certain amount of reduction in service.)

Comparative studies of charging systems have also been carried out in the United States by the management consulting firm of George Fry and Associates for the Library Technology Project [now the Library Technology Program], a unit of the American Library Association, and the results of these investigations were published in LTP's *Study of Circulation Control Systems* (Chicago: 1961).

The Swedish and American investigations were made by more or less the same methods and along the same general lines, although there were minor differences. The Swedish investigations included a total of ten variations of five different charging systems, while the American investigations included 33 different charging systems or variations of charging systems. Of these, 23 were used in public libraries.

The American investigation classified the circulation systems into four groups:

Group 1. Book card systems that do not require borrower participation.

Group 2. Book card systems that do require borrower participation.

Group 3. Transaction card systems that do not require borrower participation.

Group 4. Transaction card systems that do require borrower participation.

The circulation systems, which according to the American investigation show the most economical operation within each group (that is, can be done with the least total cost per volume circulated), are also included in the Swedish investigation. There are only slight differences in the results of the two studies, partly due, no doubt, to the fact that the investigations did follow slightly different paths.

The charging systems in each of the above groups that show the most economical operation are:

Group 1. Newark. (In the American study called "Newark Staff Charge-Numerical.")

Group 2. Detroit. (In the American study called "Newark Self Charge-Signature.")

Group 3. Photocharging.

Group 4. Wayne County. (In the American study called "Self Charge Transaction.")

Of the photocharging systems, the Swedish investigation included Recordak Junior and the Remington Rand Bibliotekskamera, and revealed that the Remington Rand system operating costs are slightly less than the Recordak Junior system. In the American investigation, Recordak Junior and Regiscope (not included in the Swedish study) proved to be the most economical among the photocharging systems investigated while the Remington Rand Champion was slightly less so. (The Remington Rand Bibliotekskamera was not included in the American investigation.) However, the differences in the operating costs of the various photocharging systems were small in both the American and the Swedish investigations.

The necessary equipment and procedures for using the four charging systems that showed that most favorable economic results in each group (according to the Swedish report) are as follows:

Newark system

The Newark system requires the following equipment:

Alphabetical and numerical borrowers' card files. Each registered borrower is entered on one card in each file. The cards contain personal data (name, address, occupation, birth date), and a borrower's number.

A borrower's card for each registered reader. The borrower's card is furnished to the reader and contains his name, address, and borrower's number and (in the pure Newark system) a place for date stamping the charge and discharge of the book issued. The Newark system exists in several variations, in one of which (here called variant A) the borrower's card is not stamped during charging and discharging, but serves only as an identity card.

In the pure Newark system the books are provided with (1) book cards containing the classification number, author, title, volume and copy number, and a space for date stamping the circulation charge, (2) book pockets containing the same information as the book cards, but without a place for stamping, and (3) pasted-in date slips with places for stamping when the book is charged out. The pasted-in date slip can be replaced by date cards, which are stamped in advance and placed in the book pockets when the book is charged out (this system is here called variant B).

At the circulation counter, a pencil with date stamp and a stamp pad (in the pure Newark and variant A), or a pencil without the date stamp or pad (variant B), are used. Circulation counter space is required for the file of books charged out (the filing tub is known as "the wash basin" in Danish library jargon), and for the borrowers' file.

The procedure is as follows: In charging, the reader hands the book and his borrower's card to the staff member who stamps either the date charged out or the date due on the date slip in the book, on the book card, and on the borrower's card, and writes the number of the borrower's card on the book card. In variant A, the borrower's card is not stamped, and in variant B, a prestamped date due card is put in the book pocket. The book and borrower's card are returned to the reader, and the book card is placed in a preliminary sorting drawer. Later, all the book cards that make up the circulation for the day are sorted and then filed in the "wash basin" behind a guide card which has the date (either charge out date or due date) stamped on it.

Upon return of the book, the staff member checks the most recent stamp on the date slip to see if the book is overdue. If it is, the fine is computed and paid. The borrower's card is then stamped under the date returned heading (except, of course, in variant A), and given back to the reader. By means of the last stamp on the date slip (date card in variant B) and information about the book obtained from the book pocket, the book card is taken out of the circulation file and placed in the book pocket (in variant B the date due card is taken out of the book at the same time). If the book is not reserved it can then be reshelved.

When a book becomes overdue, the reader's registration card is located in the numerical file by using the borrower's number on the book card, and the overdue notice is written and sent out.

For reserves, a reserve notice is written up. The book card of the reserved book is then located in the circulation file and marked with a clip or a tab, and the reserve notice is placed in a special file. When the requested book is returned and the book card replaced in it, the clip or tab indicates that the reserve card file is to be checked. A notice is then mailed to the reader and the book is then set aside until it is called for by the reader.

173

The daily circulation statistics are counted by tallying the cards of the books circulated and can be broken down by classification number, or in other ways, in as detailed a manner as desired.

Detroit system

The Detroit system requires much the same equipment as the Newark system. There are, however, the following differences:

The borrower's card has no place for stamping the charge and discharge, but serves solely as an identity card (as in the Newark system variant A).

The books are not provided with date slips. These are replaced by prestamped loose date due cards (as in the Newark system variant B).

Writing positions for the borrowers must be located near the circulation counter.

The procedure is as follows: In charging, the reader himself writes the number shown on his borrower's (identity) card in the first empty space of the book card and then hands the book, book card, and borrower's card to the staff member at the circulation counter who checks to see that the correct borrower's number was written on the book card, inserts a prestamped date due card in the book pocket, and returns the book and borrower's card to the reader. The book card is then placed in the preliminary sort drawer. Subsequent processing of the book card is the same as in the Newark system. In variant A of the Detroit system, prestamped date due cards are placed at the reader's writing positions at or near the circulation counter, and the reader himself places them in the pocket of each book charged out. In variant B of the system, pasted-in date slips are used instead of date cards, and the library staff member stamps the date slip when checking the borrower's number on the book card.

The discharging process functions in the same way as in the pure Newark system except that borrower's card is not stamped on returning the book, and the book card is searched from a date card and not from a date slip. (However, variant B of the Detroit system has stamped date due slips.)

The overdue, reserve, and statistical routines are the same as in the Newark system.

Photocharging systems

The photocharging systems require the following apparatus and equipment:

A microfilm camera, possibly with a built-in reader, at the circulation counter. (If the reader is not a part of the camera it must be available in the office where the overdue notices are written.)

Transaction cards with serial numbers and issue or due dates (these may be punched or edge-notched cards), and wooden or metal containers for the transaction cards.

Book cards may be used in photocharging systems, but generally they are not because the information about the book is given on the book pocket and the pocket is photographed during the charging process.

In photocharging systems, borrower's cards are prepared and used simply as identity cards, without a space for stamping. Borrower's files are not used.

The procedure is as follows: In charging, the reader's identity card is photographed together with the transaction card and book information from either the book card, or the book pocket with the identity card and the transaction card inserted. The photographed cards are then turned over to the reader with the book, and the film is later developed and stored.

Discharging is done by removing the transaction card. If the book is overdue, the fine is computed and paid. The transaction card is sorted in numerical order by days, either by hand, by needle, or by machine (if punched cards are used). Before being shelved the book is checked to see if it has been reserved.

On the date on which a batch of books becomes overdue, the numerically sorted transaction cards from that date in the file are checked (by machine, if punched cards are used), and the missing numbers are noted. These missing numbers represent overdue books. The developed film is put on a reader and turned to the numbers of the missing transaction cards. Overdue notices are then written from the filmed record of the borrower's identity card.

Reserves are handled in the same way as in book card charging systems. The reserved titles are entered on lists or placed in a reserve file. The returned books are checked against the reserved lists or reserve files to see if the books have been reserved. If so, they are set aside and processed as in the book card charging systems.

The daily number of books circulated can be determined from the serial numbers of the first and last transaction cards. Detailed statistics can be obtained only through samples. The developed film is usually used for obtaining such samples, but counts can also be made as the books are charged out or returned.

A thorough review of the procedures of photocharging is given in *Fotonotering. En Vejledning* (A Guide to Photocharging), by Viggo Bredsdorff, Christian Götzsche, and Johannes Pedersen (Dansk bibliografisk kontor: 1962).

Wayne County system

The Wayne County system requires the following equipment:

Transaction cards, charge slips, borrowers' identity cards, consecutive numbering machines, and a container for transaction cards.

Writing positions for the borrowers must be accessible near the circulation counter.

The procedure is as follows: In charging, the reader writes his name, address, and the author and title of the book in shortened form on a charge slip. The short form of the author and title are also indicated on the book pocket. The staff members at the circulation counter stamp the charge slip with the numbering machine so that each title on the slip has a serial number. The transaction card, which is numbered and dated in advance, is then placed in the book. The transaction card number is the same as the number on the charge slip. The charge slips are kept until the books are returned.

Discharge, overdue, reserve, and statistics are handled the same way as in the photocharging systems. However, the overdue notices are written from the charge slips.

Method and bases of the Swedish and American investigations

The Swedish as well as the American investigations included measurements of the time and the total costs involved to service each book charged.

Measurements of the working time used per book circulated were made by M-T-M (Method-Time-Measurement) studies in both investigations. In M-T-M studies, times are measured and predetermined in advance for each individual element of motion in the work operations. In these studies, therefore, the use of working time per unit (per book recorded as having been circulated) may be computed without carrying out the work in practice each time the method is used. Also, in this way the calculations of the working time are independent of individual differences in the speed of the workers who perform the work under investigation. M-T-M studies are therefore particularly well suited for comparative investigations of different working methods.

The four charging systems described above were included in the Swedish as well as the American investigation, but there are minor differences between the definitions of the individual charging systems in the Swedish and the American studies. The following routines were included in the Swedish investigation: charging out books at the circulation counter, sorting book cards in the book card systems, receiving returned books and the work associated with this (inserting book cards, etc.), overdues, reserves, registering borrowers and maintaining the borrowers' file, and writing book cards. The same routines were included in the American investigation except for the writing of book cards in the book card systems.

Investigations must be made on the basis of assumptions decided upon in advance. Among the assumptions of the Swedish investigation were that 50 percent of the borrowers hand over the books at the counter opened and ready for charging; that 2.5 percent of the total circulation would be overdue; that the number of reserves would correspond to 1 percent of the total circulation; that book cards would be used an average of 50 times; and that 25 percent of the accessions would be acquired through the Swedish collective binding service. The American assumptions did not completely correspond to those of the Swedish study. In the American investigation it was assumed, for example, that only 1.8 percent of the total circulation would be overdue, and that the reserves would correspond to only 0.6 percent of the total circulation.

If the circulation systems investigated had been defined exactly the same in both the Swedish and American studies, and if the assumptions had been identical, the results in general would have been in quite close agreement. Because of their different definitions of the charging systems and their different assumptions, however, there are minor variations in the results of the two investigations.

Results of the investigations

The results of the Swedish investigation of the staff time taken up in the various charging systems per book circulated are shown in Table 39. The figures shown include an increment of 25 percent for interruptions, etc.

Table 39. Staff time for circulation control using different systems (Swedish investigation)

Circulation system	Per volume circulated (minutes)
Newark with borrower's card	0.631
Newark with identity card	0.555
Detroit with date card	0.415
Detroit with date slip	0.468
Recordak Junior (without book card)	0.312
Remington Rand Bibliotekskamera	0.278
Wayne County	0.336

The corresponding results of the American investigation, also including an increment of 25 percent for interruptions, etc., are shown in Table 40.

The costs of using the different circulation systems were calculated on somewhat different bases in the Swedish and the American investigations. There were differences in the equipment, material, and hourly salary

Table 40. Staff time for circulation control using different systems (American investigation)

Circulation system	Per 1,000 volumes circulated (hours)
Newark	10.1
Detroit	8.6
Recordak Junior	5.3
Regiscope	5.3
Remington Rand Champion	6.2
Wayne County	5.3

costs used, and also differences in the way the results were computed.

Cost estimates of the Newark system were not made in the Swedish study, as this system was considered to be too time-consuming to be recommended for use in the Swedish full-time libraries.

In the Swedish investigation, material costs per volume circulated included: book cards, date cards, film (including developing), postage, overdue notices, charge slips, reserve file cards, reserve cards, and transaction cards. Costs per borrower included identity cards and borrower registration cards.

The Swedish study was computed on the basis of an hourly salary of 5.89 Swedish kronor,[1] and the total costs for salaries, material, equipment and apparatus, and depreciation and interest payments, are shown in Table 41.

The result of the cost calculations in the report of the American investigation are shown in Table 42. These calculations were also based on hourly salaries, material costs per circulated volume, and depreciation and interest of equipment and apparatus.

The cost estimates of the Swedish work simplification studies were based on the purchase of new equipment regardless of which system was selected. The same applies to the American estimates shown in Table 42.

The American report also contains comparative estimates made when the old equipment and apparatus is liquidated at the highest possible price after a change to another system. An example of these estimates is shown in the totals given in Table 43. The figures in this table give the annual cost of maintaining a present (Newark, in this case) system compared to the cost of changing to each of the four other systems in one library with an annual circulation of 100,000 volumes and

1[About $1.12, the Swedish krona being approximately equivalent to 19c in U.S. currency.]

Table 41. Total daily costs for circulation control work (Swedish investigation) in Swedish kronor

Volumes circulated per day	Detroit	Recordak	Remington Rand	Wayne County
100	6.61	7.51	6.94	6.19
200	12.17	12.45	11.49	11.18
300	17.73	17.39	16.04	16.17
400	23.34	22.35	20.58	21.16
500	28.85	27.27	25.14	26.15
600	34.41	32.21	29.69	31.14
700	39.97	37.15	34.24	36.13
800	45.53	42.09	38.79	41.12
900	51.09	47.03	43.34	46.11
1000	56.65	51.97	47.89	51.10

Note: Daily circulation can be converted to yearly circulation by multiplying by 300.

Table 42. Relative cost of four circulation systems at different salary levels and volume of circulation (American investigation)

Hourly salaries (in dollars)	Annual circulation	Newark	Detroit	Photo-charging	Wayne County
1.00	Up to 90,000	3	2	4	1
1.00	90,000 - 400,000	4	2	3	1
1.50	Up to 35,000	3	2	4	1
1.50	35,000 - 90,000	4	2	3	1
1.50	90,000 - 400,000	4	3	2	1
2.00	Up to 25,000	3	2	4	1
2.00	25,000 - 45,000	4	2	3	1
2.00	45,000 - 400,000	4	3	2	1

Note: The circulation systems are numbered so that the least expensive system has the lowest number (1), and the most expensive system the highest number (4), for each of the hourly salary rates and each circulation range given.

Table 43. Annual costs of circulation control (American investigation) in U.S. dollars

Present system	Other systems			
Newark	Detroit	Recordak	Regiscope	Wayne County
1,576	1,338	1,318	1,382	1,116

salary costs of $1.50 per hour for circulation work. In this library, changing to any of the four other systems would be economically favorable, with the change to the Wayne County system being the most economical.

Cost estimates based on the Swedish investigations

The results of the cost estimates of the Swedish and American investigations cannot be used directly as the basis for selection of circulation systems in Danish full-time libraries. Salaries, as well as material, equipment, and apparatus costs in Denmark do not correspond to the comparable costs in Sweden and the United States. However, some cost estimates in Danish full-time libraries can be made based on the results of the Swedish and American studies. The examples below are based on the results of the Swedish investigation.

The factors included in estimating the costs of maintaining circulation control are:

1. Investment costs, that is, expenses for equipment and apparatus.

2. Material costs, that is, expenses for forms and other materials and supplies used in connection with the daily circulation work.

3. Salary costs.

The investment costs will depend upon whether new equipment and apparatus must be acquired, or whether serviceable, fully depreciated equipment is available for the system currently in use.

If completely serviceable and depreciated equipment is available for a Newark or Detroit system currently in use, investment costs to maintain one of these systems, or to change from one of these systems (or from a variant of these systems), to another of these systems (or to another variant of these systems), may be set at zero. The investment costs necessary to change from a Newark or a Detroit system to a photocharging system are estimated in Table 44.

The investment costs for steel cabinets as well as for punched card stock increases with rising circulation, of course, and the investment costs given are about the lowest possible at present prices. It will be seen that costs for the circulation counter have not been included as photocharging systems make less demands on the circulation counter than book card systems. (In practice, however, some expense in rebuilding or renovating the counter can hardly be avoided.) The cost of a typewriter is also not included as a typewriter will be used regardless of which system is employed. Finally, the cost of a microfilm reader is not included because most of the full-time libraries, regardless of which charging system they use, may be expected to acquire such a reader as a result of the increasing circulation of microfilm to the public libraries by research and special libraries. The cost estimates in Table 44 assume the use of a counter and typewriter currently in use with a Newark or

Table 44.   Danish investment costs for changing from a book card circulation system to Remington Rand Bibliotekskamera system (in kroner)

Equipment and apparatus	Investment
Remington Rand Bibliotekskamera	5,075.00
Cassetts for camera	970.00
Steel cabinets for punched cards (at least one for each daily circulation of 500 volumes)	1,550.00
Punched card stock (for daily circulation of 500 volumes)	1,500.00
	9,095.00
Sales tax	655.00
Total	9,750.00

Detroit circulation system. The sale of excess equipment and apparatus is not included in the estimates as it was in the corresponding American estimates.

In case wornout circulation equipment and apparatus must be discarded and new equipment and apparatus acquired (possibly in connection with moving to new quarters), the investment costs may be estimated as shown in Table 45.

Table 45.   Danish investment costs in setting up a Newark, Detroit, or Remington Rand Bibliotekskamera circulation system (in kroner)

Equipment and apparatus	Investment		
	Newark	Detroit	Photocharging
Transferred from Table 44	0.00	0.00	9,095.00
Circulation counter	1,675.00	1,675.00	1,675.00
Table for circulation file	1,000.00	1,000.00	—
Writing positions for borrowers	—	750.00	—
	2,675.00	3,425.00	10,770.00
Sales tax	193.00	247.00	775.00
Total	2,868.00	3,672.00	11,545.00

The figures in this table are based on the lowest priced standard equipment. The cost for the circulation counter, for example, is set at the price of the cheapest counter available from Bibliotekscentralen.

The costs of forms and other material used in daily circulation work will be subject to frequent changes, but Table 46 shows the costs as taken from the Swedish work simplification study, converted to Danish kroner.

Table 46. Costs for forms and other material (converted to Danish kroner)

	Cost per volume circulated	
Newark	Detroit	Photocharging
0.0061	0.0061	0.0136

The hourly salaries for circulation control work vary widely in full-time libraries. In these estimates the salary rate applicable to clerical assistants with some business school training has been used for circulation control work, although most of the full-time libraries can probably count on lower average salary costs per hour for this work.

The staff time required per volume circulated according to the Swedish study is shown in Table 47.

Table 47. Staff time required for circulation control using different systems (Swedish investigation). Includes 25 percent addition for interruptions

System	Service time in minutes per volume circulated
Newark with identity card	0.694
Detroit with date card	0.519
Remington Rand Bibliotekskamera	0.348

The costs of maintaining an existing Newark or Detroit charging system, or of changing to a photocharging system (Remington Rand Bibliotekskamera), may be calculated when usable and depreciated equipment is used (Table 48), and when new equipment and apparatus are acquired (Table 49).

Under the assumptions used in making these estimates, a change from the Newark system with identity card to the Remington Rand Bibliotekskamera system will be economically feasible when daily circulation exceeds about 130 volumes (corresponding to a yearly circulation of about 40,000 volumes), and a change from the Detroit system with date card to the Remington Rand Bibliotekskamera system will be economically feasible when the daily circulation exceeds about 340 volumes (corresponding to a yearly circulation of over 100,000 volumes). These figures assume that the circulation equipment in use under the book card system may continue to be used in photocharging and that it

Table 48. Daily costs for circulation control when depreciated equipment for a book card circulation system is used (in kroner)

Daily circulation	Costs	Newark with identity card	Detroit with date card	Remington Rand Bibliotekskamera
100	Investment	0.00	0.00	4.06
	Forms, etc.	0.61	0.61	1.36
	Salaries	7.74	5.79	3.88
	Total	8.35	6.40	9.30
200	Investment	0.00	0.00	4.06
	Forms, etc.	1.22	1.22	2.72
	Salaries	15.48	11.58	7.76
	Total	16.70	12.80	14.54
300	Investment	0.00	0.00	4.06
	Forms, etc.	1.83	1.83	4.08
	Salaries	23.22	17.37	11.64
	Total	25.05	19.20	19.78

Table 49. Daily costs for circulation control when new equipment is used (in kroner)

Daily circulation	Costs	Newark with identity card	Detroit with date card	Remington Rand Bibliotekskamera
100	Investment	1.20	1.53	4.81
	Forms, etc.	0.61	0.61	1.36
	Salaries	7.74	5.79	3.88
	Total	9.55	7.93	10.05
200	Investment	1.20	1.53	4.81
	Forms, etc.	1.22	1.22	2.72
	Salaries	15.48	11.58	7.76
	Total	17.90	14.33	15.29
300	Investment	1.20	1.53	4.81
	Forms, etc.	1.83	1.83	4.08
	Salaries	23.22	17.37	11.64
	Total	26.25	20.73	20.53

is fully depreciated. In case new equipment must be acquired, the change from the Newark system with identity card to the Remington Rand Bibliotekskamera system is economically feasible when the daily circulation exceeds about 120 volumes (corresponding to a yearly circulation of about 35,000 volumes), and the change from the Detroit system with date card to the Remington Rand Bibliotekskamera system is economically feasible when the daily circulation exceeds about 280 volumes (corresponding to a yearly circulation of about 85,000 volumes). A change from the Newark to the Detroit system is always economically advantageous, regardless of the circulation.

Indeterminate factors

Regardless of what basis is used for making cost estimates the estimates will always include a number of indeterminate factors of greater or lesser significance.

1. In figuring the staff time per volume circulated, no account was taken in either the Swedish or the American M-T-M studies of help which may have to be given to the borrowers by the circulation staff in those parts of the charging procedure that are supposedly done by the borrowers themselves. The time shown in the studies is therefore somewhat less than it is in actual practice. This factor will affect the Detroit and Wayne County systems more than the Newark and photocharging systems—which do not assume borrower participation.

2. M-T-M studies are carried out on the basis of a series of assumptions. To the extent that these assumptions do not correspond to conditions in libraries, the results of the investigations will differ from the actual staff time required per circulated volume. Accurate estimates of the effect of this factor cannot be made, but a larger number of reserves than 1 percent of the total circulation, and a larger number of overdues than 2½ percent of the total circulation, as assumed in the Swedish study, for example, will affect the costs of the photocharging systems and the Wayne County system more than the Newark and Detroit systems.

3. The results of the investigations presume that "fill-in" work is available for the staff while on duty at the circulation desk so that the working time saved in changing from a charging system that requires a certain staff time per circulated volume to a system that requires less staff time may be used entirely for other work. If this is not the case, the actual costs in using the different circulation systems will differ considerably from the results of the investigations.

4. Interest and depreciation are of great importance in the cost estimates, and regardless of which basis is used in estimating these factors, the serviceability time of the individual items of equipment and apparatus

cannot be calculated in such a way that it will correspond exactly to their actual serviceability time. An accurate estimate of the amount of the depreciation and interest would require that the write-off time be determined for each individual item of equipment and apparatus. For example, it should be noted that neither the American nor the Swedish investigations considered that charging systems which require borrower participation need not only more writing places for the patrons in the vicinity of the circulation counter, but also a larger circulation department area in general, and thus greater space costs, than the charging systems that do not require borrower participation.

The extent of the above factors cannot be estimated with complete accuracy, and investigations have not been made even of their approximate extent. However, the Swedish and the American investigation of charging systems are probably as thorough and accurate as is possible today. The results of these investigations concerning the service time per volume circulated should therefore form the basis for the selection of circulation control systems in Denmark. The cost estimates which must be considered in the selection of the charging system must also, however, be made on the basis of the situation in the individual library.

Choice of circulation system

The selection of the circulation system should not be based solely on the economic advantages of the system, of course, but also on the quality of service which can be offered to the library patrons.

The Wayne County system demands so much participation from the borrower in the charging routine that this system cannot be recommended for general use in the public libraries. It can, however, be used with advantage as an emergency system in libraries which use a photocharging system (the latter system being sensitive to operational disturbances such as electric power failures).

Therefore the selection of charging systems should be made between the Newark, Detroit, and the photocharging systems.

The pure Newark system has the following advantages:

1. The borrowers do not need to take part in the charging routine.

2. In reserving books it can be quickly determined if the book is lost, and the book can then be requested from another library. (In transaction card systems it can only be determined that a book is missing or unavailable when it does not show up during a check for reserves in the course of a loan period which is usually one month.)

3. The borrower can see each time his borrower's card is stamped whether all the books taken out have been returned.

The pure Detroit system has the following advantages:

1. In reserving books it can be quickly determined if a reserved book

is lost, and the book can then be requested from another library.

2. Counter service (charging and discharging), is faster than in both the Newark system and the photocharging systems, and the risk of delay at the circulation counter is therefore less.

All the book card systems have the advantage over the photocharging systems of providing detailed circulation statistics more easily. The value of circulation statistics is considered by many to be negligible, however, so that the importance of this advantage may be questionable.

The photocharging systems have the following advantages:

1. The borrowers do not need to take part in the charging routine.

2. The photocharging systems result in faster charging, and the risk of delays at the circulation counter are less than with the Newark system (but more than with the Detroit system).

3. The possibilities for making mistakes in charging are less than in a book card system.

Taking into account both economic and service factors, the Work Simplification Committee recommends that a photocharging system be established in libraries whenever the circulation per service point makes it economically feasible. Libraries where the change to photocharging is not considered economically feasible should choose between the pure Detroit system, variant A of the Detroit system (in which prestamped date cards are available at the writing positions and are put in the books by the borrowers), and the Newark system with the modifications contained in its variations A and B (in which identity cards are used instead of borrower's cards and prestamped date cards are used instead of date slips).

The Detroit system and its variant A are distinguished from the modified Newark system only in that the Detroit system requires participation of the borrower in charging. The modified Newark system requires less staff time per circulated book than the Newark system with identity card. It does, however, require more staff time than the Detroit system and its variant A.

PROPOSALS CONCERNING ASSISTANCE
TO READERS AND CIRCULATION CONTROL

The Work Simplification Committee further recommends:

58. That reader's advisory service and circulation control be completely separated.

59. That a high quality of assistance to readers be a goal in all libraries, and that the time of the librarians required for keeping up with the literature ("orientation time") required to achieve this quality be carefully considered and provided for.

60. That changes in circulation control and all the elements of work connected with it be considered on the basis of the investigations reported in the Swedish work simplification study, *Organisation och arbetsmetoder vid kommunala bibliotek,* and that the recommendations in Chapters 6 and 7 of that report be followed with the exception of the recommendations for discontinuing the reservation of nonfiction books and for the selection of circulation systems.

61. That a photocharging system be established if and when it is considered economically feasible.

62. That the Detroit system or its variant A, or the Newark system with the modifications contained in its variants A and B, be used if a change to a photocharging system is not economically feasible.

16 Proposals concerning distribution of the work load among categories of staff

The tasks of the full-time libraries are made up of processes and elements of work that make widely varying demands on staff members. These tasks must therefore be divided among different categories of staff in accordance with the education, training, and skills required to carry them out.

Analyses of the present composition of library work and the distribution of the work load among the categories of staff members with various backgrounds of education and training were necessary before changes and improvements could be proposed. The Work Simplification Committee has carried out such analyses by means of the work surveys of 1961 and 1962. The methods and results of these surveys are contained in Chapters 7 to 9 of this report. The conclusions and recommendations of the Committee regarding the distribution of library work among the various categories of staff are set forth in this chapter.

CLASSIFICATION OF LIBRARY WORK

A proper distribution of library duties among the various categories of staff will ensure that the demands made upon the workers who are to undertake these duties will correspond to the greatest possible extent to their education and to their qualifications for doing the job. A necessary first step is therefore that these duties be divided into groups which correspond to the various levels of training and education of the staff members who are responsible for carrying them out.

From this point of view, library work may be divided into the following four groups:

I. Library work that assumes professional training. For example:

1. Book selection and care.

2. Assisting readers and public relations work.

3. Professional cataloging and classification of titles that are not cataloged by Bibliotekscentralen, bibliographical verification, and the preparation of book lists.

4. Certain supervisory duties and making policy decisions on book selection, acquisitions, binding, cataloging, etc.

5. Work for the library board and library planning, including the preparation of budgets.

6. Attendance at professional meetings and training courses.

7. (For the county libraries): consultation with the part-time libraries within their districts.

II. Library work that assumes office training supplemented by fairly extensive library training. For example:

1. Technical processing work, including the authors' report and inventorying the book stock.

2. The less difficult cataloging, and bibliographical verification.

3. Supervisory duties in technical processing.

4. Cooperation in organizing the work of the library.

5. Attendance at professional meetings and training courses.

III. Library work that assumes office training supplemented by less extensive library training. For example:

1. Carrying out and directing circulation work.

2. Participating in certain technical processing activities.

3. Keeping financial records.

4. Performance of clerical duties.

5. Cooperation in organizing the work of the library.

6. Attendance at professional meetings and training courses.

IV. Library work that does not assume any professional library training, but only brief in-service instruction. For example:

1. Routine work connected with circulation.

2. Sorting and filing.

3. Adding plastic covers to books.

4. Packing, and messenger and transportation service.

The above descriptions include only regular library work, and not custodial services or porter or cloakroom duty. The categories of staff which would be responsible for or assigned to the four broad classifications above are the following:

I. Librarians (code symbol B).

II. Library assistants (code symbol K1).

III. Clerical assistants (code symbol K2).

IV. Other staff (code symbol M).

In the distribution of the individual activities among the above four staff categories the most essential criterion must be that the demands made upon the worker should correspond to his or her professional training. In addition, however, economic factors must be considered. In the proposal made by the Work Simplification Committee for distribution of the activities among the categories of staff (see Table 50), consideration is given to the fact that the librarians are generally the most expensive manpower, followed by library and clerical assistants, and that the "other staff" members are the least expensive.

In Table 50, some activities are divided into a number of sub-activities, as not all parts of the same activity need always be done by the same type of staff. For some activities and sub-activities, the daily supervision (and possibly part of the performance) can be done by one type of staff while other types of staff would do the greatest part of the actual work. For example, most of the technical processing work ought to be done under the daily supervision and direction of K1 staff, while the rest of this work should be done by K2 and M staff. As another example, circulation work in general should be directed by K2 staff, with most of the actual work undertaken by M staff.

No rigid position has been taken in the Committee's proposal as to the details of the organizational structure of the departments of individual libraries, or on general problems of supervision and performance. Therefore in Table 50, the column "Directed by" indicates only those activities or sub-activities that should be done under constant daily supervision and direction. For activities or sub-activities that can be done independently, or without constant supervision, simply on the basis of orders or brief instructions from staff in another category, nothing is shown in the "Directed by" column. (An example of this is the typing by K1 staff of the final copy of the book selection proposals which were prepared by librarians in activity 1.) Individual libraries may, of course, feel that other, or different, activities need this kind of supervision, or that the supervision should be done by personnel other than those shown in the table.

Distribution of work as recommended in Table 50 depends, of course, upon the personal qualifications of the individual staff members and their professional education, but the training received at the library in which the staff member is employed is also important. Therefore, the work distribution proposed is based on the assumption that a sufficiently long period of employment for all staff categories may be depended upon so that a sufficient amount of training in the library can be made.

Staff category M, for example, is assumed to consist of part-time high school, college, or other students, or full-time young people who expect to begin other training. For these staff members an employment period

Table 50. Proposal for the distribution of library work among the categories of staff

	Activity	To be performed by	To be directed by
1	Orientation.		
	Preparation for book selection, including keeping up with reviews, etc.	B	
	Typing of book proposals, etc.	K1	
	Filing work.	K2	K1
2	Newspaper reviews.		
	Filing of copies of reviews received on subscription from Bibliotekscentralen.	M	K1
3	Internal reviews (prepared within the library).		
	Preparation.	B	
	Typing final copies.	K1	
4	Control to prevent duplicate purchase orders.	K1	
5	Want lists.		
	Decision on titles to be included in want lists.	B	
	Typing lists.	K1	
6	Approval books.		
	Decision on ordering and distribution to participants in book selection.	B	
	Ordering and recording of distribution.	K1+K2	K1
7	Book selection.		
	Decision on book purchase and distribution of purchases to departments of the library, deciding on gifts of books, discussion and deliberation of form of book selection.	B	
11	Verification of titles and dealers, etc., for book purchasing.		
	General verification.	K1	
	Difficult bibliographical verification.	B	
12	Ordering books, including writing work slip for sets of titles for which catalog card sets cannot be obtained from Bibliotekscentralen.	K1	

	Activity	To be performed by	To be directed by
13	Receiving books, including checking delivery against work slips, entering in continuations file, returning unsatisfactory used books, etc.	K1+K2	K1
14	Collation: decision on returning used books in unsatisfactory condition.	B	
21	Writing book cards, pockets, shelf list cards.	K2	K1
22	Accessions list.	To be eliminated	
23	Stamping accessions.	To be eliminated	
24	Accessions statistics.	K2	K1
25	Arranging, filing, taking out shelf list cards and work slips in shelf list and files.	M	K1
29	Additions to shelf list cards.	K1	
31	Books to bindery.		
	Selecting binder and type of binding.	B	
	Preparation for book binder.	K1	
32	Bindery list.	To be eliminated	
33	Receiving books from bindery.	K1+K2	K1
34	Binding control work.	K1+K2	K1
35	Final preparation of bound books, including adding copy number and adding book plates (if any).	K1+K2	K1
36	Reinforcing books and pamphlets with plastic covers.	M	K1
37	Final preparation of books not bound, including adding classification number, pasting book pocket, adding copy number to book card, pocket, and shelf list card, adding cardboard covers to unbound serial sets.	K1+K2	K1
39	Other.		
	Distribution of new books to departments of the library according to work slip.	K1	
	Inserting pages in loose leaf volumes.	K1	
	Deliberation and discussion of binding practices.	B+K1	

Activity	To be performed by	To be directed by
41 Classifying done without immediate association with cataloging.	B	
42 Ordering and receiving printed sets of catalog cards.	K1	
43 Adapting printed catalog cards.	To be eliminated	
44 Preparing manuscript slips for catalog cards.	B	
For more simplified cataloging.	K1	B
45 Copying catalog cards from manuscript.	K2	K1
46 Writing catalog cards without manuscript.	Included in 44	
47 Arranging and filing of printed slips and catalog cards in files and catalogs.	M	K1
48 Changes or corrections in card catalogs as result of changes in catalog rules or cataloging practice.		
Preparing manuscript copy.	B	
Making changes.	K1	
49 Other.		
Distribution of catalog cards to departments and catalogs.	K1	
Additions and changes on cards because of purchase of new editions, new volumes, continuations, etc.	K1	B
New guide cards and reference apparatus.	B+K1	B
Removal of old periodical analytics.	K1+K2	B
Cataloging of pictures and photographs.	B+K1	
Analytics and genre cards for books previously cataloged.	B+K1+K2	
Cataloging with printed cards.	To be eliminated	
Discussion of cataloging practices.	B+K1	
Revision of class divisions.	B	
51 Surveying book stock for repair, rebinding, storage, and withdrawal.	B	
52 Repairs, including rewriting book cards, etc.	K2	K1
53 Rebinding.		
Work with special lots of books sent for rebinding.	K1	

	Activity	To be performed by	To be directed by
54	Withdrawal, including taking up shelf list and catalog cards.	K1+K2	K1
55	Storage and other permanent transfer of books from one department to another, including changes in card catalogs resulting from such transfers.	B+K1	B
59	Selection of books from, or for, summer deposit.	B	
61	Registration of readers. Making registrations, issuing borrowers' cards.	K2	
	Introduction to library meetings.	B	
64	Preparing cards for alphabetical and numerical borrowers' registration files.	K2	
65	Renewals.	M	K2
66	Arranging cards in borrowers' files.	M	K2
67	Reissuing borrowers' cards.	K2	
68	Correction of address, occupation, name, or transfer of borrower from one department or branch to another.	K2	
69	Other. Arranging, withdrawing deposited borrowers' cards.	M	
	Issuing and cancelling temporary borrowers' cards.	K2	
	Arranging new borrowers' numbers.	K2	
	Circulation statistics concerned with borrowers.	K2	
	Correspondence (with patrons registered twice, for example).	K2	B
71	Charging, discharging, renewing books, including stamping date card.	M	K2
72	Inserting book cards in returned books ("slipping"), straightening out mixed-up cards, etc.	M	K2

194

Activity	To be performed by	To be directed by
73 Shelving and reshelving in reading rooms, stacks, summer deposits, and special collections.	M	K2
74 Reading shelves.	M	K2
75 Preparing circulation counter for opening hour, and clearing up reading room at closing time.		
Assisting readers.	B	
Circulation counter work and straightening up.	M	K2
76 Tallying and arranging circulation statistics.	M	K2
77 Overdue notices.	K2	
78 Messenger work.		
Writing call slips.	K2	
Fetching the books.	M	
79 Other.		
Duty at reader's advisor counter.	B	
General duty at circulation counter.	K2+M	
Individual reminder letters and replacement questions.	K2	B
Searching for missing books.	K2+M	K2
81 Advising or assisting readers, including all forms of information for readers, handling reserves and requests for purchase, requests for preparation of reading lists, help in using catalogs, help in selection of reading material, and all forms of reference work (however, see 91).	B	
Telephone information on library hours, etc.	B+K1+K2+M	
84 Reserves.		
Preparing reserve cards and checking shelf list for number of copies.	K2	
Tabbing book cards in the circulation file and checking returned books for reservations.	M	K2

	Activity	To be performed by	To be directed by
85	Verification, including bibliographic work in connection with obtaining material from other libraries and verification of requests.	B	
	More simple verification.	K1	B
86	Interlibrary loan.		
	Loan of material from and to other libraries and individual loans between the main library and branches; includes writing special book cards and notices to libraries and borrowers concerning interlibrary loans.	B+K1	B
88	Introduction to the library for groups and school classes, including preparation for this work.	B	
89.1	Work with book deposits, including regular deposits and class sets and "traveling" deposits (to hospitals and nursing homes, for example).		
	Selection and assembling.	B	
	Delivery and correspondence.	K2	
91	Preparation of bibliographies and reading lists as requested from readers.		
	Preparation.	B	
	Typing final copy.	K2	
92	Issuing, stamping, setting out of periodicals and newspapers.	K2	
93	Arranging, storing, withdrawing of back issues of periodicals and newspapers.	K2	
94	Special catalogs, including "style" files, periodical indexes, etc. for reading room.		
	Manuscript.	B	
	Copying.	K1	B
95	Clipping collections.		
	Selection of clippings: as in book selection.	B	
	Clipping and arranging of articles and pictures.	K1	B

Activity	To be performed by	To be directed by
Mounting of such clippings.	M	B
96 Statistics of library visitors.		
Running count of visitors.	To be eliminated	
Special investigations.	K2	B
101 Arrangements of exhibitions in the library.	B+K2	B
102 Preparing signs and posters.	K2	B
103 Preparing catalogs and book lists.		
Compiling manuscript slips.	B	
Writing, duplicating, work in connection with printing.	K2	B
104 Arrangements of exhibitions outside the library.		
Making arrangements.	B	
Correspondence involved.	K2	B
Preparatory work involved.	M	B
105 Arrangements for other activities, inside or outside the library, including meetings, lectures, literary evenings, study circles.		
Making arrangements.	B	
Correspondence involved.	K2	B
Additional work involved—moving furniture, etc.	M	B
106 Writing and posting lists of new books.	K1+K2	K1
107 Story hours, book talks, etc.	B	
108 Articles, interviews for newspapers, magazines.		
Preparation.	B	
Typing final copies.	K2	B
109 Other.		
Mailing or distributing interest cards, book lists, and catalogs to readers, waiting rooms, information centers, etc.	K2	B
Correspondence concerning publicity, public relations.	B	
Typing of correspondence.	K2	B
109.1 Children's book week.	Does not take place every year	

	Activity	To be performed by	To be directed by
111	Book purchase proposals for part-time libraries.		
	Preparation.	B	
	Copying and duplication.	K2	B
112	Budget proposals for part-time libraries.		
	Preparation.	B	
	Final copying and duplication.	K2	
113	Review of book proposals and budgets at meetings in part-time libraries or the county library.	B	
114	Driving bookmobile.	Discontinued in present form	
115	Maintenance of special bookmobile collections, including class set collections.	Discontinued in present form (see under the activities for processing work)	
118	Advice and consultation on library technical services.	B	
119	Other.		
	Participation in inspection trips.	B	
	Review and reorganization of part-time libraries.	B+K1	B
121	Library board meetings.		
	Preparation and secretarial work.	B	
	Financial estimates and correspondence work in connection with organizing board meetings.	K2	B
122	Professional meetings and courses.	B+K1+K2	
123	Preparation of budgets.		
	Preparation.	B+K1+K2	
	Working out estimates and preparing final copy.	K2	B
124	Accounts and auditing.	K2	B
125	Personnel.		
	Preparing work schedules.	B+K1+K2	
	Work in connection with appointment and termination of employment of staff.	B	
	Staff meetings, work with staff association, etc.	B+K1+K2+M	

198

Activity	To be performed by	To be directed by
126 Maintenance of premises, furniture, and equipment.	B+K2	B
127 Planning of new activities, new construction, reorganization of work, etc.	B	
Participation in planning involving processing work.	K1	
Participation in planning involving circulation and accounting.	K2	
128 Office work and general administrative work, includes staff information work of general nature.	B+K1+K2+M	
Operating telephone switchboard.	K2	
Purchase and disposal of office material.	K1+K2	B
129.1 Authors' report.	K1+K2	K1
129.2 Inventorying book stock.	K1+K2	K1
135 Orientation in recently purchased library material.	B	
136 Introduction and guidance of library trainees and new staff members.		
General introduction and introduction to library work as a whole.	B	
Introduction to processing work.	K1	
Introduction to circulation and bookkeeping work.	K2	
139 Packing and shipping work, messenger service and delivery work.	M	

of not less than a year is necessary if they are to be used for duties other than such things as packing, messenger and transport service, or photocharging work.

The three other staff groups are assumed to consist of individuals who will need longer periods of employment and training.

Keeping the accounts and routine office work by the clerical staff depend almost entirely on training in office methods and procedures, and requires only very limited in-service training. Supervision of circulation work, however, and certain duties in the technical processing activities require specialized skills which can be acquired only after a fairly lengthy period of employment and training in the library. It would not usually be necessary to supplement this training with extensive library training courses. However, participation in brief courses or meetings that deal with problems of supervision and new working methods must be considered to be of considerable value for these staff members.

The basis of the professional training of the library assistants also consists of training in office methods and procedures, but the carrying out of duties in the technical processing services and the undertaking of cataloging and bibliographical verification work require fairly extensive additional training in techniques unique to library work. In some libraries, this training has taken place as part of the daily routine, but it would probably be better to organize this training so that at least part of it could be done through special courses arranged by the Royal Danish School of Librarianship. These courses would not completely eliminate the need for in-service training of library assistants in the individual libraries, but they would relieve the libraries of a considerable part of such training.

In the proposed work distribution plan, the categories of library and clerical trainees have been disregarded. This is because it is not possible, based solely on professional qualifications, to assign these staff members specific duties. The duties which they are assigned should be chosen because of their training or educational value and not because of their financial advisability from the library's point of view. The traineeship program requires that library and clerical trainees take part in most of the library's activities, but the process of introducing these trainees into certain other library activities demands so much of the trained staff members' time, that from a financial point of view these same activities could be performed more efficiently and more economically by the trained staff members alone.

DISTRIBUTION OF THE LIBRARY WORK LOAD AMONG THE CATEGORIES OF STAFF

Besides the activities that would be completely eliminated [these activities would make up about 4.61 percent of the present total work load] as a result of putting the Work Simplification Committee's proposals into effect, a number of other activities would be affected to a greater or lesser degree. The extent of some of these activities after the proposed changes can be estimated with some degree of accuracy (see Table 51). (Note that in this table, the expression "percent of total working time" has been replaced by the expression "time unit.")

The savings in manpower to be made in the activities listed in Table 51 have been estimated on the following basis:

Activity 2: Only about half of the full-time libraries today clip reviews

Table 51. **Estimate of the extent and distribution among the categories of staff of certain activities after carrying out the proposals for the new working methods (in time units)**

Activity	Total before change in method	Total after change in method	Librar- ians	After change: work to be performed by		
				Library assistants	Clerical assistants	Other staff
2	0.49	0.25	—	0.05	—	0.20
13	0.54	0.30	—	0.15	0.15	—
21	2.88	1.28	—	0.28	1.00	—
31	0.35	0.15	0.02	0.13	—	—
42	0.56	0.16	—	0.16	—	—
Total	4.82	2.14	0.02	0.77	1.15	0.20
Reduction		2.68	0.01	0.82	1.65	0.20

from the newspapers. The Committee recommends that newspaper reviews should be used for book selection in all full-time libraries. If all libraries were to use them, the number of time units would thereby be doubled from 0.49 to almost 1.00. With a subscription for these reviews from Bibliotekscentralen, however, the clipping work would no longer be necessary and the filing work would be reduced considerably. Therefore, the future manpower need is estimated at 25 percent of the 1.00 time unit.

Activity 13: During recent years, only about 15 percent of the accessions of the full-time libraries have been bought through the cooperative binding service. With a complete utilization of this service this percentage can be increased to between 50 and 75. The work of receiving books from booksellers would thus be reduced considerably. The reduction in necessary manpower shown in the table is a conservative estimate.

Activity 21: With complete use of the cooperative binding service and the purchase of book card-pocket-shelf list card sets from Biblioteks-centralen, this activity may be reduced to simply writing union shelf list cards. However, this activity will also include, at least during the first few years until Bibliotekscentralen has built up a stock of these sets for older books, writing the book cards, pockets, and shelf list cards for the older titles purchased by the libraries. The estimate of the future extent of this activity shown in the table is for the period before such a stock of cards has been built up by Bibliotekscentralen.

Activity 31: The future manpower need is estimated conservatively on the basis of complete utilization of the cooperative binding service.

Activity 42: The proposed new order procedure for ordering sets of printed catalog cards, sets of book card-pocket-shelf list cards, or single shelf list cards would facilitate this work to such an extent that it would be practically eliminated. Here, again, the future manpower needs are estimated quite conservatively, and include ordering book card-pocket-shelf list card sets (or single shelf list cards) as well as catalog cards.

To these savings in manpower in technical processing, savings in circulation control should be added. In the Swedish study of public library working methods, *Organisation och arbetsmetoder vid kommunala bibliotek*, the savings in manpower in changing from the Newark system to the Detroit system with date card, or from the Detroit system with date slip to a photocharging system, were estimated to be about 40 percent in the following activities: "work at the circulation counter," "registration of borrowers," "overdues," and "circulation statistics." These activities correspond more or less to the following (work survey) activities of this investigation: 64, 65, 66, 67, 68, 69, 71, 72, 76, 77, 78, 79, and 84. In the Swedish study, these activities required a total of 24.39 time units. The corresponding Danish activities required a total of 21.57 time units. A change to a less time-consuming circulation system will not, of course, reduce the need for manpower in each of these activities by the same amount. For example, a change to a photocharging system will actually increase the manpower need for reserves (Danish work survey activity 84).

The total current manpower needs in each of the staff categories concerned with the circulation control activities just mentioned are shown in Table 52, together with the reduced manpower needs after changing to a less time-consuming circulation system. (It was assumed in the table that the reduction in staff time would be distributed equally among the staff groups involved.)

In Table 53, the estimated ideal distribution of staff in the average library of 1961-62 after carrying out the recommendations of the Work

Table 52. Manpower needs in circulation control activities 64, 65, 66, 67, 68, 69, 71, 77, 78, 79, and 84 (in time units)

	Total	Librarians	Library assistants	Clerical assistants	Other staff
Before change to less time-consuming circulation system	21.57	0.25	—	5.13	16.19
Reduction of 40 percent	8.63	0.10	—	2.05	6.48
After change to less time-consuming circulation system	12.94	0.15	—	3.08	9.71

Table 53. **Ideal and actual composition of staff in the average library of 1961-62 (percent)**

Staff category	Ideal composition of staff in the average library of 1961-62	Actual composition of staff as of January 1, 1962
Librarians	38	51
Library trainees	0	7
Library assistants	12	} 19
Clerical assistants	21	
Clerical trainees	0	7
Other staff	29	16
Total	100	100

Simplification Committee is compared with the actual distribution of the staff in the full-time libraries as a group as of January 1, 1962.

This estimate of the ideal staff distribution is based on a number of uncertain factors. It is, for example, based on the conditions in a hypothetical average library, and on the library work load of 1961-62 which has, of course, increased considerably since that time.

The uncertainty of this calculation also results, to a lesser extent, from the fact that some activities are divided into sub-activities the extent of which is only estimated, and that the effect of the changes on these activities and their distribution among the various staff categories is also only an estimation.

The hypothetical ideal library in the table is the average of the 14 libraries that took part in the work survey of 1961. Of these 14 libraries, 6 were county libraries, 3 were suburban libraries, and 5 were "other full-time libraries."

There are great differences in the size, extent of activity, and resources of these libraries and in the quantity and quality of their services. These factors affect the work load of the individual libraries in a number of ways. The work load of the hypothetical average library will therefore differ from the work load in any one of the 14 libraries which participated in the work survey, and also from any one of the non-participating full-time libraries.

The average size, extent of activity, resources, and quantity and quality of the services of the 14 work survey libraries are, however, quite close to the averages of the full-time libraries as a group. Therefore, while the work load of the hypothetical average library may be expected to differ more or less from the work load of any particular full-time library, it will be very similar to that of the existing full-time libraries as a group.

Because the work load of the individual library does differ from that of the hypothetical average library, its ideal staff composition will also differ somewhat, and the final composition of its staff will, of course, have to be adjusted to its own work load.

Table 54 shows both the total manpower needs and the ideal staff composition in the hypothetical average library (based on the work load of 1961-62) if the recommendations of the Work Simplification Committee are carried out.

The estimated ideal staff composition does not include trainees, however, and for this reason alone it cannot be completely attained. The Committee did not seek to fit library and clerical trainees into its recommendations for the distribution of work among the categories of staff because the office work training program (for clerical trainees) is undergoing extensive changes at the present time, while changes in the training program for library trainees are also being prepared.

With the above reservations, the estimated ideal staff composition may be used as a guide as long as the library work load does not differ greatly from the work load during the investigation in 1961-62. It is, however, to be expected that rather substantial changes will occur in the next few years.

Some of the changes will take place as a direct consequence of implementing the proposals of the Committee. For example, a separation of circulation control and assistance to readers will mean that the share of

Table 54. **Total manpower needs and ideal staff composition after carrying out the changes in working methods proposed by the Work Simplification Committee (in time units)**

	Total	Librarians	Library assistants	Clerical assistants	Other staff
Total library work load (excluding activities deleted)	95.39	31.77	11.19	21.28	31.15
Reductions caused by changes in technical processing work	2.68	0.01	0.82	1.65	0.20
Reductions caused by changes in circulation control work	8.63	0.10	—	2.05	6.48
Total library work load after carrying out proposed changes	84.08	31.66	10.37	17.58	24.47

assistance to readers in the total library work load will increase, and, after such an increase, the professional library staff may have to make up a larger percentage of the entire staff than that shown in the estimated ideal staff composition.

Other and very significant changes will take place as a result of the development full-time libraries are going through at present. Among the more important of these changes are:

1. The already far-reaching changes in book selection activities as a consequence of constantly more diversified literature needs, and the resulting increase in the number of titles the libraries must consider and select for their collections.

2. The increasing need for library materials of all kinds is bringing about a greater requirement for reader's advisory service and interlibrary loans.

3. The increasing interest in public relations activity.

4. The enlargement of the school libraries and the increased processing work of the public libraries as a result of their cooperation with the school libraries.

5. The increasing cooperation of the libraries with other educational institutions such as teacher training institutes, high schools, colleges, vocational schools, and adult educational associations.

6. The establishment of new service facilities, such as music departments and local history archives.

7. The change in the nature of, and the increase in, the consultation work of the county libraries for the part-time libraries as a result of the growth of the latter.

The new Public Libraries Act of 1964 has itself brought about changes in many of these areas. The changes are occurring not only because the library law directs or encourages them, however, but also because of the development that all educational and cultural institutions are undergoing today due to the constantly increasing demands placed upon them by the public.

All of these changes make it rather difficult to make long range estimates of the composition of an ideal library staff; they will affect not only the size of the staff required, but also its composition, since the proliferation of the activities of libraries and the extension of their service facilities will result in more demand for professional librarians than for personnel in other staff categories.

Thus a fixed distribution of the categories of staff on a long range basis is not possible. On the other hand, the estimated ideal staff composition of the hypothetical average library may be used, at least to some extent, as a guide in libraries where the work load today corresponds more or less to that of the average library. In addition, the distribution of library activities among the categories of staff as shown in Tables 51 and 52 may be used as a basis for estimating the changes in the extent of individual activities and their distribution among the various types of staff, and provide at least some basis for working out a reasonable scheme of staff distribution. However, such estimates will inevitably require certain adjustments, particularly in those libraries that make use of library and clerical trainees.

The Work Simplification Committee must particularly caution the very small full-time libraries against trying to conform exactly to the estimated ideal staff composition of the average library. In these libraries, assistance to readers frequently makes up a greater part of the library work load than in the average library. Also, these small libraries must use a greater part of their working time for book selection than the average library, if they wish to maintain a high quality of book selection. As an example of changes in the ideal staff composition that can be caused solely by a difference in the share of the total work time used for assistance to readers and book selection from that used in the average library, the ideal staff composition has been calculated for one library in which assistance to readers corresponds to 20 time units as against 11 time units in the average library, and where book selection takes up 10 time units as against 4.5 time units in the average library. The effects of these differences are shown in Table 55.

Table 55. Ideal staff composition (percent)

	Average library of 1961-62	Library in which assistance to readers and book selection activities is significantly greater than the average
Librarians	37.66	46.83
Library assistants	12.33	10.52
Clerical assistants	20.91	17.83
Other staff	29.10	24.82

The Committee must conclude that absolute standards for the composition of the staff for the full-time libraries cannot be established. The distribution of work among the categories of staff will be influenced by the size of the library, its work load, the quantity and quality of its services, and its ability to obtain staff members with sufficient qualifications within the different categories. Workers within all categories must be selected with the greatest care. Before each appointment is made, the content of the job to be filled should be carefully evaluated with the purpose of selecting the applicant who appears to have the correct qualifications for it. The appointment of over-qualified as well as under-qualified staff should be avoided whenever possible.

ESTIMATE OF STAFF NEEDS

Because of the developments now going on in library work, the Committee does not consider it possible to establish exact standards for the size of library staff. For one thing, such standards would become quickly outdated.

With the present composition of library work, the Committee does, however, consider it possible to estimate the staff size of the individual library as the sum of the manpower needed to carry out the following four groups of duties:

1. Total processing work, including book selection, "registering" (the complex of activities involved in adding materials to the library collections and making them available for use), and book conservation or care.

2. The "outgoing" or public service activities which include assistance to readers, circulation control, and public relations.

3. Administrative work.

4. County library work.

The staff requirements for each of these four groups of activities may be estimated on the basis of the present work load and the present quantity and quality of library services.

The manpower needs of the total processing services as defined above depend directly on the size of the book budget. The total manpower needs for total processing in non-county libraries may be estimated at one staff unit (with a work week of 42 hours) per 32,000 kroner of the book budget with the working methods used during 1961-62, and at one staff unit per book budget of 35,800 kroner after carrying out the proposals of the Committee. According to these proposals, the new staff unit should consist of 0.39 librarians, 0.33 library assistants, 0.21 clerical assistants, and 0.07 "other staff."

Manpower needs for technical processing, excluding book selection activities, may be estimated at one staff unit (with a 42-hour work week) per book budget of 40,300 kroner before carrying out the Committee's recommendations, and at one staff unit per book budget of 46,000 kroner afterwards. According to these recommendations, the new staff unit should consist of 0.26 librarians, 0.39 library assistants, 0.27 clerical assistants, and 0.08 "other staff."

The basis for the above staff requirements is the manpower requirements of the average library. As mentioned in Chapter 12, the manpower needs per volume purchased are not the same in libraries of varying size. In large libraries (which buy a considerable number of titles for which printed catalog cards are not available from Bibliotekscentralen), the figures cited are undoubtedly inadequate.

The staff requirements for the "outgoing" activities depend directly on the size of the circulation. In libraries that have not changed to a less time-consuming charging system, the staff needs for the total "outgoing" activities may be estimated at one staff unit per annual circulation of 23,675 volumes from departments served by regular library staff (that is, excluding school libraries served by school librarians and by assistants in school library departments). According to the proposals of the Committee, this staff unit should consist of 0.32 librarians, 0.03 library assistants, 0.18 clerical assistants, and 0.47 "other staff." In libraries which have changed to a less time-consuming circulation system (photocharging, for example), the staff needs may be estimated at one staff unit per annual circulation of 28,400 volumes from departments serviced by regular library staff. This staff unit should consist of 0.39 librarians, 0.03 library assistants, 0.17 clerical assistants, and 0.41 "other staff."

For circulation control work alone (activities 71-79, Table 50), the staff needs may be estimated at one staff unit per annual circulation of 43,900 volumes from departments served by regular library staff when photocharging is not used. The staff unit should consist of 0.03 librarians, 0.18 clerical assistants, and 0.79 "other staff." In libraries which use photocharging the staff requirements for this work may be estimated at one staff unit per annual circulation of 63,200 volumes from departments served by regular library staff. This staff unit should be made up of 0.03 librarians, 0.15 clerical assistants, and 0.82 "other staff."

The staff requirements for administrative work depend directly on the extent of the other main tasks, and should be estimated in relation to the staff need for those tasks. If the administrative work is considered to include activities 121-137 in Table 50, the staff requirements for this work may be estimated at 19.6 percent of the staff required for the other main tasks before carrying out the recommendations of the Committee, and at 24.2 percent of the staff needs of the other tasks after carrying out the recommendations. Included in these figures is the staff required for messenger service and transportation. This staff would make up 6.1 percent of the staff required for the other tasks before carrying out the proposals of the Committee, and 7.5 percent after carrying out the proposals. If messenger service and transportation are included, each staff unit for administrative work should consist of 0.30 librarians, 0.08 library assistants, 0.31 clerical assistants, and 0.31 "other staff."

The staff needs for county library work depend upon the number of part-time libraries that need assistance, and the number of books purchased by the part-time libraries that must be processed in the county library departments of the county libraries. Since there is no firm basis for estimating the manpower needs for this task, and as the extent and composition of the duties presumably will soon change significantly, the Committee did not attempt to make such an estimate.

The estimated figures for the staff needs given above are based upon the present quality and quantity of library service and the composition of the work load in the average library, and in making them the Committee had to make certain assumptions and extrapolations in order to simplify its calculations.

For those libraries that want to offer better or more extensive service than the average library of 1961-62, the figures cited for staff requirements must be adjusted. For example. if it is desired to carry out more thorough (and therefore time-consuming) book selection than that of the average library, certain adjustments must be made in the number of staff units allocated to both book selection and technical processing if the total budget is to remain the same.

The figures cited may be used as a practical aid in estimating the staff needs of the libraries when the necessary adjustments are made. They cannot, however, be used as absolute or final standards. Fundamental changes, such as an increased number of titles which the libraries must deal with in book selection, for example, or in an increased need of readers for assistance will mean that manpower needs must be revised and that the basis for the estimates must be changed completely.

PROPOSALS CONCERNING WORK DISTRIBUTION

The Work Simplification Committee finally recommends:

63. That the distribution of the work among the categories of staff be made to conform as nearly as possible with the proposal for the classification of work shown in Table 50 after due consideration of the difficulties arising from part-time employment of librarians and library and clerical assistants.

64. That the Royal Danish School of Librarianship establish a program of courses for library assistants in the public libraries.

65. That the Committee's estimations of staff requirements be adjusted to meet the conditions resulting from increased library services and the differences between the work load of the average library in 1961-62 and the library of today.

17 Conclusion

The Work Simplification Committee has not attempted to investigate, or to discuss in this report, all areas of public library activity. Accordingly, this report is concerned only with selected tasks, and with the distribution of library work among the different categories of library staff.

The Committee decided not to conduct an investigation that would include all the tasks that make up library work primarily because it felt that it would be able to carry out more thorough investigations within the areas selected for study than otherwise would have been the case. In addition, in refraining from investigating the tasks which the Swedish Work Simplification Committee has already studied most thoroughly (circulation control, in particular), it has been possible for the reports of these two work simplification committees to supplement each other. Consequently, the Danish Work Simplification Committee recommends that Danish full-time libraries make use of the report of the Swedish Work Simplification Committee, *Organisation och arbetsmetoder vid kommunala bibliotek,* in addition to the present report.

During the period in which the Danish Work Simplification Committee has been active, some problems of work simplification have been treated by other individuals and committees. Therefore, the Committee has been able to omit consideration of these problems from its investigations and has only very briefly discussed such matters in this report. The following publications therefore ought to be used in the libraries along with the present report:

1. Bredsdorff, Viggo, Götzsche, Christian, and Pedersen, Johannes. *Fotonotering. En Vejledning (A Guide to Photocharging)*. Copenhagen: Dansk bibliografisk kontor, 1962.

2. Hovman, Ole, Jacobsen, Marie Helene, and Koch, Ole. *Systematisk emnekatalogisering (Systematic Subject Cataloging)*. Copenhagen: Bibliotekscentralen, 1962.

3. Koch, Ole. *Blanket og skrivemaskine: Vejledning i rationel maskinskrivning med eksempler fra bibliotekspraksis (The Printed Form and the Typewriter: A Guide for Effective Use with Examples from Library Practice)*. Copenhagen: Bibliotekscentralen, 1964.

Furthermore, in Chapter 15 of the present report, the Work Simplification Committee has used, in addition to the Swedish Work Simplification Committee report, *Study of Circulation Control Systems,* published in 1961 by the Library Technology Project (now the Library Technology Program) of the American Library Association, as the basis for its discussion of circulation control methods. The American investigation used more or less the same methods as used in the investigation of the Swedish Work Simplification Committee and it established conclusions that differ only slightly from those of that committee. Therefore, the American report may be used in the Danish full-time libraries as a more detailed, but optional, supplement to the Swedish report.

Work simplification is not a process which can be carried out once and for all. On the contrary, work simplification must be a continuous process. The growth and development of library activities, as well as the constant improvement of the techniques for simplifying work, necessitate continual analyses of the tasks of the libraries as a foundation for improvements in library organization, procedures, working methods, and work distribution. The Work Simplification Committee has accordingly proposed that the State Library Inspection establish a permanent work simplification section with the mission of undertaking investigations of the library tasks that have not been investigated by the Committee itself, and of performing new studies of those that were investigated by the Committee whenever it appears that such studies would lead to further improvements in the organization, procedures, working methods, or distribution of library work. At the same time, such a work simplification section would be able to offer guidance and advice to the individual libraries concerning the implementation of the recommendations of the Work Simplification Committee and of any recommendations which it may itself make in the future.

It is not possible, of course, to foresee all the consequences of the present recommendations of the Committee; carrying out these recommendations may achieve effects not foreseen or taken into account in this report. Libraries and library work will also be influenced by the Public Libraries Act of 1964, by the report of the (government appointed) Committee of Building Standards (1965), by the increased importance of education, the increasing necessity for the diffusion of knowledge and

211

information throughout the community, and by many other factors, including the activity of the future work simplification section of the State Library Inspection. However, the Committee does wish to call attention to some certain and some probable effects and consequences of a practical nature that may be expected to follow from this report.

A more careful distribution of activities among the categories of staff will mean that the practical training of library trainees will no longer aim at enabling them to perform all library work, but only that work which requires professional training. Practical knowledge of other duties will be required only to the extent that it ensures an overall understanding by the trainees of the main library tasks and the relationship between these tasks, so that they can enter into harmonious cooperation with workers of the other staff groups upon completion of their probationary period. This new objective for the practical phase of the education of library trainees may also affect the in-service part of the training for student librarians, and may result in a shorter period of practical training than that currently considered necessary. At the same time, the quality of the professional training necessary for these staff members to carry out their primary tasks must be improved.

The nature of the duties which have been assigned to librarians in this report indicates that the future training of librarians must meet the following needs:

1. Training in the regular professional library fields of book selection and assistance to readers.

The main objective of the training of librarians up until now has been to achieve the skills necessary for book selection and assistance to readers. Recent developments in the libraries will strengthen the requirement for training in both of these functions.

2. Training in the fields of administration, organization, and work supervision.

There is a greater need for training in the field of administration, organization, and work supervision. There should be more training in this area for all librarians, and even more thorough training for those librarians concentrating on this area as their particular area of specialization.

The need for training in this field has until the present time been met in part by the Royal Danish School of Librarianship and in part by the Scandinavian Advanced School for Public Librarians. The introductory treatment of subjects in this field by the School of Librarianship has included the organization of library service, cooperation between individual libraries and institutions, and the administration of the individual library, such as budget preparation and the application for state grants. Training in this field by the Scandinavian Advanced School for Public Librarians is, of course, more thorough, and includes, over and above the instruction offered at the School of Librarianship, the organization of the library system, cooperation between municipal councils, library boards, library directors and library staff, and problems of general supervision and the delegation of authority. The general principles and theory of organization and administration are also dealt with to a certain extent in the Scandinavian Advanced School. The problems of practical work supervision, however, are not currently taken up at the School of Librarianship and only to a slight extent at the Scandinavian Advanced School.

The report of the Work Simplification Committee recommends a strengthening of the introductory courses in administration, including courses in practical work supervision, for all students at the School of Librarianship. It also recommends a strengthening of the more detailed courses in this field for those librarians who intend to specialize in it.

In addition, the report of the Committee recommends the participation by library directors in these courses, and the establishment of special courses in work supervision for library and clerical assistants.

3. Training in specialized areas of librarianship.

The needs for specialized training have become intensified as a result of the increasing complexity of library work, and the School of Librarianship is attempting to meet these needs by offering more courses oriented toward special subject fields. The Committee in its report has emphasized the idea that, with the increased utilization of centralized cataloging, classification and cataloging will and should become a speciality. The nonspecialist librarian will need to continue to be able to use printed catalogs and card catalogs effectively, but the actual preparation of printed and card catalogs will in future become a specialized skill for comparatively few librarians, mostly in the larger full-time libraries.

Carrying out the proposals of the Committee will result in greatly increased activity for Bibliotekscentralen and Indbindingscentralen, and in an extension of their services to libraries. Enlarging the cataloging service of Bibliotekscentralen through the increased production of printed sets of catalog cards will mean that competence in classifying and cataloging will probably no longer be maintained by librarians in the small and medium-sized full-time libraries, and that the need for advice in this area from Bibliotekscentralen, particularly for these libraries, will increase. It is anticipated that a demand will arise for the small and medium-sized full-time libraries to be able to send in those few books for which Bibliotekscentralen does not produce printed cards for cataloging, and, in due course, for complete processing. The diminishing number of staff members with the ability to classify and catalog will mean that the establishment by Bibliotekscentralen of a processing department analogous to the American regional processing centers will become desirable for an ever-larger group of full-time libraries. Bibliotekscentralen should start such a department as soon as possible as a part of the implementation of the proposals of the Work Simplification Committee. Thereafter only the largest full-time libraries will have classification and cataloging work to such an extent that they will need experts in this field of specialization on their own staffs.

Among the most significant effects of carrying out the recommendations of the Commitee will be the better and more economical use of manpower in the libraries. The carrying out of these proposals should result in the release of staff for the performance of pressing tasks which have hitherto been neglected. The demands for increased library service are so great that the implementation of the proposals of the Committee will probably not lead to a net decrease in staff, but it will undoubtedly result in a more gradual increase than otherwise would have been the case.

It should be pointed out that the proposals of the Committee can only be carried out by increases in the budget allocated to libraries for printed materials, due to the necessary increased use of prepared sets of catalog cards, printed sets of work forms, book cards, book pockets, and shelf list cards from Bibliotekscentralen. While these increased expenses will not even approximately offset the savings to be made in manpower, they are fairly large.

To the extent that they are carried out by the libraries, the recommendations of the Committee will also lead to an increased standardization of the technical processing services, with less latitude for local variations both in the performance of this work and in its results. However, carrying out these recommendations would not diminish in any way the personal character of service in individual libraries or prevent individual contributions toward solving important library tasks. On the contrary, library staff workers would be released from performing specialized tasks that can more often than not be done with less effort and with better results by central institutions or according to standardized methods. The time and effort saved could then be used in areas where the significance of the personal contribution to the quality of library service is greater.

In the long run, the significance of what has been done by the Committee depends entirely upon the extent to which the basic ideas of work simplification are accepted by boards of trustees and library staffs. The basic ideas of work simplification are simple. They are based upon making a clear definition of each task to be done and a clear statement of the objective to be accomplished by it. The stated objective is then to be sought by the most simple and direct processes possible. The key phrases are "primary objectives," "work simplification," "work

214

distribution," and "careful planning." In choosing between tasks which cannot all be done to complete satisfaction with the financial and personnel resources available, those tasks which have the greatest importance for accomplishing the main purposes of the libraries must take priority.

The Committee attaches great importance to the implementation of its specific recommendations, but it believes that even greater results may be achieved by the mere acceptance of the ideas of work simplification by individual staff members. These results can be attained through increased attention to the efficient organization of the work of each individual staff member and the increased participation of those individuals in planning and carrying out large-scale reorganizations, either in individual libraries or in groups of cooperating libraries. As an example of possible work simplification through cooperation among several libraries, some thought might be given to the establishment of a common center for overdues for those libraries of Greater Copenhagen that use photocharging. This might well lead to reducing the costs of handling this work. An investigation might reveal that, through large-volume operations, the photoreproduction of overdue notices direct from film might be possible.

Due to considerations of economy, and also because of the limited time available to it, the Committee has chosen to concentrate on proposing reorganizations of work that do not depart too radically from current library practices. Therefore, the use of electronic data processing equipment has not been considered by the Committee. Investigations of the application of electronic data processing in the public libraries, however, must be undertaken quite soon. It is to be expected, for example, that the proposed work simplification section of the State Library Inspection will start as soon as possible to consider the possibilities for producing catalogs that can be brought up to date frequently by means of electronic equipment to replace the present card catalogs.

One additional area it may be desirable to consider is telecommunications. The Committee did not investigate the present use of telecommunications in the full-time libraries, as the increasing use of teletype equipment by large full-time libraries already appears clearly capable of bringing about great improvements in interlibrary loans and quick-reference services. Investigation of additional possibilities for using telecommunications in the full-time libraries, however, may become of great importance in the future.

The Work Simplification Committee deems it essential that, over and above its continuing investigations and guidance for libraries in the fields of processing procedures and the methods and distribution of work, the future work simplification section of the State Library Inspection also undertake investigations of problems involving internal library organization. It should, in due course, extend its consulting techniques to include the use of such aids as organization charts, work distribution plans, job descriptions, work specifications, and written instructions.

Notes and Appendices

The notes and appendices include:

1. General notes to the tables and diagrams in Part I of the report.

2. Appendices to Part II of the report. Appendices 1 and 2 are associated with Chapters 7-9 on the composition of the present library work load and its distribution among the categories of staff. Appendices 3, 4, and 4A are associated with Chapters 10-12 on the present procedures and methods of processing work.

3. Appendices to Part III of the report. Appendices 3, 5, 5A, 6, 6A, 7, and 7A are associated with Chapter 14 on the proposals of the Work Simplification Committee concerning new procedures and working methods.

217

General Notes to Tables
and Diagrams in Part I

FULL-TIME LIBRARIES

The tables include data from the following libraries:

County libraries (less Gentofte):

Assens	Horsens	Odense	Sønderborg
Esbjerg	Kalundborg	Randers	Thisted
Haderslev	Kolding	Roskilde	Tønder
Helsingør	Køge (after 1948)	Rønne	Vejle
Hjørring	Lemvig	Silkeborg	Viborg
Hobro (after 1948)	Nakskov (after 1948)	Skive	Åbenrå
Holbaek	Nykøbing F.	Slagelse	Ålborg
Holsterbro	Naestved	Svendborg	Århus

Large city libraries

Copenhagen   Frederiksberg   Gentofte

Suburban libraries, which in 1960-61 included:

Ballerup	Herlev	Tårnby
Birkerød	Hvidovre	Tåstrup
Brøndbyerne	Hørsholm	Vejlby-Risskov
Dragør	Lyngby	Viby J.
Gladsaxe	Rødovre	Vaerløse
Glostrup	Søllerød	Åby

(In 1945-46 Vejgård was also included.)

219

Other full-time libraries, which in 1960-61 included:

Bjerringbro	Hillerød	Rødby
Bov	Kjellerup	Samsø
Brønderslev	Korsør	Saxkjøbing
Fredericia	Løgstør	Skagen
Frederikshavn	Maribo	Skanderborg
Frederikssund	Middelfart	Skjern
Frederiksvaerk	Níløse-Stenlille	Stege
Fåborg	Nyborg	Store Heddinge
Grenå	Nykøbing M.	Struer
Grindsted	Nørresundby	Tikøb
Hadsten	Odder	Varde
Hadsund	Ribe	Vejen
Haslev	Ringkøbing	Vordingborg
Herning	Ringsted	

(In 1945-46 Hobro, Køge, and Nakskov were also included. In the personnel count as of April 1, 1962, Bramminge and Farum were included, and in the personnel count taken as of April 1, 1963, Kistrup and Sorø were also included.)

In the tables showing the figures for book stock, circulation, and finances, the public libraries cited above are included from the first fiscal year in which they had a full-time staff. In the tables showing staff figures, libraries are included as of the first count made on April 1 after the appointment of a full-time staff. Figures for the independent children's libraries are always included when the public library located in their municipality is included, regardless of whether or not the children's library is administered separately from the public library.

LIBRARY DISTRICTS

In general, the home municipality is considered to be the area which a library serves. Where written agreements exist concerning service to one or more municipalities other than the home municipality, such other municipalities are included in the library districts. The Samsø Library is considered to cover Besser, Kolby, Onsbjerg, and Tranebjerg. The Stege Library is considered to cover Stege, Stege Landsogn, Damsholt, Elmelunde, Keldby, and Nyord.

POPULATION

The population figures used in the tables are based on the number of registered inhabitants as of April 1, 1946, 1951, 1956, and 1961. Source: *Kommunal årbog (Municipal Yearbook)*.

BOOK STOCK

The number of volumes throughout are those figures as of March 31, 1946, 1951, 1956, and 1961, as given in the libraries' requests for state grants.

CIRCULATION

Circulated volumes include all loans from public libraries as well as children's libraries, including branches of both, and also hospital libraries, libraries at military installations, circulation departments in schools, etc.

FINANCES

Total income figures include municipal grants from the home municipality (including grants agreed upon between municipalities, or council appropriations), state and other grants, and all other income, but do not include surplus or deficits from the previous fiscal year.

State and municipal grants cited throughout are those grants paid out in the fiscal years 1945-46, 1950-51, 1955-56, and 1960-61.

State grants include the general basic grants and also special grants for county libraries, bookmobiles, and military installations, but not reimbursements for equipment (such reimbursements are not included in the financial statements of the libraries, and are not included in the total income of the libraries).

Municipal grants include only grants from municipalities which have their own libraries. Grants from municipalities for the provision of library service from other municipalities with whom they have written agreements and from the counties are not, however, included.

The book funds cited in the tables include the same items as in the individual library financial reports: funds used for the purchase of books, periodicals and newspapers, and for binding. The salary budget includes salaries and social security taxes for the individual staff members, including school librarians, but excluding maintenance staff and the compensation of school librarians in terms of exchange hours. During the entire period 1945-60, the latter form of payment was used in very few places outside of Copenhagen and Frederiksberg.

Financial figures per circulated volume of the county libraries include loans to libraries and patrons outside the geographical boundaries of their districts.

The price index is computed from the price index of 1914, as revised in

January 1, 1946, 1951, 1956, and 1961. The index of January 1, 1946 is used as the base (100).

STAFF

All figures for library staff are based on the annual reports submitted to the State Library Inspection and are the library staffs (excluding school librarians and janitorial staff) as of April 1 each year, converted to full-time equivalents. Since 1957, the State Library Inspection statistics of library personnel have included the trainees attending the first-year course of the Royal Danish School of Librarianship. It is estimated that one-third of the total number of trainees were not working at the libraries as of April 1 during the years 1957-61. Therefore the number of trainees for these years has been reduced by one-third. The remaining number has been further reduced by two-sevenths due to the fact that trainees spend two hours of the working day studying.

The staff figures upon which the population and circulation per staff unit figures are based are the staff figures as of April 1, 1950, 1955, and 1960. The circulation figures used in these calculations include non-resident loans of the county libraries and loans to other libraries including the part-time libraries.

Written instructions to participants in the work survey of September-October, 1961

TIME AND WORK UNIT MEASUREMENT STUDY
DURING SEPTEMBER-OCTOBER, 1961

An important part of the two-year investigation of public library work which is to be undertaken beginning August 1, 1961, is the survey of the daily work in 15 selected libraries from Monday, September 18, through Saturday, October 14, 1961, inclusive.[1]

All staff members of the 15 libraries are to take part in the study except school librarians and janitorial staff.

The work survey means extra work for all participants, but its successful completion will provide an important basis for the further progress of the investigations of the Work Simplification Committee.

The Committee therefore asks for the active cooperation of all staff members in the selected libraries.

Running notation

The work survey is to be made by the daily reporting of the work performed by each individual participant. This is to be done on special forms.

The forms to be used for the daily count and the weekly totals are identical. [For a sample form see page 228.]

The forms used for the daily running count are to be dated in the blank for "Date/Week" and the word "Week" is to be crossed out. If the report for one day requires more than one form, the forms are to be arranged in

[1] [As was pointed out by the author in Chapter 7, one library withdrew during the course of the survey, and only 14 libraries actually completed the work.]

chronological order. Column 1 is to be filled in according to Code A (which immediately follows these instructions). The next three columns are to be filled in according to Code B (following Code A). In column 5, the starting and finishing times are to be entered for each task reported. These first five headings are to be filled in as the work is completed, that is, each time a change is made from one task to another. Columns 6-10 can be filled in at the end of the day. Column 6, "Time in minutes," can even be completed during idle moments, or when tallying and completing the weekly form.

Columns 7-10 are to be filled in by check marks, or "x's." A mark is to be placed in columns 7-9 (collectively marked "Code C") according to the type of work done: "performance" (column 7), "inspection" or "control" (column 8), and "direction" or "guidance" (column 9). Column 9 should be understood in the restricted sense of planning, decision-making, and instructing, and never the actual performance of the task concerned. (For example, deciding how many printed cards are to be ordered in cataloging certain titles comes under activity 42 of Code B and column 9, "Direction," of Code C is to be marked.) For an explanation of column 10, "Estimated time," see below. Column 11, "Revision," is reserved for the Committee's use, and is not to be used by the libraries.

The reporting of work done is to be complete; all the time in the working day must, as far as possible, be accounted for. As a rule, however, time of less than 5 minutes is not to be reported.

Estimated time

Time is to be separately estimated for each individual task if several tasks were carried out more or less simultaneously during a given time period, and the exact time spent on each task could not be shown. The procedure is as follows: In the daily report the work is to be noted under a single activity code number with an identifying mark in column 10, "Estimated time." When the day's work is completed, an estimate is to be made of how much of the time thus recorded was used for each of the two or more activities that were reported under the one code number in the daily notation. Three lines below the last running entry for the day these activities are now to be listed individually with the estimated time shown in column 6 and the identifying mark shown in column 10. In estimating the separate activities, column 5, showing the time of day, cannot, of course, be filled in for these activities. Estimated time is to be figured as carefully as possible (and it should be remembered that in doing work that one does not care for, it is natural to believe that more time is required than is actually the case) .

Main groups

If the time for performing several sub-activities under the same Code B

224

heading cannot be separately estimated, the main code heading is to be used. If possible, however, the numbers of the subordinate headings are also to be given.

Work that can be classed within a main heading but not under one of the specific subheadings is to be entered under the last number in the main heading, i.e., the 9-heading (a number ending in 9, meaning "other"—see Code B), and a description of the specific type of activity carried out is to be entered in column 3.

In doubtful cases, where there is a question of which Code C column (7, 8, or 9) should be checked, a 9-heading can always be used and the task specifically described in column 3.

Telephone calls are to be entered under the subject activity. There is no special code number for this activity as such.

Correspondence is to be entered under the 9-subheadings except in 120 where it is to be placed in the appropriate specific subheading. In column 3, a distinction is always to be made between writing (1) drafts, (2) letters (directly without drafts), or (3) final copies from drafts. Dictating is entered as (1), and taking dictation as (3).

Reading room activities are to be entered in main heading 90 (or in 81 or 83) regardless of whether the work took place in a reading room or some other location.

County library work is entered under the appropriate code heading with the notation O in the Code A column. However, the special main heading 110 may be used for the specific county library tasks specified under that heading. Code numbers 116 and 117 are to be used only if the activities cannot be entered in the other code numbers to which they are referred under those numbers.

Neither the location where the work is done nor where the staff member is on duty at the time determines conclusively the code number under which an activity is to be entered. For example, if a person is scheduled for circulation duty during a slack period, but used this time for reading publishers' circulars in preparation for a book selection meeting, this time is to be entered under activity code number 1, "Orientation," and not under code numbers 60-89.

Code numbers that include work not done in your library are not to be used.

If material is produced which serves several functions, and each of these functions comes under different code numbers, the work is to be entered under the number for which the material was first used. (For example, if a copy of a book order list is also used as an accession list or bindery list, preparation of the list is entered in activity 12, and not in 22 or 32.)

Corrections are entered under the code number of the work corrected. (However, see code number 79.)

Overtime is to be recorded in the same way as work done during normal working hours.

Work units

The number of work units is to be entered in column 4 for those activities for which units are specified in Code B. Work units may also be given, if this is not particularly inconvenient, even where they are not specified in the Code. In such instances, the type of unit (volumes, titles, or whatever) should be shown as well as the number of units.

The number of work units is to be shown only for work actually performed, not for inspection work or "direction." That is, if the number of work units is given, then Code C must be checked in column 7, "Performed."

If two or more staff members jointly do a task that is to be reported in work units, and it cannot be determined how many units each person did, only one of the persons should record the number of units, while the others should refer to the form of the person reporting the work done by entering the initials of this person in the amount column (column 4) of their own forms.

The number of units should be entered only when the work is finished. This is the best way to avoid double counts.

Time used for totaling work units, when this is not done immediately, and when such time would not otherwise be accounted for, is to be entered under code number 131, "Work for the investigation."

Daily and weekly totals

On every daily form, column 6, "Time in minutes," is to be totaled at the end of the day, and the total is to be double-checked to be sure that the sum corresponds to the length of the actual working day, with additions or deductions for any overtime, time off, etc.

For each week the total time spent on each activity is to be reported on a separate form in numerical order by code number. Columns 2, 3, 4, 6, and 10 of these forms are to be filled in. Column 3 is to be filled in with the description from Code B in brief form (for group 9 use only "other," for example). Column 10 is to be marked only if there are one or more estimated times in the totals. Column 6, "Time in minutes," is to be totaled at the end of the week and, in the heading at the top of the form "Date/Week," the word "Date" is to be lined out and the week (numbered from 1 to 4) of the work survey is to be entered in that space.

Changes in working methods

Finally, changes in work procedures that may result from the work survey itself must be avoided or postponed until the survey is completed, no matter how desirable they may seem at the time—either because they may result in increased efficiency, or because in making them it would be easier to fit a procedure into Code B and simplify making out the report.

Trial runs
It is suggested that every staff member of the participating libraries become thoroughly familiar with Code A, Code B, and these instructions. Each person should thoroughly familiarize himself in particular with those numbers of Code B that he himself will be using. It is strongly recommended that the recording of the work to be done be practiced beforehand for a couple of days so that any questions that may come up may be answered before the actual work count begins. In this way the recording done later by every person will be greatly improved.

Return of forms
As the forms with the weekly totals are completed, they should be sent to the Work Simplification Committee together with the work sheets for the daily records. The Committee wants to receive the original drafts and not copies. Therefore the original work sheets should be made as legible as possible (corrections should be lined out), and the weekly totals should be typed if possible.

Example of completing a form
On the next page is an example of how a form might be completed by a hypothetical Niels Nielsen, a cataloger in a medium-sized library.

The heading "Library," "Name and position," and "Date/Week" can be filled out in advance, possibly typed.

In this hypothetical situation, Niels Nielsen has circulation duty from 0900 to 1000 hours with a library trainee who shall be called Anna Andersen. He first goes through the mail for circulation inquiries, and then makes out the reserve cards from the previous day (adding any missing names, addresses, and call numbers, and noting on the cards how many copies of the reserved books the library has). The reserve cards are then taken over by Anna Andersen, who goes through the circulation file and clips the book cards. As Niels Nielsen does not complete the reserve process himself, no work units are entered in column 4 of his form, and he refers to Anna Andersen's form by placing her initials in that column.

The library opens at 1000 hours. The circulation counter then is taken over by another librarian, while Niels Nielsen, after correcting mistakes on circulation records, goes to work in the catalog department.

At 1019 hours Niels Nielsen works on ordering printed catalog cards. He then works on adapting and completing printed catalog cards, being interrupted several times to instruct trainees serving in the catalog department. The instructions are concerned first with ordering printed cards, and later

| Library Oldtown | Name and position *Niels Nielsen, Librarian* Dept. or special task *Cataloger* | | | | | | | | Date/~~Week~~ | |

1	2	3	4	5	6	7	8	9	10	11
Code A	Code B No.	Code B ACTIVITY	No. of work units	Time from — to	Time in minutes	Performance	Inspection	Direction	Est. time	Revision
✓	128	Check mail for circulation inquiries	—	9:03 –9:09	6	×				
✓	84	Reserve cards (complete writing of, etc.)	A.A.	9:09–9:34	25	×				
✓	79	Correction of exchanged cards	—	9:34–10:12	38	×				
×	137	Personal	—	10:12–10:19	7					
✓	42	Ordering of printed catalog cards	—	10:19–10:31	12			×		
✓	43	Completing printed catalog cards	18	10:31–12:01	90	×			x¹	
✓	42	Checking orders for printed catalog cards	—	13:01–13:15	14		×			
✓	43	Completing printed catalog cards	12	13:15–13:46	31	×				
✓	21	Instruction on writing of book cards, etc.	—	13:46–13:54	8			×		
✓	79	Take over circulation, receive instructions, check counter for reserves, etc.	—	13:54–14:07	13	×				
✓	47	Check filing of catalog cards in card catalog	—	14:07–14:49	42		×		x²	
✓	71/81	Work at circulation counter	—	14:49–15:14	25	×			x³	
×	137	Coffee break	—	15:14–15:26	12					
✓	71/81	Work at circulation counter	—	15:26–16:10	44	×			x⁴	
✓	47	Check filing of catalog cards in card catalog	—	16:10–16:18	8		×			
✓	71/81	Work at circulation counter	—	16:18–17:07	49	×			x⁵	
×	131	Completion of this form	—	17:07–17:14	7	×				
					431					
✓	43	Completing printed catalog cards	18	—	68	×			x¹	
✓	42	Instruction on ordering of printed catalog cards	—	—	14			×	x¹	
✓	21	Instruction on writing of book cards, etc.	—	—	8			×	x¹	
✓	47	Check filing of catalog cards in card catalog	—	—	35		×		x²	
✓	71	Charging, discharging, renewing of books	—	—	7	×			x²	
✓	71	" " " " "	—	—	15	×			x³	
✓	81	Guidance to borrowers	—	—	10	×			x³	
✓	71	Charging, discharging, renewing of books	—	—	12	×			x⁴	
✓	81	Guidance to borrowers	—	—	32	×			x⁴	
✓	71	Charging, discharging, renewing of books	—	—	9	×			x⁵	
✓	81	Guidance to borrowers	—	—	40	×			x⁵	

Note: Remember every day: Code B, Code C, and any estimated time periods!

228

with writing out book cards, etc. for new books.

After lunch Niels Nielsen checks to see that the ordering of the printed cards has been done correctly. He then continues adapting printed cards for a while.

Before going back to the circulation department Niels Nielsen shows the trainees in the catalog department the work to be done during the afternoon (1346-1354 hours).

Niels Nielsen is to take over circulation at 1400 hours, but he arrives at 1354 hours to find out about the work in progress and to look over the reserve cards and other forms at the counter.

As things are quite slow at the circulation desk, Niels Nielsen checks the filing of the catalog cards in the card catalog (1407-1449 hours).

Niels Nielsen is interrupted in this work a couple of times by service at the counter, charging and delivering books. After 1449 hours, Niels Nielsen is completely occupied charging books at the counter and advising readers.

At 1514, Niels Nielsen is relieved for his coffee break.

After this (from 1526 hours on), the activity is continuous, but as a trainee has been at the circulation counter since 1500 hours, Niels Nielsen has been mainly concerned with advising readers and has only charged out a few books.

At 1610 the circulation counter is again quiet and Niels Nielsen tries to check some of the catalog cards in the card catalog. The calm did not last very long, however, and from 1618 to 1707 hours, Niels Nielsen was again busy advising readers and charging out books.

After being relieved from circulation duty, Niels Nielsen enters those notations on the form which could not have been entered at the time the work was done and for which he did not have time earlier in the day.

CODE A FOR THE WORK SURVEY
OF SEPTEMBER-OCTOBER, 1961

X General.

V Public library (adult departments except O, S, G, K, and F).

B Children's library.

O County library work.

S Hospital library work.

G Work at or for old people's homes.

K Military installation library work.

F Branch work (except S, G, and K. Can be combined with V as FV or with B as FB if the branch serves only adults or children).

On the daily/weekly report form, column 1 (also marked Code A) is to be filled in with one of the letter abbreviations given above.

Work done is not to be further subdivided by departments. Work for a special collection in a public library, for example, is simply reported as V.

Code X is to be used if work in two or more of the above classes is done at the same time. If possible, an estimate should be made of how large a part of the working time is spent on each separate class. (For example, in charging books to both adults and children at a common circulation counter, X is to be noted in column 1, and if possible an estimate is later to be made of how much of the working time was used for charging out books for children and how much for charging out books for adults.) The procedure for entering estimated time is given in the Instructions.

CODE B FOR THE WORK SURVEY
OF SEPTEMBER-OCTOBER, 1961

Activities   **Work units**

0 *Book selection.*

1 Orientation (in *Det danske bogmarked;* books received on approval; publishers' circulars, etc.; taking part in the campaign known as "Introduction to the Book Season") .

2 Clipping and arranging newspaper reviews.

3 Preparation of reviews for books received on approval and other books being considered for purchase.

4 Check against duplicate orders.

5 Preparing want lists, want slips, desiderata file.

6 Ordering and return of books sent on approval.

7 Decision on purchase (individual decisions or decisions made at book selection meeting).

9 Other. Description to be made on form.

10 *Book purchase.*

11 Verifying title, dealer, etc.

12 Ordering.

13 Receiving books (unpacking, checking packing slip [accounting control under 124], checking order list, entering in continuations file) .

14 Collation of second-hand books.

230

Activities	Work units
19 Other. Description to be made on form.	
20 *Accession.*	
21 Preparing book cards, pockets, date slips, shelf list cards.	cards, pockets, etc.
22 Preparing accessions list.	
23 Stamping in accessions and making notations in books.	vols.
24 Accession statistics.	vols.
25 Sorting and filing cards in files and shelf list.	
29 Other. Description to be made on form.	
30 *Binding and preparation for circulation, etc.*	
31 Preparing books (including periodicals) for binding. (Deciding type of binding, choosing bindery, etc.)	vols.
32 Preparing binding lists, etc.	
33 Receiving books from bindery.	vols.
34 Control of binding.	vols.
35 Final preparation of bound books. (Includes adding book plates and series slips.)	vols.
36 Reinforcing books, pamphlets, etc., with plastic covers.	vols.
37 Final preparation of books (including pamphlets) not to be bound. (Adding call number, pasting date slip, book pocket, etc.)	vols.
39 Other. Description to be made on form.	
40 *Classification and cataloging.*	
41 Classification of books for which printed catalog cards are not available or are not used.	titles
42 Ordering, receiving, and arranging printed catalog cards.	
43 Completing printed catalog cards.	titles
44 Cataloging without printed catalog cards (preparing manuscript slips).	
45 Copying catalog cards from manuscript.	titles
46 Preparing catalog cards without use of printed cards and manuscript slips.	

Activities	Work units

47 Alphabetizing and sorting printed slips and cards, then filing in catalogs.

48 Corrections because of changes in catalog rules and practice. (Includes corresponding correction of call numbers.)

49 Other. Description to be made on form.

50 *Book care and conservation.*

51 Surveying book stock with regard to repair, rebinding, storage, withdrawal. (In both stacks and books set aside at circulation counter.)

52 Repair. (Rewriting book cards, etc.)   vols.

53 Rebinding. (If this can be differentiated, otherwise enter under 30-39.)

54 Withdrawal. Includes removing shelf list and catalog cards, stamping books, sending them to be pulped, etc.

55 Storage and other transfer from one department to another. (Includes corrections in catalogs caused by such changes.)   titles

59 Other. Description to be made on form.

60 *Registration of readers.*

61 Receiving registrations, issuing borrowers' cards, introduction to the library.   borrowers

62 Receiving registrations, issuing borrowers' cards.   borrowers

63 Introduction to the library (62 and 63 are subgroups under 61 and are to be used where such a division can be made).   borrowers

64 Preparing registration file (alphabetical and numerical).   borrowers

65 Renewals of borrowers' cards.   borrowers

66 Arranging cards in registration file (s).

67 Rewriting borrowers' cards.   cards

68 Correcting addresses, occupations, names.   borrowers

69 Other. Description to be made on form.

Activities	Work units

70   *Circulation control.*

71   Charging, discharging, renewing.

72   Putting cards in discharged books, that is, "slipping books." — vols.

73   Shelving (in stacks, special collections, summer deposits, reading rooms) .

74   Shelf reading.

75   Preparing the circulation counter for work before the library opens and clearing up at closing time.

76   Arranging and tabulating circulation statistics (referred to as "statistics") . — vols. (Only for "daily statistics." Monthly counts, etc., only measured in time, not volumes)

77   Writing of recalls and overdue notices. — notices

78   Messenger slips. — slips (when picking up books; the writing of the slips only measured in time)

79   Other. Description to be made on form. (Includes special correspondence about return of books, searching for missing books, correction of exchanged cards.)

80   *Advising readers.*

81   Advising readers. (Includes all forms of information for readers, accepting reservations and requests for purchase, receiving requests for book lists, help in using catalogs, aid in choice of reading, and all forms of reference work. However, see 91.)

82   Assisting readers in circulation department.

83   Assisting readers in reading room.

84   Reserves. (See 81-82, here only enter preparing reserve cards and clipping book cards. For requests from parish libraries see 116.) — reservations

85   Bibliographic work in connection with obtaining material from other libraries. (Verification of requests.) — requests

Activities	Work units
86 Interlibrary loan. Loan of material from and to other libraries. (Includes writing "book cards," etc., if any, and notices to libraries and readers about interlibrary loans. Requests from parish libraries entered here as O under Code A; see also 116.)	requests (notices and "book cards" to be measured in terms of time.)
87 Packing (and unpacking) and sending books to and from other libraries.	
88 Introducing the library to groups and school classes. (Also includes preparatory work.)	groups/classes (preparatory work, however, to be measured in time spent)
89 Other. Description to be made on form. (Includes taking books from stacks if this can be separated from 81-83, also "class sets" and "free reading" sets for schools, deposits to youth clubs, etc.)	
90 *Reading room work.* (For advising readers, use 81 and 83.)	
91 Preparing bibliographies and book lists on special request. (See also 103.)	bibliographies/lists
92 Charge, set out, discharge newspapers and periodicals.	
93 Sorting and storing old issues of periodicals and newspapers.	
94 Special card catalogs in reading room. (Preparing, keeping up "style" file, newspaper indexes, etc. Do not enter here work under general cataloging; use 40-49.)	
95 Clipping files. (Does not include book reviews [use 3] but does include local history and material on the library.)	
96 Statistics of reading room visits (estimated).	visitors
99 Other. Description to be made on form.	
100 *Public relations.*	
101 Arrangement of exhibitions in libraries.	
102 Preparation of signs and posters.	

Activities   **Work units**

103 Preparing catalogs and book lists. (Includes annotated book lists, for example.) (See also 91.)

104 Arrangement of exhibitions outside the library.

105 Other arrangements inside and outside the library.

106 Writing and posting lists of recently purchased books.

107 Story hours, book talks, etc.

108 Preparation of articles and interviews for newspapers.

109 Other. Description to be made on form.

110 *County library work* (see also other groups + O under Code A).

111 Preparing book purchase proposals (for parish libraries).   proposals

112 Preparing budgets (for parish libraries).   budgets

113 Review of book proposals and budgets at meetings in parish libraries or at the county library.   meetings

114 Driving bookmobiles.

115 Maintaining and arranging special bookmobile collection.

116 Individual requests from parish libraries. (Usually under 86 + O under Code A, and actual reservation of books not in collection to be entered in 84 + O under Code A. This group number is to be used only when work cannot be included in groups cited.)   requests (by title or subject)

117 Cataloging for parish libraries. (Usually under groups 20-30-40 + O under Code A. This group to be used only when work cannot be included in groups cited.)

118 Advice on library technical services.

119 Other. Description to be made on form.

120 *Administration.*

121 Board meetings.

Activities

Work units

122 Other meetings and travel to meetings (except meetings that come under numbers 1, 7, 113, and 125).

123 Budget preparation.

124 Bookkeeping and auditing.

125 Personnel. (Scheduling, hiring staff, staff meetings, but not book selection meetings.) (See 7.) Description to be made on form.

126 Maintenance of premises, furniture, and equipment.

127 Planning. (New activities, new buildings, reorganization of work, etc. General day-to-day planning entered under subject with check in Code C, columns 7, 8, and 9.)

128 General office and administrative work. (Correspondence that cannot be allocated to other groups, telephone switchboard operation, purchase of office material, etc.)

129 Other. Description to be made on form. (Includes visits of foreign colleagues on study trips, report on library use of works of Danish authors, taking inventory of book stock.)

130 *Other.*

131 Work for the investigation.

132 Vacation and time off.

133 Illness.

134 Unproductive time (waiting, transportation during working hours, etc.)

135 Keeping up with newly purchased literature and professional reading. Book review meetings. (Does not include reading outside of working hours.)

136 Assisting trainees and new staff members. (In addition to general supervision and instruction.)

137 Personal time. (Private visits, telephone calls, use of restroom, coffee breaks, etc.)

139 Other. Description to be made on form. (Cloakroom duty, chauffeuring, etc.)

Written instructions to the participants in the
work survey of 1961 who later submitted
estimates of their annual work load

ESTIMATED REPORT OF THE ANNUAL WORKING TIME

Enclosed are two copies of the statement of your working time during the
four-week survey completed during 1961. Within the next two weeks we
would like to have one copy of this statement returned with your estimate
of the distribution of your annual working time among the activities listed
in Code B.

Purpose of the year's estimate
The period during which the four-week work survey was made was selected
on the basis that the working time for the largest number of the general
library activities studied would be more or less normal for the year during
that period. We were well aware, of course, that this would not be true of
all activities. The reason for having this estimate of the distribution of
working time made for an entire year, therefore, is to correct as much as
possible the errors which are undoubtedly included in the results of the
work survey. Those errors are due to, among other things, the fact that
certain activities are carried out only once a year or at infrequent intervals—
such as preparing budgets (123), closing the accounts (124), preparing the
annual report (128), making out the report of library use of works by
Danish authors (129.1), the yearly review of the registration file (69), taking
inventory of the book stock (129.2), etc. In this year's estimate you are
asked not to estimate a normal year based on your recollection of the work
done over a period of several years, but rather to reconstruct as closely as
possible the distribution of your working time according to the activities

listed in Code B during the year immediately past (with corrections, of course, for such irregularities as extensive absences due to illness, etc.). The year's estimate includes only *working time* not *amount of work*. Your estimate should be entered in the column farthest to the right ("Year") and is to be given in *minutes*. [The reference here is to the special form used in making the yearly estimate. That form is not shown in this report.]

Library pages, etc.

Library pages, messengers, and other persons who are concerned with very few activities, and whose work is of a rather routine nature, can, if their work was normal during the period of the work survey, easily prepare an annual estimate. The figures in minutes from the work survey period are to be divided by four and then multiplied by the number of weeks you have worked during the year. If your work is exactly the type described above, you can skip the following instructions and simply look over the corrections and additions to Code B at the end of these instructions to see if any of them have any bearing on your yearly estimate. One stipulation for using the method just described is that you did not do, at one or more periods during the year, work that is not included in your regular weekly duties.

Method of procedure

If your work is more varied, it will probably be easier and safer to estimate the year's work in the following sequence:

1. Total time during the year that must be accounted for.
2. The extent of the regular (or almost regular) activities.
3. The extent of the activities that were normal (or almost normal) during the work survey.
4. The extent of the remaining activities.

Total of the year's estimate

Assuming that there are 303 working days in one year (365 days minus Sundays and holidays), your year's estimate will consist of a total of 303 times the number of minutes you work every day. If your work week is 42 hours, your daily working time is 7 hours or 420 minutes, and your yearly working time is 420 × 303—approximately 127,000 minutes. Your yearly working time can be calculated in a similar manner if you are employed part-time or your number of hours per week is other than 42. If you have not held your present position for a year, or if you are to leave your present post before the end of the year, it is requested nevertheless that you estimate the work and time distribution of the position for the entire year. Persons in such a situation may possibly be guided by colleagues or supervisors about the work entailed in the position. Library trainees who attended the basic course of the Royal Danish School of Librarianship during the first half of 1961 are asked to estimate their annual working time as if they had been working at the library during the entire year. Staff with substitute appointments, pages employed only during the winter (and who cannot use the simple procedure for pages, etc. described above), and others ·employed temporarily, should be told by their supervisors how much of the year their position should be considered as occupied, and thus how much time their annual estimate should cover. The total for the year's estimate is to be entered on page 4 of the yearly estimate form, under the column headed "Year."

Fixed, or regular activities

The following activities will in general have a fairly fixed character:

Work for the investigation (131), which is to be stipulated in minutes from the four-week work survey, plus the number of minutes used for totaling the fourth week if this total had not already been entered by Saturday of the fourth week.

Vacation and time off (132) will presumably also be easy to determine, but it should be noted that time off which is used to attend meetings or other activities is to be entered under other code numbers. (Introduction to the Book Season under number 1, or DLA Annual Meeting under number 122, for example.)

It is most practical to estimate illness (133) immediately.

Study time for library and business school (clerical) trainees (139.1) will, in general, be the number of working days (303 minus vacation and sick leave) times 120 minutes.

Driving bookmobiles (114) will, for most of the county librarians and others who share this work, presumably be so regular that the number of minutes spent "on the road" during the year can easily be calculated.

Activities that were normal during the work survey

Those activities that were of normal or almost normal extent during the work survey can be calculated in the following way:

Vacation and sick leave are to be subtracted from the yearly 303 weekdays and the result divided by the number of working days (24) during the work survey, after deducting from this number any possible vacation or sick leave days taken during the survey. The result of this division is then to be rounded to a whole number and the time spent on activities which were of normal duration during the work survey is to be multiplied by this figure. The result is the yearly extent of such activities in minutes.

For activities that were almost normal during the work survey period, this method can still be used, as the extent of the year's activity can be worked out first according to this method and the result can then be raised or lowered by an approximated number of minutes.

239

Pure estimates

Any remaining activities that were not of normal extent, or that did not occur during the work survey, should be estimated "free hand." It will be of some help to see if the total of all these estimated amounts agrees approximately with the estimated total for the year that you have figured out in advance.

Changes in Code B for making the yearly estimate

During the review and analysis of the material gathered during the investigation it was found possible and practical to separate certain survey activities into new code numbers (89.1, 109.1, 129.1, 129.2, 139.1, 139.2, 139.3, 139.4, 140). One correction has also been made (exchanging cards is placed in 72 and not 79), and subject matter has been specified for the 9-numbers. The reason for this is that during the review of the forms completed in the work survey, it appeared that there were doubts in some instances about where to place certain duties. The following list contains those Code B activities which have been changed or clarified for making the year's estimate figures. For the code numbers to be included in your year's estimate, you are first asked to compare this list with the original Code B list.

Activity

1   Also includes time spent in keeping up with the literature in order to make book proposals to be submitted to a book selection meeting.

6   Also includes the distribution of books received on approval to members of book selection committee.

9   Discussion of and deliberation about the form of book selection. Decision on the allocation of purchase to departments of the library if this decision is not made at the same time as book selection. Deciding about gift books.

12   Also includes the handling of normal claims or complaints.

19   Discussion of and deliberation about acquisition practices. Correspondence concerned with book purchases.

21   Includes various stampings and later entries to shelf list cards to indicate that the processes in activities 30-49 have been carried out.

22   Also includes preparing and duplicating accessions lists for use within the library.

29   Making entries of new copies on joint shelf list cards.

31   Also includes conversations about binding with bindery staff or consultation with binders who pick up books for binding.

39   Deliberation, discussion, and correspondence about binding practices. Distribution of new books to departments of the library. Inserting leaves in loose-leaf works (occupation register, etc.).

41   Includes only classification not done in connection with cataloging. (In contrast to 44.)

240

49 Deliberation, discussion, and correspondence about cataloging practices. Work in connection with revising book classification. Distribution of cards to departments and catalogs. Preparing guide cards. Correcting old errors (to the extent that this is not included in 48). Cataloging using printed slips partly as manuscript. (Actual preparation of such cards under 45.) Additions and corrections to cards because of adding additional copies, annual volumes, or new editions ("copy also in reading room," for example). Removing old periodical analytics. Preparing analytics for previously cataloged books and periodicals. Cataloging pictures.

59 Book selection for summer deposit collections. (Actual transport of such collections under 139.2 and shelving or arranging under 73.)

68 Also includes transfer of readers from one department or branch to another when this transfer is done without new registration.

69 Filing and removing deposited borrowers' cards. Correspondence (with readers who have received two overdue notices, for example). Work with temporary borrowers' cards. Setting up new borrowers' numbers. Borrowers' statistics.

71 Also includes stamping date cards.

72 Also includes correction of exchanges of cards. (Moved from 79.)

73 Also includes maintenance.

75 Includes all general clearing up at circulation counter and in reading room and preparation for opening as well as actual opening and closing. (In hospitals, also includes preparation of book truck.)

79 Serving and giving directions at "librarian's desk" and circulation counter. Sending individual reminder notices and settling matters about replacements. Searching for missing books. (See also 72.)

86 In the larger libraries, also includes individual loans between main library and branches and also between children's and public libraries if this requires special arrangements. (Preparing special book cards and the like.)

87 No special changes, but see 139 and 139.2.

89 Correspondence concerning advising readers.

89.1 Work with deposit collections, that is, the selection, assembling, and sending of deposits, including regular deposit collections, "class sets," and "traveling" libraries to hospitals and old people's homes. Also includes preparation of special book cards or lists of deposits.

95 Also includes clipping and pasting pictures and articles.

96 Includes total "visitors statistics" and keeping a record of reference inquiries, if any. (Keeping a completely accurate record of visitor's statistics would probably not be possible—a reasonable estimate is all that could be required.)

99 Correspondence. Deliberation and discussion of reading room work

in general. (For periodicals selection, see code numbers under 0, *Book selection*. For clearing up reading room, see 75. For advising readers, see 83.)

109   Correspondence. Sending reader interest cards, book lists, and catalogs to readers, waiting rooms, etc. Preparing and sending pamphlets to municipalities or parishes without libraries.

109.1   All preparation for and work in connection with children's book week.

116   Delete. Use 86.

117   Omit as far as possible. (See Code B.)

119   Correspondence. Making inspection trips. Survey and reorganization of parish libraries including necessary follow-up work.

122   Also includes preparation for and participation in annual meeting of the DLA, county librarians' meetings, contact meetings, board meetings of librarian associations and other meetings connected with librarian association work, and professional committee meetings and courses.

125   Also includes making out work schedules for a single department of a large library, and all staff committee and employee representation work.

128   General office and administrative work (includes correspondence). General communication within the library ("shop talk" and preparing staff information bulletin). Telephone switchboard operation. Purchase and clearing up of office material. Rental or loan of (1) study rooms or other premises, (2) film and slide projectors, and (3) film and slides. Visits of colleagues on study trips. Answering questionnaires of a general nature.

129   Delete and enter under 128. However, see 129.1 and 129.2.

129.1   Preparation of report on library use of works by Danish authors.

129.2   Taking inventory of book stock.

134   Also enter here "stand-by time," that is, where presence is required without being able to perform regular tasks. Also, for example, temporary reading room duty by a page with the instruction to summon a librarian if necessary.

136   Includes time of trainees as well as supervisors.

137   Also includes private services for other colleagues.

139   Unspecified messenger service (to bookstores and bindery, for example). See also 87 and 139.2. Arranging and watering flowers. Work for local "friends of the library" association. Other kinds of non-private work.

139.1   Study time for library and business school (clerical) trainees.

139.2   Transportation and messenger service for books, catalog cards, and other material between departments and branches of the library. Includes picking up books from stacks, sending books and other

242

material to or from branches, for example. Packing and sending books to other libraries is entered under 87, and all other messenger service under 139. (Prefer 139 in doubtful cases or where the various forms of messenger service cannot be separated.)

139.3 Custodial and janitorial service (cleaning walks, tending furnace, etc.).

139.4 Cloakroom duty.

140 Military library work of all kinds, that is, all work that was marked with K in Code A on the daily/weekly work survey form.

As previously mentioned, you should feel free to consult with colleagues or your supervisor in preparing your estimate. You are not, however, required to do so. Your year's estimate will be treated by the Committee in the same manner as were your statements on work distribution during the work survey, and will be published simply in the form of total figures together with the yearly estimates of others, or under designations which cannot reveal your identity.

Queries about the yearly estimate of the working time and work units should be made in writing or by telephone to the Copenhagen office of the Danish Library Association—Work Simplification Committee. When completed, your year's estimate should be sent to the same office.

Symbol code and abbreviations for the flow chart diagrams in Appendices 4, 5, 6, and 7, and the tables in Appendices 4A, 5A, 6A, and 7A

Symbol Code

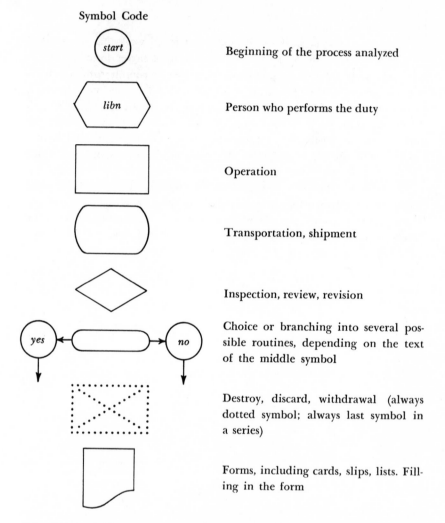

Beginning of the process analyzed

Person who performs the duty

Operation

Transportation, shipment

Inspection, review, revision

Choice or branching into several possible routines, depending on the text of the middle symbol

Destroy, discard, withdrawal (always dotted symbol; always last symbol in a series)

Forms, including cards, slips, lists. Filling in the form

Note: Italic text inside a symbol means that *nothing takes place,* but that the symbol is merely used as a heading for what follows. If a form symbol contains instructions for writing out the form, the text is in Roman type. If the text for writing out a form is inside an *operation* symbol, however, it contains only the name of the form in italic.

A symbol in a dotted line (• • • • • • • • •) means a *final operation* for a process or material. Symbols in broken lines (— — — — — — —) indicate processes carried out only under certain specified conditions. Symbols in a broken and dotted line (—•—•—•—•—) indicate a final operation carried out only under certain specified conditions.

Symbol Code

Two forms, one of which is a carbon copy of the other

Filing or storing

Direction of the process

Connection between two processes (conferences, for instance)

Indicates processed material (this symbol is used where the material is separated into different routines and where it may be difficult to tell which material moves in which direction)

Operation of no interest (or which takes place outside the library) here omitted

Operation of no interest (or which takes place outside the library) here summarized

Process continues, but the rest is of no interest

Material waits and enters the process again at the number indicated (used to avoid long connecting lines)

Material enters the process again from number given (used to avoid long connecting lines)

245

Abbreviations for the forms in Appendices 4 and 4A

F0	work slip
F1	temporary shelf list card
F2	book card
F3	extra book card for bookmobile collection
F4	extra shelf list card for bookmobile collection, hospital collection, etc.
F5	shelf list card
F6	blank book pocket

Abbreviations for the forms in Appendices 5, 5A, 6, and 6A

B1-4	work slip set from Bibliotekscentralen
B1	slip to show book on order, or in process
B2	order slip for the cooperative binding service of Indbindingscentralen (or for bookseller)
B3	order slip for printed catalog cards from Bibliotekscentralen
B4	work slip for the processing department

Abbreviations for the forms in Appendices 7 and 7A

F1-3	work slip set
F1	slip to show book on order, or in process
F2	order slip for the bookseller
F3	work slip for the processing department

Abbreviations for the text inside the flow chart symbols in Appendices 4, 5, 6, and 7, and for the tables in Appendices 4A, 5A, 6A, and 7A

acc	accession (s)
alpha	alphabetical, alphabetically, alphabetize
Bc	Bibliotekscentralen
b-c-p-s	book card-pocket-shelf list card set
bk (s)	book (s)
bk p	book pocket (s)
bkc	book card (s)
bkpg	bookkeeping
BV	*Bogens Verden*
cat (s)	catalog (s)
cc	catalog card (s)
circ	circulation
class	classified
classn	classification
cler	clerical staff

DBK	Dansk Bibliografisk Kontor (former name of Biblioteks-centralen)
DdB	*Det danske bogmarked*
dept (s)	department (s)
deptl	departmental
distr	distributed
hlibn	head librarian
Ibc	Indbindingscentralen
lib	library
libn (s)	librarian (s)
ms	manuscript
nec	necessary
no.	number
o.p.	order period (Indbindingscentralen)
pcc	printed catalog card (s)
pcsl	printed catalog slip (s)
recd	received
ref	reference
rev	review (s)
sel	selection
sl	shelf list (s)
slc	shelf list card (s)
subj	subject
subscr	subscription
tr	trainee
vol	volume

Appendix 4A

Information on forms, etc. used in library CF 2

Library: CF 2	F0	Order list to bk-seller	F1	F2	F3	F4	F5	Ms card	Order list for pcc	Ms cards for trac-ings	Bind-ery list	Pock-et label	"List of new books"	Series slips	Book
Author	1	1	1	1	1	1	1	1			1	1	1		
Title	1	1	1	1	1	1	1	1			1	1	1	1	
Edition/impression	1	(1)	1				1	1							
Year of publication	1	1	1			1	1	1					(1)		
Publisher	1	1	(1)				1								
No. of pages								(1)							
No. of vols.	(1)	(1)	(1)	2	2	(1)		(1)			(1)		(1)		
Vol no.	1	1	1	2	2	1	1	(1)			1		1	1	2
Classn no.			2	2	2	2	2	1			1	1	1		
No. of copies	1	1	2	2	2	2	2	1			1		(1)	(1)	2
Copy no.			2	2	2	2	2					1			2
Name of lib									1[1]						1
Dept. of lib	1							1					1[1]		
Dealer (bkseller)	1						1							1[1]	
Date ordered	1														
Date recd	2														

Item	Values
Date notified out of print	2
Price (retail)	1 1
Binder	3
Date sent to bindery	3
Date recd from bindery	4
Binding price	4
Pcc no.	1
Date pcc ordered	1^1
No. of pcc	1
Tracings	1
Item in series	1
Acc no.	1 1
Month entered	1
Bk dealer's discount	1
New guide card or subj ref card, if nec.	1
Type of binding	1^1 3^2

Note: The number 1 in a column indicates that information is entered on the form, list, or book the first time information is added to them in the library. Number 2 indicates that information is entered on the form, list, or book the second time information is added in the library. Numbers 3 and 4 indicate that information is added the third or fourth time.

(1) indicates that the information is added only in certain instances.

[1] As a heading.

[2] Removed after binding.

Information on forms, etc. according to new procedure I

Library without photocharging	B1	B2	B3	B4	slc	book	bk p	bkc
Author	x	x		x	x		x	x
Title	x	x		x	x		x	x
Edition/Impression	x	x		x	x			
Year of publication	x	x		x	x			
Publisher	x	x		x	x			
No. of pages	x	x		x	x			
No. of vols								
Vol no.	x	x		x	x		x	x
Classn no.	x	x		x	x		x	x
No. of copies		1		1				
Copy no.					2		1	1
Name of lib		1	1			1		
Dept. of lib				1				
Dealer (bkseller)		1						
Date ordered								
Date recd								
Date notified out of print								
Price (retail)	x	x		x	x			
Binder								
Date sent to bindery								
Date recd from bindery								
Binding price				x				
Pcc no.	x	x	x	x				
Date pcc ordered								
No. of pcc								
Tracings								
Item in a series							x	
Acc no.								
Month entered								
Bk dealer's discount								
New guide card or subj ref card, if nec								
Type of binding								
Ibc order period		x		x				
No. of slc								
No. of b-c-p-s								
No. of cc sets			1					
Invoice date of bk				(2)	(1)			

Note: Items marked x are printed on the form and not entered by the library. Items marked with number 1 in a column are entered on form first time information is added to the form in the library. Items marked with number 2 are entered on form second time information is added to the form in the library. Information marked with (1) or (2) ought not to be entered on the forms if it can be avoided.

Information on forms, etc. according to new procedure II

Library without photocharging	B1	B2	B3	B4	slc	book	bk p	bkc
Author	x	x		x	x		x	x
Title	x	x		x	x		x	x
Edition/Impression	x	x		x	x			
Year of publication	x	x		x	x			
Publisher	x	x		x	x			
No. of pages	x	x		x	x			
No. of vols								
Vol no.	x	x		x	x		x	x
Classn no.	x	x		x	x		x	x
No. of copies		1		1				
Copy no.					2		1	1
Name of lib		1	1			1		
Dept. of lib				1				
Dealer (bkseller)								
Date ordered								
Date recd								
Date notified out of print								
Price (retail)	x	x		x	x			
Binder								
Date sent to bindery								
Date recd from bindery								
Binding price								
Pcc no.	x	x	x	x				
Date pcc ordered								
No. of pcc								
Tracings								
Item in a series							x	
Acc no.								
Month entered								
Bk dealer's discount								
New guide card or subj ref card, if necessary								
Type of binding								
Ibc order period								
No. of slc								
No. of b-c-p-s			1					
No. of cc sets			1					
Invoice date of bk				(2)	(1)			

Note: Items marked x are printed on the form and not entered by the library. Items marked with number 1 in a column are entered on form first time information is added to the form in the library. Items marked with number 2 are entered on form second time information is added to the form in the library. Items marked with (1) or (2) ought not to be added to the forms, if it can be avoided.

Information on forms, etc. according to new procedure III

Library without photocharging	F1	F2	F3	slc	bk	bk p	bkc
Author	1	x	x	1		1	1
Title	1	x	x	1		1	1
Edition/Impression	1	x	x	1			
Year of publication	1	x	x	1			
Publisher	1	x	x	1			
No. of pages	1	x	x	1			
No. of vols							
Vol no.	1	x	x	1		1	1
Classn no.	1	x	x	1		1	1
No. of copies	2	1	1				
Copy no.				1		1	1
Name of lib		1			1		
Dept of lib			1				
Dealer (bkseller)							
Date ordered							
Date recd							
Date notified out of print							
Price (retail)	1	x	x				
Binder							
Date sent to bindery							
Date recd from bindery							
Binding price							
Pcc no.							
Date pcc ordered							
No. of pcc							
Tracings							
Item in a series						1	
Acc no.							
Month entered							
Bk dealer's discount							
New guide card or subj ref card, if necessary							
Type of binding							
Ibc order period							
No. of slc							
No. of b-c-p-s							
No. of cc sets							
Invoice date of bk			(2)	(2)			

Note: Items marked x are carbon copies made from filling in F1. Items marked with a number 1 in a column are entered on form first time information is added to the form in the library. Items marked with number 2 are entered on form second time information is added to the form in the library. Items marked with (1) or (2) ought not to be added to the form, if it can be avoided.

The text paper used in this book is "Permalife," a stable
and enduring paper developed under a grant from the Council
on Library Resources, Inc., and produced by the
Standard Paper Manufacturing Company, Richmond, Virginia.